Getting It Together
Black Businessmen in America

Getting It Together

Black Businessmen in America

John Seder and Berkeley G. Burrell

Harcourt Brace Jovanovich, Inc. / *New York*

This book
is dedicated to
poor people
all over the world

Contents

List of Illustrations

(Between pages 110 and 111)

Preface

Only within the past decade have white Americans become aware of the enormous gap between what black people have achieved and public knowledge of those achievements. A serious national effort is required to rewrite our history from these new perspectives, to set the record straight. An important part of this task is a reassessment of the role of black businessmen in American life. This book attempts to contribute to this reassessment by telling the story of a few of these remarkable human beings.

Of the many cruelties that have been committed against black men throughout the history of Western "civilization," not the least is the failure until recently to keep written records of their accomplishments or even of their existence. As late as the 1920s, many counties in several Southern states did not issue birth certificates for black babies, and so there are millions of Americans today who are not sure how old they are. The occasion of their birth was considered by the authorities to be an event of such complete insignificance that it did not deserve notation on public records. Similarly, the achievements of black men in the ancient African kingdoms and elsewhere have gone largely unchronicled. The material in the first four chapters on the early endeavors of black entrepreneurs is therefore incomplete, being based on fragmentary historical data and, in some cases, legend.

Information about successful black businessmen of today is incomplete for a different reason. No census or tabulation of entrepreneurs—whether black or white—can ever be complete or completely accurate; even if this were not so, any figures would be out of date within days. The world of business moves too fast. Small companies expand and move, old ones fail or are sold and their names changed. And, despite the handicaps that black men encounter in the 1970s in America, new black businesses continually come into being. All over this troubled land, ambitious black men lie awake in the small hours planning their plans and dreaming their entrepreneurial dreams. Tomorrow's John Johnson or Dempsey Travis is probably a man we have never heard of who is now working for the Post Office, going to school at night and making a bank deposit every week as Edward Davis did during the Depression. These restless and energetic men do not hold still long enough for anybody to tabulate them.

The men we have written about may not be the first or the most important or the most successful in their particular industries and cities; but each in his own way has experienced the trauma of being black and running his own business in the United States. Each had the courage to knock on doors that had never been opened to black men and to try what everybody said couldn't be done. While all of them are warm and friendly human beings, they also possess something of that "loner" quality that is required of those who blaze new trails and sail uncharted waters.

Our particular thanks—together with our esteem, respect and good wishes for continuing and even greater successes —go to these sixteen strong men who allowed us to tell their stories and, with two exceptions, permitted us to interview them to the point of fatigue and interrogate them to the point of irritation or beyond.

We also acknowledge with thanks the assistance of the following, each of whom made his own unique contribution to this book and whom we list in the order of the English alphabet: Edwin Barber, Fannie M. Burrell, *Business Week*, Richard Clarke, David S. Cunningham, Peter C. Demetri, Melvin Doxie, *Fortune*, David D. Jones, Francis Kelly, Peggy Kinchen, Richard D. Kuhn, Preston L. Lambert, Dr. Arthur C. Logan, Marion Logan, W. Ware Lynch, Hedi Butler Nelson, Dunbar McLaurin, Commissioner Major R. Owens, Patricia Rainford, David Rice, Emmett Riordan, William Rowe, William Sims, Dolphin Thompson and Cyril D. Tyson. And, last but not least, our wives, Pat Burrell and Liz Seder—only they know how much they contributed to make this book possible.

BERKELEY G. BURRELL
JOHN SEDER

January 14, 1971

Introduction

Throughout more than forty years in business and public life, I have noted the alarming lack of minority Americans among the owners of business enterprises operating in our country. While this is an important concern to me and to many others, it has seldom received the attention it deserves either from the government or from the larger business community. However, in my capacity as Secretary of Commerce, and in carrying out my assignment from President Nixon to lead the government's program for minority business, I have attempted to marshal the resources of the government and the private sector to strengthen this important element of American free enterprise—the minority businessman.

One of the things I have discovered is a virtual void in the literature about minorities in business. Until recently, the subject was largely ignored by publishers and, therefore, by the public at large. I was happy to discover upon further investigation that a large and important group of black businessmen is represented by an organization that is now over seventy years old—the National Business League. Founded in 1900, the league has worked steadily and effectively toward better business practices and the encouragement of black-white business co-operation. The National Business League's leadership, from Booker T. Washington to Berkeley G. Burrell, co-author of this book, has been outstanding. My admiration for the man and for the organization has grown steadily since my first contacts with both when I was with the Eisenhower Administration. Thus, I am happy to introduce this book and to wish it a long and effective life.

Only by knowing the past—who we are, where we came from—can we understand the present and direct the future. It is thus understandable and appropriate that the authors have begun by discussing business history in Africa, thereby establishing a formal base upon which every black man can stand. This section leads naturally into the profiles of contemporary business leaders in the black community. These men have learned by hard work and experience what business in America is all about. Each of the sixteen has enriched not only his own life, but that of others around him by "getting it together" in a uniquely American way.

The American dream of free enterprise has been denied for too long to the 16 per cent of our people represented by the minorities. It is my dream, as well as my responsibility, to see that other black men and indeed all minorities have their full share of American prosperity. I urge everyone to take heart from these examples of the first steps toward economic participation by blacks as owners. Although much remains to be done, out of the roots of the past black Americans can fashion their rightful part of American opportunity. This book can help. It deserves to become a landmark in the literature of business, and of black people in America.

MAURICE H. STANS
SECRETARY OF COMMERCE

Washington, D.C.
January 20, 1971

Getting It Together

Black Businessmen in America

1

In Ancient Africa and the Colonies

During the early Christian era, while others of their race were being sold into slavery, black merchants carried on trade in India, China and Europe. Thus, by the beginning of the Islamic era, black people had been introduced—both as merchants and as merchandise—into many "white" countries. It was during these early times that three powerful states emerged in West Africa—Ghana, Mali and Songhay. They compared favorably in political organization with their European counterparts and were clearly superior in several respects.

The power and wealth of these early "black powers" derived from the trans-Saharan trade in gold. Caravans of hundreds of camels made the trip from the north laden with wheat, sugar, fruit, textiles and salt. These were ex-

changed for gold, rubber, ivory and slaves, all in great demand in the north. In the power politics of the time, the
country that controlled the gold mines controlled West
Africa.

The earliest recorded mention of Ghana appeared in Arab
writings about A.D. 800, but other evidence indicates that
the country originated a century or two earlier. Flourishing
in the ninth and tenth centuries, it reached the peak of its
power in the early part of the eleventh century as one of
the main sources of gold for North Africa and Europe.

Its principal city, Kumbi-Kumbi, was an important commercial center whose rulers imposed taxes on imports and
exports to amass great fortunes. Under the rule of Ten-
kaminen, Ghana also subdued the surrounding territories to
assure the safety of the trade routes.

By the end of the eleventh century, however, severe
droughts and a series of invasions by Moslem fanatics had
combined to send Ghana into a period of economic decline.
From that point on it succumbed to waves of conquerors,
and the torch of Sudanese civilization passed to Mali, which
had grown from a small Mandingo state in the seventh
century into a strongly organized kingdom. Mali's most
notable ruler was Gonga Musa, who promoted and systema-
tized the development of weaving, construction and gold
mining among a people who had been predominantly agri-
cultural.

Since many of these peoples practiced the religion of
Islam, it was customary to use the royal pilgrimages to
Mecca to display the wealth of the kingdoms and attract
trade. Musa's pilgrimage was one of the most elaborate,
comprising an entourage of 60,000 people, including 12,000
servants, and more than twelve tons of gold. It is said that
he once gave away so much gold in Cairo that he upset the
Egyptian market. These pilgrimages also served to attract
scholars and architects who were brought back from Mecca
to build lavish temples at Timbuktu, Kengaba and other
cities. When Musa died, in the fourteenth century, he left a
flourishing economy, a thriving foreign trade and a stable
government—all in a period when Europe had not yet
awakened from the Middle Ages.

But the fifteenth century saw the decline of Mali, its power challenged and eventually eclipsed by Songhay, which for centuries had been a small and inconsequential kingdom whose rulers were vassals of Musa and his successors. The Sonni dynasty of Songhay produced an aggressive lineage of kings. The seventeenth and last of the line, Sonni Ali, conquered Timbuktu and made the Songhay Empire the most powerful ever seen in West Africa. Songhay's political and commercial dominance had been firmly established by the time Sonni Ali died in 1492.

In 1493, the Sonnis were overthrown by Askia Mohammed, known as Askia the Great, who became Songhay's most brilliant ruler. During his reign, which lasted until 1529, he concentrated on strengthening the empire, making his people prosperous, and encouraging learning. Songhay then included most of West Africa, an area larger than all of Europe, extending from Lake Chad westward to the Atlantic.

Askia's pilgrimage to Mecca was motivated by more practical concerns than homage to Allah or an ostentatious display of wealth. His retinue of scholars and statesmen sought contact with mathematicians, scientists and other experts in order to learn how to improve the administration of government, codify the laws, foster industry and trade, and raise the intellectual level of the country.

During this great age of Songhay, many reforms were instituted. A uniform system of weights and measures was established, sales were inspected, banking and credit were improved. The markets of Timbuktu and Gao were visited regularly by traders from Europe and Asia. Commerce thrived, and with it came prosperity.

Under Askia's reign, Timbuktu, a city of more than 100,000, was celebrated throughout the medieval world for its luxury and gaiety. It also remained an intellectual center of the first magnitude where, according to a sixteenth-century observer, more profit was made from the book trade than from any other line of business. (It is probably the only city in history that could make this claim.) Its University of Sankore was known throughout the civilized world.

In the latter part of the sixteenth century, the Songhay

Empire weakened under attacks by Moors and Spanish renegades. Timbuktu and the civilization of which it was the highest expression declined in the seventeenth century, bringing to an end the reign of the great West African states. Although some lesser states retained their identities, the dissolution of the Songhay Empire was in general accompanied by a return of the various peoples to tribal living.

Contrary to popular myth, the West African tribesmen were not ignorant savages. While agriculture was the basis of economic life, each tribe also had its own corps of craftsmen, whose skill in textile weaving, pottery, woodworking and metallurgy would later be utilized on the Southern plantations. Although barter was the principal means of exchange, a money system based on the cowrie shell was in use before European penetration. Moreover, the tribes had complex socio-economic institutions, ranging from extended family groupings to village states and territorial empires, which constituted a well-organized social and governmental system. These West African tribesmen, and the people of the kingdoms of the ancient Sudan, were the ancestors of most American blacks.

The first blacks to arrive in America came to Jamestown in 1619, not as slaves but as servants indentured for a period of twenty-five years. Originally they enjoyed the same status as white indentured servants, with one crucial difference—they could not run away and "pass" as free men. It was not long before the need for labor became so great that Virginia effected the perpetual servitude of blacks; thus slavery made its insidious way into American life.

One of the main arguments for slavery—that the blacks were "heathen"—was nothing more than a rationalization. To the Southern colonies slavery was first and foremost an economic institution introduced to solve an economic problem. Virginia's solution quickly spread to other Southern colonies and gradually took on legal sanction. Virginia laws recognized slavery in 1661; Maryland followed in 1664, the Carolinas in 1673.

The North had no great need for slave labor, but in the plantation colonies of the South, where rice, tobacco, sugar cane and cotton were becoming important crops, slavery met the growing demand for field hands. Because of the shortage of skilled white labor, slaves were also trained in the handicraft trades. Many of them, already capable craftsmen in Africa, readily adapted to specialization as coopers and carpenters, shoemakers and tailors, bricklayers, painters and plasterers.

Plantation artisans were selected from among the slaves on the basis of intelligence and skill. They developed a pride in their craft and their status in the plantation economy. In a few areas, where they were permitted to hire out their time and talents, some succeeded in earning enough to buy their freedom. Skilled slave labor largely accounted for the rise of plantation manufacturers; thus, the slave craftsman had an important place in the commercial development of the Southern colonies. For example, his barrels and staves for exported staples and his leather were used both at home and abroad.

In the Northern colonies, although slaves generally had menial tasks, a substantial number learned trades. They could be found in every skilled craft, including goldsmithing, cabinetmaking, ropemaking and carpentry. Black artisans became so expert that their white counterparts in Boston, New York and Philadelphia sought to have them barred from these occupations. Slaves helped to build the large fishing and whaling ships of New England and also helped man them. The women became proficient in knitting, spinning and weaving.

By about 1750, slavery had become an integral part of the maturing economic system in all of the thirteen colonies. The white colonists soon grew apprehensive about the activities of the growing black population, only a small part of whom were free, and their anxiety was reflected in the enactment of rigid slave codes. For example, a law passed by New York's Colonial Assembly provided that "no servant or slave shall give, sell or truck any commodity whatsoever during the term of his service." Further action taken in 1702 rendered all bargains or contracts with slaves null and void and prevented trading with any slave without his owner's consent. The nature of the trade carried on by slaves and servants was indicated by New York City's regulations, which forbade the sale of large quantities of "boiled corn, peaches, pears, apples and other kinds of fruits."

Blacks attempted to evade these prohibitions by selling in their homes or on the streets. In 1740, the Common Council declared this activity a public nuisance and health hazard, punishable by public flogging. Yet there were no such restrictions when the same produce came to market in the city by order of the masters of these slaves and servants. Over the years there were elaborate efforts through colonial legislation to stifle attempts by blacks to make any business transactions from which they would realize a profit.

The very existence of these restrictive laws demonstrates that slavery could not destroy black men's initiative in conducting trade. In spite of having been wrenched away from their homelands by force, having much of their basic cultural orientation suppressed, being forbidden to mingle in groups and generally put into situations where communication and self-assertion were all but impossible—some blacks rose and declared their freedom as men. There are a number of accounts of business activities in seventeenth- and eighteenth-century North America by enterprising slaves whose names went unrecorded.

The earliest known black American businessman was Emanuel Bernoon, an emancipated slave formerly owned by Gabriel Bernoon of Providence, Rhode Island. He bought his freedom in about 1730 and opened first a catering service and later the first ale and oyster house in Providence. Both proved to be successful ventures; his experience as a servant had given him valuable insights into the mechanics of running an eating and drinking establishment. When Emanuel Bernoon died in 1769, he left an estate of more than £540.

Another early entrepreneur was Amos Fortune, who was born in Africa around 1710 and brought here as a slave while still a boy. At the age of about sixty he bought his freedom and homesteaded in Massachusetts. Then, in 1781, already past seventy, he set himself up in the tanning business in Jaffrey, New Hampshire. As the business prospered, he became one of the town's leading citizens, employing both black and white apprentices. Fortune died in 1801.

As the eighteenth century wore on, American colonists themselves found out what it was like to live under prohibitive laws. When they finally revolted, most white Americans failed to notice one of history's greatest paradoxes—colonies with half a million slaves decided to go to war in support of the equality of all men and the "unalienable Rights . . . [to] Life, Liberty, and the pursuit of Happiness"!

The inconsistency of their position as slaveholders and oppressed colonists did not elude all of the revolutionary generation. Among others, Thomas Paine, Benjamin Franklin and Thomas Jefferson bitterly denounced slavery and the slave trade. The revolutionary rhetoric was not lost on blacks, either—many slaves petitioned the courts for their freedom as a "natural right."

Black patriots made significant contributions to the American Revolution, including the valiant martyrdom of Crispus Attucks, and this service strengthened the antislavery sentiment. More than 100,000 blacks received their freedom as a direct result of the war. Through a combination of legislative decrees and the acts of individual slaveholders infected by the spirit of the Declaration of Independence, slavery officially died in the North.

2

Before Emancipation

The conciliatory spirit of the Revolutionary War was short lived and deceptive, for the attitude of American society towards blacks in the early years of the Republic was charged with the character of slavery. The moral indignation of the new abolitionist movement was confined to isolated groups and areas, one of which was New England. But while writers and orators delivered their tirades in that abolitionist stronghold, New England merchants continued to sell African black men into Southern slavery.

In both North and South, the black man struggled to secure a measure of economic independence in an atmosphere of subordination, subservience and contempt for his personality. Although Northern blacks were under generally less severe restrictions and suffered less outright cruelty, they fared no better economically than those in the South. In a way, their situation was worse—a slaveowner usually at least fed his slaves. Even the abolitionists were silent on the issue of employing blacks in the higher pursuits of labor. Competition with Northern whites in even the most menial jobs made it very difficult for free blacks to earn a livelihood. Thus entrepreneurship was often a last-resort endeavor.

Among the free blacks who sought economic independence in the post-Revolutionary period, Paul Cuffe was one of the earliest and most outstanding. He was born in New Bedford, Massachusetts, in 1759 of an African freedman father and an Indian mother. Possessing very little formal education, he was nevertheless determined to make his way in that settlement of seafarers and soon excelled in mathematics and navigation.

In a brave and significant act during the Revolutionary War, Cuffe and one of his brothers refused to pay tax in Massachusetts on the grounds that they and all other blacks were denied the right to vote. Their protest went all the way to the state legislature, which honored their suit by passing a law granting free blacks full citizenship with all accompanying rights and privileges.

Cuffe had gone to sea at sixteen. Five years later, in 1780, he began to build and operate his own ships, starting with a small open boat of less than ten tons, which made regular runs to New York and points farther south. By 1806, he had moved into the fleet class with one large ship, two brigs and several small vessels; he also had sizable holdings of real estate. His operations later extended to the West Indies and England.

Along the way he joined the Quakers, becoming deeply interested in improving the lot of his fellow blacks. He went to Sierra Leone on one of his ships in 1811 to investigate the possibilities of establishing free black colonies in Africa. Three years later he took thirty-eight people to Sierra Leone in an unsuccessful attempt at colonization that cost him almost $4,000. Paul Cuffe died in 1817, leaving an estate of over $20,000 from his shipping empire.

In New York, Samuel Fraunces opened a restaurant where George Washington often dined and where the New York State Chamber of Commerce was organized. Fraunces Tavern is still in business—under white ownership.

During the early 1800s, the seat of black affluence was Philadelphia. As early as 1789, free blacks ran small shops throughout the city, and by 1820 the black population of 12,000 persons owned about $250,000 worth of property. Richard Allen, founder of the African Methodist Episcopal Church, was one of these influential black leaders. He owned a boot-and-shoe store and, with his friend Absalom Jones, also a minister and businessman, he formed the Free African Society of Philadelphia. This nonsectarian religious organization operated a mutual-aid society, which marked the beginning of the black insurance business.

Perhaps the most successful Philadelphia entrepreneur was James Forten, a Revolutionary War veteran who made a fortune as a sail manufacturer. Starting as an errand boy around the docks, he learned the trade through apprenticeship to a white man who recognized young Forten's exceptional abilities. Upon the death of his mentor, Forten took over the business and expanded it until there were more than forty employees, including whites. The company continued to prosper until steam navigation came into general use.

James Forten was an active abolitionist and a close associate of William Lloyd Garrison. As a financial angel for the antislavery movement, he is credited with saving Garrison's famous paper, the *Liberator*. Forten also championed a movement to hold periodic national conventions of free blacks in order to attack the mounting problems confronting them.

By the time of Forten's death in 1842, black business in Philadelphia had succumbed to a series of setbacks. The influx of competitive European immigrants resulted in racial clashes that often erupted into riots. Black citizens in the City of Brotherly Love had been deprived of the right to vote in 1836, and subsequently the number of black businessmen and women there dropped sharply.

In Cincinnati, a black cabinetmaker named Henry Boyd built a factory for the manufacture of bedsteads when local prejudice prevented him from practicing his trade. Boyd invented a machine to produce rails for beds and obtained a patent for it in a white man's name. His furniture-making operation occupied four buildings and at one time employed fifty men.

The settlement that later became Chicago, Illinois, was founded shortly after the Revolution by a black trapper and fur trader named Jean Baptiste Point du Sable. Neighboring Indians reportedly had a saying: "The first white man to settle in Chicago was a Negro."

Black merchants also ventured into the newly opened Western territories. William Alexander Leidesdorff, who became a rancher, merchant and land speculator in California, was born in the Virgin Islands, the son of a Danish planter and an African mother. At an early age he was sent to New Orleans to work in the office of his brothers, who were in the cotton business. When the brothers died, leaving him a fortune, Leidesdorff adventurously sold his property, bought a 106-ton schooner and set sail for San Francisco Bay, which he reached months later after a hazardous voyage around Cape Horn. This same ship made several voyages to Hawaii in Leidesdorff's export-import business.

Pre–gold-rush California, thinly populated and still under Mexican domination, was coveted by both the United States and England. Leidesdorff was able to capitalize on this international intrigue. He had himself appointed American consul in California, and then became naturalized as a Mexican citizen. He entertained officials from both countries in his impressive home, and was able to wheel and deal his way to fortune. He built stores and a warehouse in San Francisco, the latter on a street bearing his name. In 1844, he obtained a grant of 35,000 acres of land on a bank of the American River.

The political intrigue ended when the U.S. Marines landed and captured Monterey in 1846, but Leidesdorff continued to expand his holdings. In 1847, he launched the first steamship to pass through the Golden Gate; when he died a year later, at the age of thirty-eight, his estate totaled about $1,000,000.

In the South, the majority of blacks were slaves and could neither trade freely nor purchase goods. But a few were free and their presence was a constant embarrassment to the slaveholders, for it seemed to undermine the very foundation upon which slavery was built, the alleged inferiority of blacks. Southern whites considered it in their best interest to keep them "in their place."

A rash of restrictive laws affected the legal and property rights—even freedom of movement—of free blacks. Some states passed specific economic proscriptions. In 1805, Maryland prohibited free blacks from selling corn, wheat or tobacco without a license. A North Carolina law of 1831 required licenses, which were difficult if not impossible to obtain, for all free black traders and peddlers. Other legislation barred them from certain trades and occupations.

Nevertheless, a few black men had a natural business acumen that enabled them to achieve success in the Southern states. Lunsford Lane, a servant for a wealthy citizen in Raleigh, also ran errands for merchants and he learned much by observing their business operations. Since the state legislature met in Raleigh and its members were heavy smokers, he started a business to supply them with pipes and tobacco. Later he expanded to cover a large part of the state.

With his profits Lane bought freedom. Since that was still illegal in North Carolina, he went to New York with his master's agent to complete the transaction. Returning to Raleigh, he continued his tobacco business and opened a general merchandise store and lumberyard. Although he grew quite wealthy and counted the well-to-do people of Raleigh among his patrons, he was unpopular among poor whites, who demanded that he be expelled from the state under a law forbidding free blacks from other states to reside in North Carolina. Finally, all of his property was take from him by force and he was tarred and feathered and driven out of town.

An earlier North Carolina businessman, John C. Stanley, had been freed by a legislative act in 1798. He was a prosperous barber who invested in plantations and bought and freed many blacks. It is reported that his net worth of more than $40,000 made him one of the wealthiest men in Craven County, North Carolina.

Black entrepreneurship emerged even in Washington, which was perhaps the most notorious slave market in the country until 1850. William Wormley was a wealthy man who owned and operated the largest livery stable in Washington. Unfortunately, Wormley's health and business declined after repeated acts of vandalism and persecution following the riots of 1835.

A number of free black merchants prospered in Louisiana, where they owned sugar and cotton plantations—with slaves—and a variety of thriving businesses. By 1860, their property was said to be worth more than $15,000,000. Thomy Lafon, a New Orleans cotton broker, had accumulated half a million dollars at the time of his death and had contributed so much to the city that the state legislature ordered a bust of him to be carved and placed in the state museum.

Thus there was black entrepreneurship in the United States even before the Civil War. The outstanding achievements of these black men in a hostile society were testimonials to their exceptional shrewdness and determination. But they were not only unusual; they were few in number. The fact that the vast majority of the black population lived in bondage made it impossible for free black men to develop a broad business class.

3

After Emancipation

Abraham Lincoln's Emancipation Proclamation, which freed only the Southern slaves and which he acknowledged to be primarily a military expedient aimed at undermining the South's position, took effect on January 1, 1863. Northern slaves were not freed until early 1865, on the eve of victory. After the war, the newly emancipated blacks fought an uphill battle to participate in a shattered national economy. The grant of freedom did not and could not alter the conditioning of a slave society or the dearth of capital, experience and training. A strong entrepreneurial tradition and inclination was lacking among the freedmen, and the number of blacks in business in the years just after the Civil War was not substantially greater than before.

Emancipation understandably made less change in the status of blacks in business in the North than in the South.

With the exception of the grant of civil rights, which had generally been withheld, Northern blacks had nothing new in their lives. The vigorous postwar industrial development of the North and West left behind the small local pursuits of the black businessman. Barbers, caterers and restaurant keepers continued to eke out meager incomes, just as they had before the war.

There were, however, some exceptional entrepreneurial efforts in the North and Border States. One, the Chesapeake and Marine Railway and Dry Dock Company, was organized in 1865 by a group of blacks in Baltimore. Created to protect black mechanics from the competition and prejudice of their white counterparts, it was capitalized at $40,000. By 1870 the company was prosperous enough to buy a shipyard, but profits began to decline in 1877 and it went out of business in 1883.

In the South, the release of 4,000,000 people from bondage had enormous implications for the economy. White Southerners grudgingly accepted emancipation, but they had no interest in helping the freedmen achieve economic independence; indeed, they fought any attempt to raise the black race out of poverty. Legal and monetary difficulties were created for any black man who sought to engage in business in competition with whites. They were even driven out of those industries and crafts that they had mastered as slaves. In fact, the activities of black businessmen were limited and experimental until almost 1900.

Still, there were, as always, important exceptions. As early as 1866, James Tate was running a fine grocery in Atlanta. Elijah Cook was the highly prosperous proprietor of an undertaking establishment in Montgomery. A store owned by Samuel Harris in Williamsburg, Virginia, brought in over $50,000 a year. Other individually owned enterprises flourished in cities such as Charleston, New Orleans and Memphis. Southern blacks also engaged in co-operative farming ventures—a number of large plantations were owned and successfully managed by blacks who had combined their resources to purchase the property and pooled their labor to provide a work force.

The most serious blow to black economic development

after the Civil War was the collapse of the Freedmen's
Savings Bank and Trust Company, an enterprise that was
neither initiated nor managed by blacks. The bank was
authorized by an act of congress in March 1865, and it
began operating in May of that year. Its main office was
first located in New York, then moved to Washington, with
branches established in many cities throughout the South.

Although the bank was not an agency of the federal
government, it was clearly the intent of Congress to create
an institution of unimpeachable integrity. The bank was
managed by a board of trustees consisting of fifty wealthy
and prominent citizens who were presumably also dedicated
and public-spirited. These men were expected to protect the
hard-earned savings of black people, most of whom were
newly freed slaves. The trustees were required to serve
without salary. However, no security or bond was required
of the officers, and strangely enough there was no penalty
for misconduct. (Only later, when the bank was virtually
bankrupt, did Congress amend the Act of Incorporation
to provide punishment of misconduct as a misdemeanor,
with a maximum five-year sentence upon conviction.)

Black people all over the country believed Freedmen's to
be a United States government institution. Promotional
literature distributed by the bank further enforced this
belief, as did many speeches made by bank officers. Blacks
rushed in such numbers to place their deposits that by 1872
there were 70,000 depositors in thirty-four branches of the
bank. The Freedmen's Bank was controlled by white men,
and at the beginning almost all of its employees were white.
Later, increasing numbers of blacks were employed as
tellers and clerks and in lower supervisory posts. However,
almost to the end of the bank's existence, there was no
room for blacks at the top of their own major financial
institution.

Dr. Abram L. Harris gives this vivid description of the
national climate that led to the failure of the Freedmen's
Bank:

The period from 1866 to the panic of 1873 was one of reckless
speculation, over-capitalization, stock manipulation, intrigue and

bribery, and downright plundering. In this welter of corruption, high finance, and fraud, the Bank played a passive role. The persons responsible for its failure were irresponsible plunderers, typical of a large group of financial speculators who rose to ascendancy in the country's economic life during this period. Such persons welcomed any opportunity which gave them control over other people's funds that could be used in speculative, if not fraudulent, ventures. Falling into the hands of such characters, small wonder that the Bank failed.*

Recognizing the progressive weakening of the bank's condition, many of the white trustees withdrew their accounts. Others resigned, including many who had participated in authorizing the speculation that led to the difficulties. As the news spread, other depositors also began to withdraw.

In a last-ditch attempt to save the Freedmen's Bank, the trustees decided to bring in the great black orator and statesman, Frederick Douglass, to serve as president. (This was, and is, a common white tactic—to select a popular black figure to restore the confidence of the black community in a faltering venture.) It was widely believed at the time that the trustees deliberately concealed the true condition of the bank from Douglass. Blacks were also added to the board of trustees and the advisory councils of the branches. But these moves were too little and too late. Confidence in the bank had been so completely shattered within the black community that it closed its doors forever in June of 1874.

The failure was disastrous, both in its financial repercussions and in its moral consequences. It was not merely that many blacks lost faith in savings banks at a time when they desperately required them; nor was it merely that the dollars lost were needed so badly. The worst aspect was that black people were convinced that they had been deliberately swindled by the United States government.

Because they understood that the Freedmen's Bank had never been under their direction, many blacks saw the need for banks of their own. The first two were established in 1888—the Savings Bank of the Grand Fountain United Order of True Reformers in Richmond and the Capital

---

* Dr. Abram L. Harris, *The Negro as Capitalist* (Philadelphia: American Academy of Political and Social Science, 1936), p. 33.

Savings Bank in Washington. A year later, the Mutual Trust Company was organized in Chattanooga and in 1890 the Alabama Penny Savings and Loan Company was started in Birmingham. No fewer than twenty-eight banks had been started by blacks by 1905.

Most of these early financial institutions were short-lived. Starting with limited capital, they soon faltered as a result of ill-advised long-term loans, speculation and misappropriation of funds by bank officials. Although both ineptness and larceny were common in banking and business at this time regardless of the race of the owning and controlling interests, these early failures produced an unfortunate image that plagues black banks even today.

In the gold-mining boom town of Denver, a former fugitive slave named Barney Ford established the Inter-Ocean Hotel in 1873 and made it a showplace for millionaires and Presidents. Strangely, he was beleaguered all his life by townspeople convinced that his source of wealth was actually gold from a nearby hill rather than his prosperous hotel and restaurant business.

Ford was deeply concerned about the removal of voting rights for blacks from the territorial constitution and led a fight to block statehood for Colorado until they were restored. Perhaps as a result of Ford's campaign, President Andrew Johnson vetoed the Colorado-statehood bill. If he had signed it, Colorado's two Senators-designate, known to be anti-Johnson, would have provided the crucial votes to defeat Johnson in the impeachment trial and remove him from office.

Later, in 1880, a special commission was appointed to decide the winner of the bitterly contested presidential election between Samuel Tilden and Rutherford B. Hayes. Barney Ford was extremely close to the Colorado representatives on the commission, and it was widely believed that his influence produced the commission's decision in favor of Hayes by a single vote. Thus it is possible that this fugitive slave changed the course of presidential history not once but twice.

About this time, benevolent and fraternal insurance and

burial societies, under the influence and control of churches, were organized in many black communities. Ministers used the spiritual bonds of their congregations to establish mutual-aid societies, which assured dignified burial for members of the congregation and provided access to insurance coverage—something very difficult for blacks to obtain. A number of these societies evolved into national organizations. Eighteen ninety-eight saw the founding of what is now the largest black-controlled business institution in the world, the North Carolina Mutual Life Insurance Company. (Its story is told in chapter 19.) Another pioneer insurance venture was Atlanta Life Insurance Company, a stock company.

A study of black business progress was undertaken in 1899 and 1900 by Dr. W. E. B. DuBois under the auspices of Atlanta University. The study covered 1,906 enterprises with $500 or more of capital. It showed that many had evolved from the occupations dictated by slavery. House servants became barbers, restaurant keepers and caterers; field hands became gardeners, grocers, florists and millowners. Those who had been plantation craftsmen used their talents to become builders and contractors, brickmasons, painters and blacksmiths.

In 1896 the Coleman Cotton Mills were established in Concord, North Carolina, by seven black men, including R. B. Fitzgerald, E. A. Johnson and W. C. Coleman. The founders had made a feasibility study by communicating with black people all over the country to determine whether they thought that such a mill was desirable and practical. The responses were very favorable and led in some cases to substantial individual investments in the enterprise. The plant consisted of a huge three-story brick building with power facilities, adjacent structures and grounds.

Coleman Cotton Mills manufactured cotton yarns and goods using the latest equipment and machinery; its work force of about 250 people included many skilled craftsmen. Only a few black businesses of that size exist today. The company shipped goods all over the United States and to parts of Africa and several cities in England. From this mill and the efforts of one of its employees, a black master mechanic, there also grew a wool mill, established in 1901.

Among other ventures founded during the last years of the nineteenth century were Mount Alto Mining and Land Company of Virginia, a real estate brokerage and contracting firm incorporated in 1880; several large denominational publishing boards, including the National Baptist Publishing Board of Nashville, Tennessee; Wormley's Hotel in Washington, established by James Wormley, who died leaving an estate of over $100,000; a firm of truck gardeners in Charleston, South Carolina, established before 1870, which had 500 acres under extensive cultivation and shipped several carloads of produce to Northern markets each week; and the Baltimore *Afro-American* newspaper, which is now published by the second-, third- and fourth-generation descendants of the founder, John Henry Murphy, Sr.

Other businesses were built by H. C. Haynes, inventor of the Haynes Razor Strap in Chicago; James N. Vanderall and Z. T. Evans, mattress manufacturers in Orange, New Jersey, and New Orleans; John S. Hicks, owner of a bakery and ice-cream and candy plants in Erie, Pennsylvania; and Junius Graves, known as the "Negro Potato King" in Kansas in the 1880s and 1890s.

One of the most successful businesswomen, black or white, that America has produced was Mme. C. J. Walker. Born in Louisiana in 1869, she was orphaned at the age of six. She married at fourteen and at twenty was a widow with a small child to support. After moving to Saint Louis, she worked as a washerwoman and laundress and then married Charles J. Walker. Mme. Walker's claim to fame and riches was her invention of a hair-styling formula and process that included a hair softener and a special straightening comb. Later she moved to Indianapolis and founded the world's first black cosmetics company. It grew rapidly into a thriving manufacturing business with more than 2,000 sales agents, and sales-training schools in many cities. The more enterprising of the salespeople became franchised dealers for the "Walker System" of hair preparation. The company is still in business.

Another outstanding business venture still in operation is the Chicago *Defender,* founded in 1905 by Robert S. Abbott. The *Defender* has now expanded from a weekly to a daily newspaper. Operated by the three Sengstacke brothers, nephews of the founder, the *Defender* also owns the Pittsburgh *Courier,* which was started by Robert L. Vann in 1910, and two other weeklies.

The Overton Hygienic Products Company was organized in Chicago in 1911 by Anthony Overton. This company manufactures and distributes baking powder, flavor extracts and various toilet articles. Overton was involved in several other ventures including the Douglas National Bank.

Against this background of black business development, Booker T. Washington called in 1900 for the formation of the National Negro Business League. That same year more than 400 delegates, about eighty per cent of them from the South, attended the organizing convention in Boston. Washington saw to it that a large part of the convention's program was devoted to individual accounts of business achievement by black people from every section of the country, from cities and rural areas, in many fields of endeavor. These success stories, told in simple, dignified terms and recounted extensively in the newspapers, provided a powerful motivation for black men interested in careers in business.

Washington noted that wherever a black man succeeded in business, in either the North or South, he was treated with respect by the white community. He hoped that, as these examples multiplied in city after city, they would rapidly provide a solution to the race problem. Although that hope proved to be wildly optimistic, the basic idea was sound—when an individual produces what the world wants and needs, the world does not inquire as to his skin color before buying.

Washington made clear to the delegates that the league was to be open to all black businessmen in the communities —no matter how small or insignificant. His objective was to reach all of them and encourage habits of thrift, self-reliance and self-respect; he hoped that they in turn would instill such habits in the black masses so that they might become the consumer class that black business desperately needed.

As the league achieved widespread acceptance and influence in black communities throughout the nation, many local chapters were organized. The next conventions were held in Chicago in 1901, Richmond in 1902, Nashville in 1903, Indianapolis in 1904 and New York City in 1905.

During the years between 1900 and 1920, committees were formed within the structure of the league that developed into the major business and trade organizations still serving black communities across the nation. These include the National Negro Funeral Directors' Association, National Negro Press Association, National Negro Bar Association, National Negro Bankers Association, National Negro Farmers Association and National Negro Insurance Association.

4

Through World War
and Depression

While there had been a gradual northward movement of blacks after 1890, the first mass migrations from the South occurred during and immediately after World War I. Prior to 1914, the country was absorbing almost 1,000,000 immigrant laborers a year from Europe, but the war made it impossible for them to get to America. Northern industry was busy manufacturing munitions and supplies, first for the European combatants and later for the U.S. war effort, and it needed large numbers of workers. Black people moved North to take these jobs.

However, the black migrants soon became painfully aware that the black belts of the cities held no dream-fulfilling prospects. In most instances the migrants were forced to live in old houses that were the hand-me-downs of whites fleeing the black "invasion" and proved to be run-down, rat-infested, dirty and poorly provided with sanitation facilities. When the war ended, the government's need for supplies and services was cut back sharply; contracts with suppliers were canceled and many plants either closed or drastically reduced operations. This brought a worsening labor market and a return to the familiar pattern —blacks, who had been the last to be hired, were the first to be fired.

Black disenchantment found expression in the back-to-Africa movement championed by Marcus Garvey's Universal Negro Improvement Association. Garvey stressed economic self-sufficiency for blacks and urged that they establish their own retail, distribution and production outlets. He also appealed to pride of race and taught the virtues of the rich African heritage of black Americans. A brilliant organizer, political tactician and leader, Garvey had grandiose designs for a black economy. He started the Black Star Line, a steamship company, the Universal Improvement Corporation, and other ventures. All of them failed, however, perhaps because he did not seek the assistance of technical and financial experts.

Meanwhile, mass migration from the South had created a black market in Northern cities, where black workers were paid higher wages than they had been receiving in rural Southern areas. Black businesses were established to serve these people. For the year 1920 the United States Department of Commerce estimated black purchasing power at $2 billion.

Thousands of black businesses were founded in the 1920s, most but not all of them small retail and service shops. A number of insurance companies, banks and savings and loan associations came into being, many of which survived the Depression and are operating today. People's Finance Corporation, a small loan company, sprang up in Saint Louis. The Greenfield (Ohio) Bus Company manufactured bus bodies. The Cannolene Company of Atlanta manufactured cosmetics and sold them door to door and by mail. A man named H. Omohundro owned the Norfolk Mirror Company, which manufactured plate glass and stained glass as well as mirrors. There were also a number of building contractors in Norfolk.

One of the best-known businesses of the 1920s was a music-publishing house started by Harry H. Pace and the composer W. C. Handy. The white recording companies had only recently been persuaded to sign black artists and performers. However, this breakthrough was considerably tainted, for they did not allow the artists their full range of expression and talent but insisted on "molding" them in "acceptable" styles. Many of these companies refused to permit any black compositions except certain kinds of blues and minstrel numbers.

Pace felt strongly that blacks should be represented as manufacturers in the phonograph-record industry in order to provide black concert, religious and jazz artists with the proper material, media and setting for their talents. He also believed that such a company could be a sound financial venture providing a good return to the investors. He dreamed of records sung, played, recorded and manufactured by black people.

The white record companies, recognizing the threat of this showcase for black talent, threw up obstacles in Pace's path. When Pace attempted to purchase a record-pressing plant, a large white company bought it just to keep him out. Eventually, he was forced to resign as president of Pace and Handy in order to free the company from threatened reprisals. Nevertheless, the company managed to record a number of classical, popular, jazz and blues artists under the Black Swan Label. All of these recordings are valuable classics today.

During the 1920s the National Negro Business League continued to grow in membership and influence. In the early twenties its president, Robert R. Moton, proposed the formation of a corporation that would finance business enterprises among blacks. This National Negro Finance Corporation came into being in 1924 with pledges of $150,-000 of capital. Subsequently, Dr. Moton became ill; without his driving spirit the enterprise never really got off the ground.

The Colored Merchants Association (CMA) was begun

in August 1928 in Montgomery, Alabama, by twelve local black grocers headed by A. C. Brown. It was a "voluntary" chain: that is, a joining together of a number of independent store owners to act collectively. The purchase orders of the group were combined into one large unit, and wholesale grocers in Montgomery were invited to bid on the combined order. Uniform accounting systems were used as well as co-operative advertising.

Albon Holsey of Tuskegee was the national organizer for the CMA chain. He instituted an educational program among the store owners and operators stressing provision of sufficient variety of fresh stock of good quality, and at prices comparable to those of white groceries and service. Race pride was to be only an incidental factor in attracting customers under this program.

A warehouse was opened in New York City, stocking canned goods, coffee, tea and other staples with CMA labels. Under Holsey's organizational efforts, the chain found outlets in Manhattan, Brooklyn, Philadelphia, Richmond, Winston-Salem, Nashville, Detroit, Chicago, Dallas and other cities. It was just beginning to get on its feet at the time of the stock-market collapse in 1929, and was not strong enough to survive ten years of depression.

Black businesses, especially the larger ones, were devastated by the Depression. As the economic distress of the nation deepened, more and more insurance companies and commercial establishments failed and were liquidated. Those that survived cut their work forces drastically.

Across the nation thirteen black banks failed during the period, some of them after twenty years in operation. Dozens of white banks also failed in the early 1930s, and in most cases the depositors lost every penny of their savings.

While most businesses at that time were foundering, a few managed to get started: Crayton's Southern Sausage Company, the Industrial Bank of Washington, organized in 1934, and Virginia Mutual Benefit Life Insurance Company, founded in 1933.

In black communities during the Depression, emphasis shifted back to the economic boycott, the organizing of purchasing power so that blacks might obtain employment in the stores in black neighborhoods. Many communities converted these into "Buy Black—Support Your Own" plans. Chicago had exceptionally effective selective-buying programs.

The election in 1932 of Franklin D. Roosevelt offered hope to a despairing nation, especially to its black people. For the first time since Ulysses S. Grant, there was a man in the White House who seemed to have a slight perception, a tiny glimmer of understanding about what black people were enduring in this country. For the first time since the dreams of freedom were shattered in the Reconstruction era, some thought they saw light at the end of the long, long tunnel. One of the achievements of his New Deal was the opening of aid programs to black people. By 1939 the Works Progress Administration, a large federal job-creation effort, was employing a million black men on its projects throughout the country, even though it was operated in a discriminatory manner in the South.

Another significant event of the 1930s was the establishment of the Congress of Industrial Organizations, which splintered away from the highly exclusive, craft-based American Federation of Labor and created a new type of industrial union that welcomed all the workers in an industry. For the first time blacks were able to join, and by 1940 an estimated 210,000 had become members of various CIO unions.

One of the most important events of the twentieth century for black people—one which foreshadowed a new era and set an example for the 1960s—never happened at all. In 1941, A. Philip Randolph and other black leaders and national organizations called for a march on Washington to dramatize and publicize dissatisfaction with employment opportunities in defense industries. Despite booming production in these plants, blacks in most instances were hired only in the most menial, unskilled categories.

In a desperate last-minute move to head off the march, which would have involved 100,000 blacks in a powerful demonstration of unity and determination, President Roosevelt finally yielded to the demands of the sponsors and issued Executive Order 8802, which stated the federal government's policy against discrimination in employment.

The Fair Employment Practices Committee was established with a field staff to investigate violations, process complaints and hold public hearings. As a result, employment opportunities were opened for blacks and other minorities, especially in the aircraft industry and the shipyards, which were important centers of the war effort. Also, black women were hired in much larger numbers and at higher levels in government departments, agencies and bureaus.

Once again, in 1941 as in 1861, the nation turned its total energies to a terrible war—and once again black people thought that when it was over they might be free at last. Sadly, many of these dreams have been frustrated once more, but not entirely—as the stories that follow will illustrate.

5

Jesse A. Terry:
Clothing Manufacturer

"A lot of people could have given us business but they didn't think we'd survive. They thought every day would be our last day. Then they'd wake up the next morning and find us still here."

Roanoke, Alabama, near the Georgia border seventy-five miles southwest of Atlanta, has a population of about 6,000. It is very much like hundreds of other small Southern towns, except for one thing—one of its biggest businesses with over eighty people on the payroll, is Terry Manufacturing Company. Almost everybody in town remembers when Jesse A. Terry opened up shop in 1963. The unanimous opinion then was that he would not last a month.

Indeed, he had plenty of problems along the way, and more than once he had to shut down temporarily because a shipment of cloth was late in arriving. When that happened, the skeptics came alive again. But Jesse Terry always managed to open up again and stay open. Somehow he met his payroll and always paid his bills. Now the rough spots are behind him. His business is an unquestioned success; it grosses over $1,000,000 a year.

Terry Manufacturing Company makes ladies' outer garments of all kinds—dresses, coats, sweaters, jackets, blouses, shorts, slacks and uniforms. Most of its output is medium-priced street dresses and hospital uniforms. Its products are sold throughout America in small dress shops and in the stores of retailing giants such as Sears, Roebuck. During its busy seasons, the company finishes and ships over 7,000 garments a week.

Terry Manufacturing now has over 150 sewing machines of all types, including some that have been modified to do special work. This variety of equipment enables the company to handle many different types of sewing and thus keep busy throughout the year, despite the seasonal nature of the business.

Sixty-five people, all of them trained by the company at its expense, work at its sewing machines. Most of these women have previously been unemployed, many of them on welfare, or working as domestics at $10.00 to $15.00 per week. Now they earn a base wage of $1.60 an hour, the federal minimum, supplemented by a piece-formula. A number of energetic girls earn between $3.50 and $4.00 an hour during a workday running from 7:00 A.M. to 4:00 P.M. on weekdays and 7:00 A.M. to noon on Saturdays.

Jesse A. Terry grew up in the rural South at a time when lynchings were still common, when redneck night riders fired shotgun blasts into the homes of innocent people, when black men saw the power and authority of government and organized society arrayed against them, when there was nowhere to turn for help or redress of grievance—except to their own poor neighbors. He endured and suffered much, he watched, he learned, he waited. He bided his time, laid his plans and waited some more. He is a man of great patience and enormous endurance.

Despite all that he had learned, all of his native shrewdness, all of his impossibly long hours, his careful planning— Jesse Terry almost didn't make it. The odds remain stacked against black men, especially black men who want to own and operate a manufacturing business in rural Alabama.

Nothing in Jesse Terry's early life would have indicated a future in manufacturing. He was born on a farm near Roanoke in 1914, the son of a minister-farmer. The six children in the family, three boys and three girls, kept busy doing their share of the farm work. The first money Terry ever earned came from raising and selling baby chicks and from plowing gardens for neighbors.

Mrs. Terry, an expert seamstress, made much of the family's clothing and also did sewing for neighbors to bring in extra money. She used the old type of sewing machine powered by a foot pedal. "She would ask me to pedal for her," recalled Terry, "and I was glad to do it because I was interested in what she was making. So I would do the pedaling and keep the machine going. I tried to pay careful attention to when it should start and when it should stop. Every now and then I would take a chance and get up there and sew some—and that's the way I learned. I started pedaling when I was eight or nine, and by the time I was twelve I could put things together pretty well."

When Terry finished the local segregated high school, he ended his formal education. He spent some time farming and made an unsuccessful effort to establish himself as an upholsterer. Then, in 1940, he went to Dayton to work for the Air Force at Wright Patterson Field, making parachutes and all types of uniforms and clothing. "That was a complete education in making clothes, because we would start with nothing but an idea and follow it through to the finished garment."

Starting as a sewing-machine operator, he was promoted several times and eventually became a supervisor of more than fifty employees. During his years in Dayton, Terry made a number of acquaintances who were later associated with garment-manufacturing companies and proved very helpful to him when he started his business.

After World War II, Jesse Terry returned to Roanoke and opened an upholstery business. With his wife and three or four other employees he made and reupholstered furniture for customers as far away as fifty and seventy-five miles.

"I was an antique upholsterer. Much of my business came

from wealthy families in the town of Newnan, Georgia. I became very well known there, and after a while I considered it more or less my town; the wealthy people there depended on me to take care of their furniture. Several of them would have their furniture done over every year. Some even changed patterns with the seasons." In addition to being recommended by satisfied customers, Terry made friends with a number of interior decorators who would see that he was retained as part of their decorating plan.

As a consequence, when Jesse Terry decided in 1963 to start a sewing business, he had excellent credentials. He obviously knew just about everything that could be known about working with needle and thread. He had demonstrated his ability to operate a small business in a successful and responsible way. He owned his own home, paid his bills on time, and had saved several thousand dollars to invest in the new enterprise.

But when he tried to find additional capital, he ran into entrenched prejudice. "I couldn't borrow a penny in this town. They didn't say I had to take less than I wanted, they just wouldn't lend me anything at all."

Finally Terry was successful in arranging a loan, guaranteed by the U.S. Small Business Administration, from a white-owned bank in the town of Wadley, fourteen miles away. "That banker had a lot of opposition within his own organization about making that loan, even though it was guaranteed by Uncle Sam. But he stayed with me all the way and was a real help in those early days. Now, of course, it's different. The presidents of these banks come to see me to ask for a deposit. They tell me to just say the word and they will lend me any amount that business procedures will allow."

One of the principal factors motivating him to start his business was the lack of good jobs for black people in Roanoke. He bought five used commercial sewing machines and recruited five women to come in for training at 4:30 or 5:00 in the afternoon, after they had finished their day's work as housemaids. At the beginning he did not pay them for taking the training. "I said, 'Look, I can't promise you a thing, but if you think you'd like to do commercial sewing, maybe we can put something together that will pay you a decent wage. At first, though, you'll have to put in your time and take a chance just like I'm doing.' Well, they were really interested, and as word got around many others expressed interest in being trained. I found that with my training they could do excellent work, so I started looking for my first order."

Any manufacturer—indeed, any businessman—has two basic problems; one is making his product and the other is selling it. Terry decided that the first problem would keep him so busy for a while that he would postpone taking on the second one. Rather than trying to build a sales organization at the beginning, he started by sewing under contract from another manufacturer. His customer would ship fabric and patterns to him and he would produce the garment as specified. He would then ship it back to be distributed through the customer's own sales organization. The profit potential in this type of contract sewing is limited, but so is the risk, since the customer has all of the selling problems.

Terry's first order was for forty dozen pairs of ladies' shorts. "There wasn't very much work to it, just two or three seams and no pockets. It was very plain, and we put it together at a low price. I think the whole order was about $400, which wasn't all we should have gotten out of it, but at that stage I just couldn't be too demanding."

The going was slow in the early days. Without a record of performance, it was hard to find orders. Fortunately, Terry had become acquainted over the years with a number of people in the clothing business who thought highly of him and were willing to take a chance on his ability to produce. "At first, we had to go on the mercies of our friends. A lot of people could have given us business but didn't think we'd survive. They thought every day would be our last day. Then they'd wake up the next morning and find us still here." Things began to come a bit easier after he had successfully delivered on his promises—his satisfied customers were his best salesmen.

In the beginning, he says, "I made all of the samples myself for showing to potential customers. My girls were good but they were still learning, and an expert in the field can tell whether or not a garment was made by an experienced operator. That's all behind us now. I'll stack our work up against anything in its price range, whether it's made on Seventh Avenue in New York or anywhere else.

"I myself can sew on any of those machines. Sometimes when we had a little problem meeting a shipping date, I would sit down at the machines and go to work sewing after the girls left at four o'clock. And when they came back at seven o'clock in the morning they found me still there. . . ."

In the early days after that small order for ladies' shorts, the company scraped along with a handful of employees and a few more small contracts. But Terry continued to train new people to prepare for bigger and better contracts. In his second year he landed his first really sizable piece of business, one that would keep twenty-five women working for many weeks. "By that time I had twenty-five I could call on. I wouldn't say they were professionals, but they were coming along well and I was confident that we could handle that order. I told them all to come in the next Monday.

"Monday arrived but the goods didn't. So I said 'Well, I'll start up next week,' but they didn't arrive then either. Now about that time a white fellow opened up a place just over the Georgia line, a few miles from here. He was the first around here that would hire black women. I think he had been watching us, because he saw that I had trained them and he put them to work.

"The cloth didn't come and didn't come, and my girls would hear their friends tell them, 'You better go on over and work for the white man; don't mess around with Terry any more, he's through. He won't ever open up again.' And fifteen of my girls did just that. When the fabric finally arrived, I had to bale it up and send it back. I had plenty of applications, but I just didn't have enough trained girls and I couldn't handle the job."

One late afternoon about three months afterward, he

saw "great clouds of smoke coming from over that way, and then I heard that the other place had burned down. One by one, those fifteen women came and asked if I would take them back. My wife said, 'No, don't take them, they'll just run off again.'

"I didn't say much at first, just waited a while. Then one day I called ten of them together and I said, 'Now, you know you don't have to make any promises, but I'd appreciate it if you'd make up your mind what you want to do.' And they said they had decided they wanted to stay with us. So I took them back and they are still here. The other five I didn't want back because they had led the gang out. That was a number of years ago and those five are still grieving."

Those early days when Terry had to take any contract he could get, even if there was little or no profit in it, are far behind him. Now he can afford to be considerably more selective. "It seems like it took a long time for people to understand that black people can turn out work and run an organization just like anybody else. But I think we finally are accepted and recognized as a successful contract-sewing business. Since I've been in business, five or six other contract-sewing plants started up in this area—all of them run by white people and all of them now out of business. There aren't too many around any more of our size. That makes things a lot easier. If I sit down with a customer and talk about a piece of work, and the price isn't enough to let us make a living, we just turn it down. I don't enjoy turning away business, but it's nice to be able to do it—we have enough good business now that we don't have to grasp at straws the way we used to."

Long before he felt securely established in contract sewing, Terry had dreamed and schemed and planned for the day when he could move into the designing, making and selling of garments under his own label. He made several modest attempts in this area, always backing away in the end, feeling that the time was not yet right. "I wasn't worried about the design and manufacture of our own label garments; it was the selling expense that bothered me. If we hire a salesman and run up a lot of expenses of his time and mine trying to sell and then find we're not accepted, that expense could just about ruin us."

Late in 1969 Terry felt strong enough to take the plunge. He retained a designer, a white woman, and hired a black salesman. In addition, he spends a good part of his own time traveling and selling. It was wise, he thinks, to wait as long as he did to start his own label. "I'm interested in making a profit, but I'm also interested in building a sound business. I didn't want to take this step sooner than I thought would be healthy."

Now he thinks he will succeed. "It used to be that you couldn't think of selling your own clothes unless you had a New York office, but that's not so true any more. There's a lot of garment activity now in places like Miami and Dallas and Atlanta. I try to keep them covered, and of course I go to New York, too."

By late 1970, Terry had reached the point where more than half of his dollar volume represented his own label. "In terms of yardage, the contract side will still be the bigger of the two, but that simply shows how much more money and profit there is in selling your own clothes."

Jesse Terry describes Terry Manufacturing as a family operation. His wife has worked closely with him from the beginning, although she is somewhat less active now. Their two older sons, Roy and Rudolph, both joined the company after graduating from Morehouse College with distinguished records. Roy Terry also took a graduate degree at the Atlanta University School of Business. Though still at Morehouse, William, the youngest son, is already handling company business in Atlanta, and will join the company after graduation.

Terry lives next door to the plant and usually makes his first appearance in the morning between 5:00 and 6:00. "I'll spend thirty or forty minutes here going over things, looking over the plant, then I'll go and get some breakfast and be back here before my people come in at 7:00. And we have things arranged so that by 9:00 A.M. I know everything that happened the day before—how many garments we made, how many we shipped, how much payroll we ran up, who was out sick. You've just got to know what's going on or else you're lost.

"And we're usually here—my sons and I—until at least 9:00 or 10:00 at night. We put in all kinds of hours. Well, we have to because we have lots to do. We have a big program."

A prominent credit-rating service reports that Terry Manufacturing pays its bills not promptly, but immediately, often COD. "You know," said Terry, "my accountant is always asking me why we pay the bills so fast. Well, the best time to pay a bill is when you have the money. And we like to get the discount for paying within thirty days. But there's another reason—when you're new I think you have to build a record. A good payment record is worth more than all the promises in the world.

"Now after we're a little better established, we can go to the normal pattern of taking time to pay. I've lived in this town all my life, and there isn't anybody here that can say I owed him money and didn't pay it. There were times years ago when I was a little late, but never badly delinquent. It's good to have that record, you see, because right now I can pick up the phone and call any place downtown and order something and they will send it right out, no questions asked. That's a good feeling."

Things are changing in Alabama—very slowly. There are many other black businessmen in Roanoke; some of them, although not so prosperous as Terry, have been in business much longer. But he is the only black member of the chamber of commerce. It is not so much that the white people of Alabama have learned to treat others like human beings; it is more a case of Money Talks.

This was clearly demonstrated on October 29, 1969, designated Jesse A. Terry Day, complete with mayoral proclamation, visiting dignitaries, formal luncheon and the presentation of a plaque. Terry startled the sponsors more than a little when he insisted that *all his employees* be invited to the banquet. The business leaders of Roanoke were willing to sit down with a black man who brings a million dollars

a year into town, but they had not expected to break bread
with the man who sweeps out the plant.

Terry Manufacturing Company makes dashikis and other
African-style garments, but this business is small and
Terry is not impressed with its potential. He thinks that
most of his products are probably bought by white people.
"I am a businessman," he says, "not a crusader. I'm not
making dresses for black women, I'm making dresses for
women. Now, at the same time, I hope that black people
will have some special pride in us, some appreciation that
this is the only black factory that has gone this far in the
mainstream.

"I want black women to take a good look at what we have
to sell, not because they're black but because they wear
clothes. As a businessman, I think I should go after any
market I see that I can serve profitably. I think a business
person should serve all the people."

In the very competitive ladies' garment business, Terry
feels that the secret of survival is to give your customers
quality and good service so that they will keep coming back
to you, even when competitors offer a slightly lower price.
Most of his sales in the early years were made to a few
large customers, either manufacturers or large distributing
organizations. He has now embarked upon an ambitious
program of developing a network of small retail outlets that
rely on him as their major supplier.

"This country seems to have an almost inexhaustible supply of women who are dying to run a dress shop," Terry
says, "and are saving up money to get started. As a rule
they don't know very much about business and need a lot
of help. So we're going to help them, and then they will sell
our garments.

"We're not going to charge them a big price for the use
of our name the way some of the franchising companies do.
We will help them lay out the store, we will prepare the
criteria and patterns, we will train them and show them
how to train their help. And, since they can't afford to hire
an experienced buyer to go to New York and buy in volume
the way the big stores do, we will supply them with mer-

chandise. If we can we'll manufacture it; otherwise we'll buy it for them. Either way, we'll see that they get style and good value so they'll stay with us. We'll charge them an initial fee for our time and effort, but after that we'll be paid for our services through the margin of profit we receive on the sale of our garments." He has been working on this plan for some time, and expects to sign up the first two or three stores in 1971.

"I think the secret of the success I've had so far," Terry says, "is that I have tried to find a way to understand and love people. I've had many opportunities to figure out ways to get revenge for the ill treatment, but I just haven't done it—I haven't taken a lot of time out to fight. I've been working steadily trying to find a way to achieve my goal.

"Some people might say that my goal is a little selfish, but then self-preservation is the first law of nature. I feel that I must get strong before I can help someone else. I have love and appreciation for my people first and then for all people everywhere. I want to help people and do something about the conditions in which they have to live, and I just haven't used any time to fight or hold anything against anybody. I find that when I sit down to talk with white people, and we get to know each other, our goals are very much the same. Most of us are just trying to get ahead.

"And, you know, you have to work. It doesn't matter who you are or where you come from, if you're going to make more than about seventy-five cents a day you'll have to work for it. One day I had an appointment to see one of the top people in another clothing manufacturing company, and before I even opened the front door I heard horseplay going on. The girl at the reception desk was kidding and carrying on with a young man. They had some soft drinks and they were having a great old time. I must have stood there five minutes and that receptionist didn't even turn around. Finally, the young man noticed me and asked who I wanted to see. . . .

"Now that told me something about that company, because the boss sets the tone of the place, and if he doesn't let people know they're expected to work he's in real trouble. When a new employee comes to work, he feels the atmosphere and acts accordingly. If it's a working place, he'll work. If it's a loafing place, he'll pick that up right away and he'll loaf, too. I never did find the man I had the appointment with, but they showed me through the plant and there wasn't much work being done there. That company failed not too long after that.

"I tell my sons and everybody else in our plant there's only one guy in the place that can take it easy, and that's me. Everybody else has got to work, and if somebody has so much free time that he can relax, you'd better let me know about it, because there's something wrong."

Asked whether he would recommend to young men that they go into business for themselves, Terry answered, "If a man is thinking about starting a business, he ought to examine carefully what business is—and also examine himself. If he wants to go into business just because he's tired of being bossed around, he's on the wrong track. When you own a business you can't just do as you please. In fact, you have a lot of bosses, you're working for a lot of people and you have to please a lot of people.

"The right way to go into business is to render a service, not with the idea of being a big man and standing on top cracking a whip. A successful businessman is a servant of the people. And he's got to be prepared to work. Too many people start with the wrong conception. They say, 'Look at that Jesse Terry, he sure has a good life, running around to Detroit last week and Miami this week, I think I'm going into business, too. . . .' Well, he'd better do a little thinking about the times I sat at a sewing machine all night long and saw the sun come up, because that's a bigger part of it than the trips."

As for spare time, Terry doesn't have any. He hasn't been fishing for years. "I get a little recreation on my business trips, an hour here or there to see friends. I get pleasure out of that. I was out of town for four days not long ago, and I guess I took three hours out to visit some old friends. . . ."

Terry is a crusader for rural development. He feels that

there are many advantages to small-town life and that not everyone should move to the big cities. Many would stay where they are if better jobs were available. He is proud that he has been able to provide over eighty jobs in Roanoke and he hopes to increase that figure by twenty before long. "One of the reasons little towns die is that usually a couple of people own everything and they go to sleep, they don't do anything with it, they don't build anything."

He also feels that black people have to be owners if they are ever to control their destinies. "Let me give you an example. That was a magnificent thing they did in Montgomery in the bus boycott, but you know, I thought they should have made an offer to take over that whole bus company and run it. That way they could put in black drivers and managers, too. I tried to tell Dr. King that, but he didn't see it. The same approach could have been used in Memphis when the sanitation men went on strike—make an offer to the city to take over the whole garbage-collecting operation on a contract basis and put all those men back to work for a black-managed company."

Terry and his wife still occupy the small frame bungalow where they have lived for more than twenty years. But they may have to move soon. The Terry Manufacturing Company began business in a small wooden building about 150 feet from the house. Within a year a concrete and cinder-block addition was built on. Two years later, another addition. And two years after that, still another. The company now has 16,000 square feet and is getting crowded again. The next addition, now being planned, will knock down Terry's modest home. He may then have to build a new one and start living like the wealthy businessman that he is.

6

Dempsey J. Travis:
Mortgage Banker

"I couldn't read or write until I was twenty-six years old."

Almost all of the more than 50 million one-family homes in the United States are mortgaged. Most of the mortgages —over $300 billion worth—are held by large lending institutions such as savings and loan associations, mutual-savings banks, commercial banks, life insurance companies and government agencies. These lenders are the principal source of home mortgage money, and even in 1970, when money was very tight and mortgages seemed almost impossible to get, they loaned over $10 billion to homeowners and home buyers.

These large financial organizations are often unfamiliar and impatient with the countless small details of a real-estate transaction—surveys, zoning problems, building permits, title insurance and the like. And a would-be homeowner on, say, the South Side of Chicago cannot possibly know that the Philadelphia Savings Fund Society might be willing to lend him money to buy a house.

The functions of handling these details and bringing the two parties together are fulfilled by a mortgage banker. He acts as an intermediary or broker between huge lending institutions and individual home buyers. Part of his job is to *originate* the mortgage; that is, to bring the borrower and the lender together, process the application and handle all of the details. In addition, he will ordinarily *service* the mortgage on a continuing basis, which means that he collects the payments every month, keeps an eye on the property and the neighborhood, makes sure that the fire insurance is not canceled, and so on.

The mortgage banker provides important services for which he is paid fees that are reasonable yet not insignificant. The originating fee is generally in the area of 1 per cent of the total amount of the mortgage. This is the base of his business, but it is somewhat unpredictable—when money is tight or home building in a slump, it may fall off badly or even completely disappear. The servicing fee is much more modest, perhaps only one-quarter of 1 per cent per year of the amount of the mortgage—but this is bread-and-butter business. Once the banker is set up to handle servicing, the monthly payments roll in year after year, in good times and bad. While the mortgage-banking business can be quite profitable, it takes a good deal of knowhow and experience to become established in it.

Of the more than 3,000 mortgage bankers in the United States who originate over $10 billion worth of mortgages every year and service well over $100 billion worth, only twenty-one are black, and twenty of these have entered the business since 1962.

The first of the twenty-one is an energetic and imaginative businessman from Chicago's South Side who decided in 1953 to become a mortgage banker. It was almost ten years before he was able to take the first preliminary steps and almost fifteen years before he was really established and allowed to join the club. It was his help and encouragement, as well as his successful example, that paved the way for the twenty brothers who followed him.

Dempsey J. Travis first took an interest in real estate in 1949. By that time he had finished college and was studying law at Chicago Kent College of Law. It happened that during an unused hour in his schedule the only course available was Principles of Real Estate. Travis never liked to waste time, so he signed up. "I figured you never can tell, I might buy a house someday," he says. "I didn't start out with the idea of being a real-estate broker—that never occurred to me. On the South Side we had never seen a black real-estate man, except for the poor guy they would hire to go around and collect rents.

"In about the second week of the course," recalls Travis, "we came to an example in the textbook in which a broker put together a $100,000 sale and collected a commission of $5,000. I couldn't believe it. Remember, this was 1949, and at that time $5,000 was more than I had made in *any ten-year period* of my life. The instructor assured me that yes indeed, the broker would normally collect $5,000 in cash as his commission on a $100,000 sale. At that precise moment I developed a very intense interest in real estate.

"I had been having second thoughts about law, anyway. I had gotten acquainted with some black lawyers, and they weren't doing very well. About the only law they practiced was matrimonial and criminal. There was no such thing as a black corporation lawyer or a black tax lawyer, and I had never heard of a black lawyer getting a retainer. I decided to switch to real estate."

After finishing the course, Travis applied for a license as a real-estate broker in Chicago. His application was approved with no particular difficulty, but the fee was $50 and he had only $25. When he offered a friend a half interest in his proposed real-estate business if he would put in the other $25, the friend declined—and has been kicking himself ever since. Travis finally scraped the money together by borrowing from his mother.

"I never will forget 1949," said Travis. "It was a very lean period. My wife and I were married in September, and she was working as a proofreader, making about $35 a week. I had one suit and one pair of shoes, and of course no car to get around in, and here I was trying to be a real-estate broker. I was borrowing office space from a lawyer whose practice was so marginal that he also had a job at the post office. Sometimes there was somebody there to answer the phone and sometimes there wasn't; if the call was for me, I often didn't get the message.

"We were invited out for Thanksgiving dinner that year, and I think our friends realized that we weren't eating very well. They had a spread of food like I've never seen, and on top of that they insisted that we take some home. We went out of there with enough stuff to last for six days.

"Finally, I thought I saw my first deal shaping up. I had made contact with a real-estate speculator who owned a twenty-four-flat building on West Jackson Boulevard, and my lawyer friend had a client who was interested in buying it. The commission was to be $2,500, and the lawyer and I would split it. That speculator must have known how hungry we were, because he bought us lunch one day and told us that the commission had to be cut to $1,500—$750 apiece. I looked at my friend and he looked at me—but we said okay.

"Then, a month or so later, this character came around again with a story about unpaid taxes that would have to come out of our commission, too. That was $900 more. We had started with $2,500 and now we were down to $600—and that was for two of us. It was a few days before Christmas—I had a new bride and I couldn't afford to buy her a candy bar—but I told him, 'Man, I'm hungry but I'm not that hungry!'

"We killed that deal right then. And from that day I have never done business with a speculator, and I tell my salesmen the same thing—get an exclusive agency agreement, with the amount of the commission specified in writing; that way you keep control of the negotiations. If you can't get that, don't waste your time with it.

"Well, it was a very bad Christmas. And January and February were worse. Then I did something really crazy. I had the feeling that I was missing telephone calls that might lead to business, so we decided that my wife would quit her job so she could answer the phone for me while I was out making rounds. Now our income was zero.

"We had to do something to put beans on the table, so I signed up to be a census taker. They assigned me some of those high-rise public-housing projects where you took your life in your hands to get into the elevator. It didn't bother me, though. I'd bang on those doors, holler 'Government!' and make the count, then go on to the next one. They paid 10¢ a name. In a few days I counted enough people to bring in almost $300.

"At last, in May of 1950, I made my first sale. It was a small building and the commission was supposed to be $900. I sat down with the lawyers who represented the buyer and the seller; they saw that I was new in the business, and I guess they thought I was an easy mark. They decided that $900 was too much for me and they should have $250 each. I said to myself, 'Here we go again.' But I had the presence of mind to suggest that we put the whole $900 in escrow with the title insurance company, and that we have a written agreement as to how it would be distributed after the sale was completed. 'Oh, no,' they said, 'we don't have to bother with that, we trust you to give us our share.'

"They were trying to cheat their own clients and conceal from them the fact that they were getting extra money out of the deal. After the deal was closed and I collected the commission one of them called me up and asked for his $250. I told him I had earned my commission and owed him nothing, that if he thought he had anything coming he could sue me. Of course, he never did. That taught me a good technique for dealing with chiselers like that—just tell them it's okay so long as everything is put in writing and all the parties to the transaction know about it, and you'll never hear any more about it. I've had dealings with those two over the years since then, and they never tried any more funny business."

Soon after making his first sale he made a second one, and after that he "never looked back." Travis has intelligence, imagination, drive, good humor, charm—and he likes people. All of these add up to make him an excellent salesman. Travis Realty Company was profitable in 1950 and every year since. It now employs more than a dozen salesmen. The continuing flow of income from real-estate-brokerage commissions has enabled the Travis organization to take on other ventures, which were unprofitable at first, and also to involve itself in nonprofit activities for the benefit of the community at large.

One of the biggest problems in selling real estate—almost as big a problem as getting the buyer and seller to agree on price—is arranging the mortgage financing. Nobody pays cash in the United States of America. The home buyer always wants to make the smallest down payment he can and get the longest possible mortgage at the lowest possible interest rate. But the seller doesn't want to get his money over twenty or twenty-five years—he wants it in cash, and right away. But in the 1950s it was almost impossible for a black man to get a home mortgage in the Chicago area. Banks would not even consider his application; neither would the Federal Housing Administration or the Veterans Administration. Until 1948, real-estate deeds and contracts usually contained a "restrictive covenant" providing that the home could not be resold to non-Caucasians.

Thousands of people in Chicago's South Side ghetto wanted to buy their own homes and had steady jobs and savings for a down payment. Many of them, unable to find mortgage financing, sold themselves into a form of twentieth-century involuntary servitude called the "land contract," which is sanctioned by the laws of the great state of Illinois, and which has been described as combining the harshest features of a lease and a mortgage without any of the advantages of either. The land contract provides that if any payment is missed, the "owner" may be summarily evicted and loses all rights in the house, even though he may have paid many thousands of dollars in principal and interest over as many as fifteen or twenty years. The duly constituted authorities in Chicago will carry out land-contract evictions *without any notice whatever,* so that a man may come home from work to find his wife and children in tears and his furniture on the sidewalk. And he will not get back a penny of what he has paid.

Why does any sensible person enter into such an agreement? Sometimes, of course, people are foolish enough to neither read the fine print nor hire a lawyer to protect their interests. But if a black man wanted to buy a home in Chicago before 1963, especially if he was an employed man of modest means who could not afford a down payment of more than 10 per cent, it was almost impossible for him to find any other financing. (Dempsey Travis has recently worked out a plan to rescue from financial slavery some of these homeowners who don't own their homes by converting their land contracts into conventional mortgages that have been bought by a number of black lending institutions.)

Travis realized that if he could find a way to work out mortgage financing, he could sell a lot of homes. By reading up on the subject he discovered what a mortgage banker was and decided to become one. In a burst of enthusiastic optimism, he organized the Sivart Mortgage Company in 1953 with $25,000 capital. He put up most of the money himself and raised the rest from his own salesmen.

"We were," he says, "ahead of our time." It was almost exactly ten years before Sivart Mortgage was able to take its next forward step. During the 1950s Travis could not find anyone in either private business or government who would enter into a serious discussion of mortgage lending to black people. Finally, in November 1962, President John F. Kennedy issued an executive order directing the federal housing agencies to cease their policies of racial discrimination in the issuance and insuring of home mortgages. Then, and only then, did things begin to move.

Travis found doors closed even in trying to learn something about mortgage banking. Courses are given at Northwestern University, but they were (and are) open only to members of the Mortgage Bankers Association, which rebuffed Travis when he attempted to join.

A minor breakthrough came about 1960, when he was asked by a black insurance company, Chicago Metropolitan

Mutual Assurance, to handle the processing and paper work in connection with some FHA mortgage insurance applications. Although the company was small and could only make twenty or twenty-five mortgage loans a year, Travis sensed that if there were ever to be a breakthrough for black people it would come in government sooner than in private business, and he decided that it was a good idea to get some experience working with the FHA.

Federal authorities may approve a mortgage banking firm as a regular originator and servicer of FHA and VA mortgages if the firm has at least $100,000 capital. In order to qualify, Travis put in $50,000 himself and managed to raise another $100,000 from a dozen black businessmen. (The capital has since been increased to $250,000.)

"I must say our investors had a lot of faith. The mortgage company had been in existence for seven years, and it hadn't done a nickel's worth of business. Furthermore, there was absolutely nothing on the horizon to indicate that it would ever get off the ground. We were in uncharted waters. We were the first—and we were all alone."

Travis persisted. He read everything he could lay his hands on about mortgage banking. Since he was not allowed to attend the school, he approached some of the white mortgage-banking firms and asked them to let him visit and learn how they operated. "They wouldn't even let me in the back door. You talk about a closed society—nothing is closed as tight as the field of commerce.

"I realized that as a single individual I would never get the doors open; so in 1961, I organized an association of black mortgage bankers—United Mortgage Bankers of America. I decided to encourage other black men to enter the field. Now this was pretty crazy. We had never banked our first mortgage, we were barred from the school, we were groping around trying to learn the business—and we set up a school to teach the business to others! It was a classic example of the blind leading the blind, but it worked. Within a few years there were three other black mortgage bankers—in Kansas City, Atlanta and Houston."

After eleven or twelve years in business and after Presi-

dent Kennedy's anti-discrimination order, Sivart Mortgage
Company finally began to bank mortgages. Its first "investor" was Equitable Savings and Loan Association of Brooklyn. ("They discounted the mortgages by 10 per cent when
they bought them, but we were grateful for anything.")
Shortly after that, the International Ladies Garment Workers Union agreed to invest $10 million with Travis and other
black mortgage bankers, with the money to be handled
through a large New York savings bank. Today, Travis has
fourteen investors—that is, lending institutions that buy
the mortgages he originates. In most cases, their prior
approval is not needed. They have developed enough confidence in his ability that they commit, in advance, to buy
whatever mortgages he sends them up to a predetermined
dollar limit.

The next problem was the banks. A mortgage banker
must have a large line of credit so he can "warehouse"
mortgages. For example, the investor may want him to
accumulate them until he has a package totaling $250,000.
This means that he has to borrow the money to carry them
for a few weeks or a few months.

"My first experience along that line was with one of the
big Loop [downtown] banks. We applied for a line of
credit, and after a lot of hassling they finally told me that
they had approved it. Wonderful! My wife and I took off on
a vacation to the Caribbean and stayed a month. All the
time we were there, I was dreaming about the big things
we would do now that we had credit.

"When we got back, I went down to the bank, and they
said yes, it was all set, there was just one little thing. Before
making the loan I had to agree to *give* them control of the
company. 'You can still sit in your office and run it, but we
want to own it.' I told them to go to hell."

Travis then started negotiations with another bank,
where he and his parents had maintained accounts for many
years. The bankers grudgingly indicated that they might
go as high as $30,000. "That was better than nothing,"
Travis recalled, "but not much better. It was about one and
a half mortgages. Here we were, with over $100,000 in

capital and approved by the U.S. government as a mortgage banker. And we weren't asking them to take any risk. Their loan to us would be secured by the pledge of first mortgages on homes, with large lending institutions having made *firm commitments* to buy those mortgages from us within a few months. And on that basis they thought it was a big deal to lend us $30,000.

"I said, 'Listen, why don't you make it $100,000?' The bank president tried to discourage me. He told me that it was very hard even for white men to build up a successful mortgage-banking business and asked what made me think I could do it. I said, 'Well, I just think I can do it. But suppose I'm wrong, I'm not asking you to take any chances, because you'll have your collateral.' We spent about six months going back and forth with them. The forms weren't filled out right and had to be done over. Every time we corrected one thing, they found something else.

"Finally, the chairman of the board called me in and announced grandly that they were going to take a great big chance and let us have a $100,000 line of credit. His manner was so condescending and his tone of voice so contemptuous that I felt just about one inch tall. And I don't like to feel one inch tall. So I just told him to forget the whole thing. I walked out of there and closed all of our accounts, and I never set foot in that bank again.

"My lawyer said, 'I think you have something wrong in your head. You spend six months sweating and struggling for this and then you kick it away in ten seconds!'

" 'No,' I told him, 'I'm not crazy. It's just that I have to live with myself. I have to look at myself when I shave in the morning. There are some things I can't do. We're right back where we started, walking the streets, with nothing but our own capital. But I'd rather walk the streets than take his money with all the humiliation and indignities that go with it.' "

One day a Chinese businessman suggested that he visit the Central National Bank. It took them only one week to approve a credit line of $50,000, and they added that if things worked out it could be increased. Within a year they had raised it to $500,000, and by 1971 Travis had a $2.2 million line of credit with Central National, the maximum they were permitted to lend to any single borrower.

The Travis organization now has a profitable real-estate-brokerage business, an insurance-brokerage business, and it services over $50 million worth of mortgages for fourteen lending institutions. In addition to originating residential mortgages, mostly for black home buyers, and placing them with lending institutions, including such huge firms as Equitable Life Assurance Society and The New York Bank for Savings, it is now originating and placing mortgages on commercial and industrial properties throughout the country—for example, a motel in Louisiana, a church in Michigan and a chemical plant in Alabama. It manages several housing developments totaling more than 2,000 apartments, owns a number of properties, and has just completed a $5,000,000 twenty-four-story apartment building at Sixty-third Street and Michigan Avenue in Chicago.

Travis is proud that he has been able to build a successful and prosperous organization. But he is also pleased to have charted a new course for black men in the mortgage-banking field. The United Mortgage Bankers of America, which he founded in 1961, now has twenty-one operating mortgage bankers as members—sixteen of these have met the $100,000 capital requirement and been approved by FHA to originate and service government-insured mortgages. It also has thirty-five other members—some of whom are title insurance companies and lending institutions. Others are real-estate brokers who hope to follow Travis's example and join the banking field.

Dempsey J. Travis was born in Chicago in 1920. His father was a laborer who always worked regularly, even though he was cut back to two days a week during the Depression. "We always had something to eat, but sometimes it was beans three times a day. My clothes were clean, but they weren't always new. I graduated from high school in a suit that had been handed down from my uncle to my father to me.

"My mother really deserves the credit for a great deal of what I have accomplished. She is the warmest, most out-going kind of person—she just loves people. She will go over and get on a bus to go downtown, and by the time she gets there she has made at least one friend. They take down each other's names and phone numbers and after that they visit back and forth. She has a whole book full of names of people she met on the bus or the elevated train."

Travis's parents started teaching him music when he was three. By the time he was thirteen, he was earning money as a musician, even though he couldn't join the union until he was sixteen. He plays the piano and violin.

"I suppose I might have stayed with music, even though it didn't pay too well," says Travis, "but I developed an interest in business while I was in the Army. In fact, quite a number of things happened to me in the Army. . . ."

He was inducted in 1942 and almost immediately became a band conductor, playing regularly at the USO center. But it wasn't long before he began to get into trouble. "The first sergeant resented the fact that I went into town every Friday and Saturday night to play with the band, and he seemed to think I ought to bring back half a pint for him. I really didn't see why I should. Things went from bad to worse—finally he took after me on something and I called him a liar, which he was, in front of the whole platoon. . . . You see, I can compromise on a lot of things, but not where personal dignity is concerned."

After the controversy, Travis was transferred to a place called Shenango, Pennsylvania. "That place was a hell hole. You stepped off the train into mud up to your knees. And the food wasn't fit to feed to pigs. I am sure they were serv-ing us horse meat."

The Army was segregated in those days, and the facilities at Shenango were Jim Crow. There was a large recreation center and movie theater for the white soldiers, but "our theater was a little cubicle. One night after the movie, we heard that one of the guys had gone into the white post exchange to try to buy a beer and they had beaten him up and knocked one of his eyes out. We were pretty sore about that, but nobody started any trouble. We were just standing around talking in front of that theater, maybe a hundred of us, partly because there was nothing else to do. There was no disturbance, though. I noticed several jeeps and trucks driving up, but I didn't pay too much attention.

"Then all of a sudden, without any warning, without anybody giving us an order to disperse or anything else, all the lights went out and *they started shooting at us.* The United States Army just deliberately opened fire on a peaceful assemblage of black men. . . ."

Travis says that the man next to him was killed instantly. He himself was shot twice. "The first shot hit me in the hip and I started to fall. It was a good thing I did, because the second shot hit me in the back just below my shoulder—if I hadn't been falling I'm sure it would have gone right into my heart."

In 1770, the British killed four white men and one black man, and that went into history books as the Boston massacre. In 1943, the U.S. Army shot at least a dozen unarmed black men and killed at least one. The FBI "investigated," but no newspaper carried a line about the Shenango massacre.

Travis was transferred a couple of times, ending up at Aberdeen Proving Grounds in Maryland. He thinks that something in his record or one of the tests he took showed the Army that he had some intelligence, "because they decided to make me a typist, even though I had never touched a typewriter. They handed me the instruction book and told me to teach myself to type. So I did. It's not that hard; all it takes is drill and practice. Besides, I had some finger dexterity from the piano."

He was made a clerk in a post exchange, then promoted after a month to assistant manager and not long after that to manager. Then he was moved to a larger PX as manager. "I had never run a business before, but I seemed to have an ability to organize and keep track of details. I did so well that they told me I had won a prize for operational and managerial excellence. They came around and took my picture and gave me a scroll, but then they said, 'Now you understand this will not be published in the paper—that's the way things are in Maryland.'

"By this time it was getting toward the end of the war, and the same United States Army that had tried its best to kill me now urged me to re-enlist! I said no thanks. I wanted to go back to school. I was discharged in time to make the February entrance class at Roosevelt University in Chicago.

"I was pretty pleased with life in those days. I had known I could make a living as a musician, but now I also knew that I had organizing and business ability. I had survived the Army, and I saw good things ahead. Then I took the entrance exam for Roosevelt . . . *and they told me I was illiterate!* They said I could barely read and write, that it was hopeless for me to try to go to college. They said I should be a plumber or a laborer of some kind."

Travis had attended the Chicago public schools. His grade school had gone on double shifts even in the early 1930s. Then he went to Du Sable High School,* where "the teachers spent most of their time out in the hall gabbing with each other while the class sat and did nothing. In twelve years of public school I can remember only three teachers that *tried* to teach us something. Du Sable High School was a jungle. There's only one good thing I can say about it— and it's a terrible thing to say—it wasn't as bad then as it is now."

Overcome by disgust and bitterness, Travis took a job as a laborer at the stockyards on Chicago's southwest side. The superintendent there noticed that he had more drive and intelligence than most laborers and advised him to better himself. "In fact, he insisted on it. He told me I could work two more weeks but that if I hadn't found a better job by then he would fire me. He said, 'Why don't you try doing income-tax returns for people? There's a real need for that and I think you can do it.' "

Taking the man at his word, Travis set himself up in business preparing income-tax returns in a storefront church run by a cousin. "I used that congregation to prac-

* Named for Jean Baptiste Point du Sable, a black fur trader and trapper who founded the city of Chicago.

tice on, and it worked out well. Even though I supposedly couldn't read or write, everybody got what was coming to him and nobody went to jail, so I began to feel a little better. In fact, I started thinking about trying college again."

After some searching, Travis found that he could enroll in night classes at Englewood Junior College without taking an entrance exam. He took courses in accounting and sociology and received a B plus in both, "and that made me feel a little better, too."

Next he tried Wilson Junior College. Although he managed to get in, he was told that he would have to take remedial reading and remedial English. Travis remembers that at the beginning of the first class, the instructor said, " 'Now I think I should start out by telling you that if you have gone this far in life and still have to be assigned to this remedial reading class, you'd just better face the fact that you're not going to make it. You've got the cards stacked against you. The statistics show that of every hundred people who come into this class, only one graduates from college. . . .' I just decided that I was going to be that one."

He had no counseling, no adviser to turn to, and he also signed up for English literature. "Now get this picture. I'm taking remedial reading and remedial English, I'm laboriously struggling through grade-school readers, figuring out one word at a time, and at the same time I'm taking English literature. I'd spend half an hour or forty-five minutes on a single page. I used to stay up until one or two o'clock in the morning, and my mother would say, 'Why don't you get some sleep?' I'd say, 'Mama, there's no time to sleep, I've got to learn to read.'

"I'd wrestle my way through Hawthorne or Thoreau or Sinclair Lewis and write a report on it, and the teacher would just look at me sadly. Wonderful man—his name was Dr. Ernst. I'd say, 'What did I do wrong?' and he'd say, 'Well, you just didn't understand what you read . . . but why don't you try it again?' And so I'd try it again.

"Then one day it all paid off—all that hard work, all that struggle. I was wrestling through a book on political science in my usual way, one word and one phrase at a time—when suddenly it clicked! It became clear, it all fell into place. The phrases fit together into sentences, the sentences fit together into paragraphs and ideas. All of a sudden I began to read just the way everybody else does. . . .

"I let out a holler and my mother came running—I think she thought I'd been shot. I said, 'Mama . . . great God A'mighty . . . *I can read!*'

"Not long after that the writing clicked, too. It had been extremely difficult, almost impossible, for me to express myself coherently, to describe anything, to make any kind of sensible argument or express an idea. If you can't grasp ideas when you read them, you certainly can't formulate and re-create them. If you can't read, you certainly can't write.

"About a week later I was trying to put together a letter to the VA complaining about the fact that I never received disability payments, even though my wounds had never healed properly. Up until then it was all I could do to get a couple of sentences written, and suddenly I found I had written five pages! I was describing, explaining, giving reasons, drawing conclusions. . . . I had learned to read, and now I had learned to write!

"I was twenty-six years old. . . ."

Travis put the secret of his success this way: "I have never placed making a dollar ahead of social good. Putting people into decent homes is pretty important, and if I get paid as a by-product, then I am being paid for service rendered. I would never involve a person in an unconscionable deal, such as a land contract, just to put money into my pocket. I have passed up a lot of chances to do that, too. I won't exploit people for my own gain. You have to decide what your principles are and stick to them.

"If your only motivation is that you want to be rich, I don't think you will make it. I think I'll make all the money I can ever spend by rendering service to the community.

"I think I deal sincerely with people. I try to identify

with them, to understand their needs and then put together something that makes sense for them, not stick them with an overpriced house that they won't be able to make the payments on just so I get a bigger commission. And it has worked. Not a single family that bought a home through us has ever lost it through foreclosure. We are proud of that.

"I think every black entrepreneur has to have a whole lot of social worker in him. And yet I've found that you can deal fairly with people and make a lot of money at the same time. Seems to me there are quite a few businessmen who don't understand that, including some in the biggest companies in this country...."

Travis normally gets up at 5:00 A.M. Four mornings a week he bicycles from the far South Side, where he lives, to Lincoln Park on the North Side and back—a total of about twenty miles. "While I'm looking at the grass and the lake, my thinking clears up. I get a lot of work done and a lot of problems solved on that bicycle path while my competitors are still asleep. When I get back to the house, I can fill out a whole notebook of things to be done." Every Saturday he has a training session for his salesmen, to teach them what he had to teach himself about the real-estate business. The meeting starts at 7:30 A.M.

Travis and his wife have no children. They live in an apartment building that he owns. His mother, now in her seventies, has an apartment there, and she still makes friends everywhere she goes, although she doesn't ride the bus as much as she used to. His hobbies are music and photography, and he does an enormous amount of reading. "Don't forget, I missed twenty-six years that I have to make up for."

Travis neither smokes nor drinks, and has had only two cups of coffee in his life. "What wakes me up in the morning is the excitement of another day. I jump out of bed because I want to get started. I don't understand why people need drugs and stimulants. Life itself—doing things— that's plenty of stimulation for me."

Although he has had more than his share of setbacks and

rebuffs, he remains cheerful and optimistic. Almost every one of the many newspaper photographs of Dempsey Travis shows him smiling or talking animatedly. "There are plenty of problems, but that doesn't mean you have to go around lookin' like a prune. . . .

"The way I see it, the number-one objective is to solve the problem. It's no good grumbling or getting mad, because that doesn't help solve the problem. I've never seen a man who was mad and was thinking. Most of the time when a man is really angry, he is destroying himself."

Having started his mortgage-banking company in 1953, Travis repeatedly applied and was repeatedly rejected for membership in the Mortgage Bankers Association. One day in 1966, he planned to inspect a building with a visitor from New York who represented a large lending institution. "He asked me to pick him up at a hotel downtown, and when I drove up I noticed that the MBA convention was going on there. As we rode out to the property he told me rather positively what interest rates would be in the months ahead. I said, 'What makes you so sure?'

"He said, 'Well, you see, one of the most important functions of the MBA convention is to give us a chance to compare notes with other guys from around the country. That way we get a feel of how building is going and the money supply and so on, and when we come out of there we have a pretty good knowledge of what the money market will be for the next six months to a year.'

"Now this really got to me. Here I was trying to be a mortgage banker, and I was completely frozen out of that club—the only place in the country where you could find out what was really going on. No black man had ever been in one of those meetings. And this was the same MBA that ran a mortgage-banking school that I had never been permitted to attend.

"There was another thing. My friend from New York had worked with me on a number of deals and he knew I knew my stuff. He also knew I was vitally interested in what was going on there, but it never occurred to him to wonder why I wasn't at that very important meeting."

Characteristically, Travis channeled his anger into direct action. He wrote a five-page letter to President Lyndon B. Johnson, describing and explaining in detail that denial of MBA membership constituted a serious handicap to him in the conduct of his business. The President assigned the matter to one of his assistants, and things started to move —slowly. Even with direct prodding from the White House, Travis found it very difficult to get the necessary recommendations from two members. One businessman said, "Dempsey, I'll sign for you but you *know* they're not gonna let you in." He got the other signature from his banker. Then the association spent several months inspecting and investigating and studying.

"I think they realized that they would have to let a black man in, but they didn't want me to be the first. I was a radical. Not long before that, I had organized a boycott of the world's largest insurance company, which collects more life-insurance premiums from black people than all the rest put together, but which had never given a black mortgage banker the time of day or made mortgages available to black home buyers. They finally did let me in, because they couldn't find any reason not to, but they saw to it that several staff guys from various insurance companies joined at the same time. They couldn't stand me being the only one."

It had taken Travis a little over thirteen years to be admitted to membership in the Mortgage Bankers Association. He immediately signed up for the mortgage-banking course and insisted that all of his senior executives also enroll in it.

The real-estate industry is so backward that it has almost total resistance to the adoption, or even the consideration, of new ideas. Things are done in a certain way because they have always been done that way; it rarely occurs to anyone to suggest an improvement. Nevertheless, there has been a good deal of discussion in recent years about a new system of handling mortgages. Perhaps more people would be willing to lend money on the security of real estate if mortgages were more *liquid*—that is, if it were possible to sell a mortgage readily. Why shouldn't mortgages be bought and sold regularly in one marketplace, just like stocks and bonds? Once again, Dempsey Travis was far ahead of his time. Years ago, he saw that this would come; in 1960, in order to start learning about it and get ready for it, he joined the National Association of Securities Dealers, the trade organization of stockbrokers.

The insurance companies, savings banks and other fiduciary institutions in the United States have assets of over $1 trillion. About one-third of this total is invested in home mortgages. Dempsey J. Travis has been directly responsible for putting black men, including himself, into positions where they can direct the investment of some of this money for the benefit of black people. By the end of 1970, he and other black mortgage bankers who had followed his lead were servicing over $300 million worth of mortgages. He probably has more *effective* financial power and leverage than any other black man in the country.

7

Edward Davis: First Black
New-Car Dealer in the U.S.

*I expect to pass through this way but once. If therefore
there be any kindness I can show or any good I can do for
my fellow beings, let me not defer or neglect it, for I shall
not pass this way again.*

*Oh, say can you see, by the dawn's early light,
What so proudly we hailed, at the twilight's last gleaming?
Whose broad stripes and bright stars, thro' the perilous
    fight,
O'er the ramparts we watched, were so gallantly streaming?
And the rackets' red glare, the bombs bursting in air,
Gave proof through the night, that our flag was still there.
Oh, say, does that star spangled banner yet wave
O'er the land of the free and the home of the brave?*

           —Signs on the wall of Edward Davis's office

The second black new-car dealer obtained his franchise
in 1966. By that time Edward Davis of Detroit had been
running his own business selling cars for almost thirty
years, had been a new-car dealer for almost twenty, and
had already had one automobile company shot out from
under him.

In 1970, at the age of fifty-seven, Davis feels that "we've
moved forward pretty steadily over the years. Once in a
while we slip back, but almost every year has been better
than the one before it. Right now, this country is in a recession, according to what I read, and one of the places
that's hardest hit is Detroit. But 1970 is going to be the best
year we ever had."

Edward Davis has great natural ability to persuade people to do what he wants them to do, which is called selling, and to make inanimate objects do what he wants them to do, which is called mechanics. As a high-school student in Detroit in 1930, he traveled ten miles a day to work at a garage. The pay was 20¢ a day for carfare plus invaluable experience. "To this day," he says, "if you tell me over the phone what your car is doing and what kind of noise it is making, I can usually tell you what is wrong with it."

Davis graduated from high school in the depths of the Depression, when there were very few jobs for white men and none at all for black men. And so he made his own job. He approached the proprietor of a gas station and said, "Why don't you let me wash cars here for your customers?" In the deal they worked out, he gave the station "the first dollar I made every day."

One of his regular car-wash customers, a supervisor at the Dodge assembly plant, liked the way the energetic young Davis worked, and offered him a regular job at Dodge. He started in the foundry and later became a machine operator at a wage of 27¢ an hour.

"When I got my first week's paycheck, something like $12.18, I went along with the other men to a check-cashing place. They took the 18¢ for cashing the check and gave me $12.00. That was the first and last time I paid to have a check cashed. The next week I opened a bank account, and after that I cashed my check at the bank. I also tried to deposit at least $2.00 or $3.00 in my account every week."

As far back as he could remember, Davis had wanted to run his own business. "I just didn't see anything else I could do when I looked at the kind of jobs that Negroes could get." While working at Dodge, he began to sell cars for a local Chrysler dealer, making $10 here and $25 there. In 1935, he left Dodge and went to work full time as a car salesman. He continued to make bank deposits every week.

He was, and is, a very good salesman. By 1936, he was making between $500 and $600 a month, which was very good money in those days—in fact, it was the price of a new car. He also took night courses in business administration at Wayne State University. "At first, my goal was to become the owner of the business where I worked. But they were so prejudiced that I couldn't stay around there."

In 1937, when Edward Davis was twenty-four and had $2,900 in the bank, he opened his own used-car business. He was completely on his own and received no help from anybody. There was no Small Business Administration in those days, no anti-discrimination legislation, no encouragement for black capitalism.

He started by selling cars that other dealers couldn't sell. He went to a number of other dealers he knew and asked each to let him have one car to put on his lot. "I said, 'When I sell it I'll pay you for it.' They knew me and they knew my word was good, so they went along with it. But of course they gave me their stiffs, the cars that had been sitting on their lots for some time because nobody else could sell them. Well, I sold them.

"When I started out, I wanted to rent a vacant building that had been acquired in a foreclosure by the bank where I had my account. It was producing no income, and they should have been eager to talk to any prospective tenant. Not only that. Since they had my account, they knew I had been saving money—they should have welcomed me with open arms. But they just didn't think I could run a business successfully, and didn't want to be bothered. They didn't really want to talk to me; they wouldn't fix it up for me or anything.

"I kept after them and they finally set a rent of $125 a month, which was way out of line. I looked at the ceiling for a moment, and then I said, 'You know, gentlemen, that comes out to X dollars a foot, and everything else in this area is going for less than half of that.' Well, that shook them up on two counts. Number one, they didn't think I knew anything about the real-estate market, and number two, they didn't know a Negro could do arithmetic in his head.

"We finally worked out a deal that I would pay $65 a month rent plus $20 a month for an option to buy the property, with the provision that if I exercised the option I would get all of the $20 and half of the $65 back to apply against the purchase price of $8,500. They figured that extra $20 a month was clear profit for them, because they didn't think there was one chance in a million that I'd ever exercise the option."

In exactly twelve months Davis came back to buy the property. He offered $2,500 in cash as a down payment and asked them to take back a mortgage of $6,000. They refused on the ground that "we don't make mortgage loans in that area." That didn't make much sense—it was all right for them to *own* a building in that area but not to make a mortgage loan to a regular rent-paying tenant. What they really meant, of course, was that they didn't make mortgage loans to black men.

They finally agreed to sell it to him on a land contract, which he paid off completely in about five years. Davis remained in that location, near downtown Detroit, until 1963.

One of his biggest problems in selling used cars was arranging installment financing for the buyers. After he made calls on two or three loan companies, he found that word had spread to the others. "I think that as soon as I left one place, the fellow would call his friends in other companies and say 'Listen, there's this colored guy who was in here and he'll probably come to see you, too. He's trying to get some used car financing—now we're not gonna give it to him and I'm sure you won't either.' "

When Davis was finally able to persuade one finance company that he was likely to stay in business, they worked out financing *with recourse,* which meant that if the customer didn't make the payments Davis would be held liable. The company had the customer's credit backstopped by Davis's guarantee. "I wouldn't wish that on anybody," Davis says, "but it was one of the greatest things that ever happened to me. I looked at those installment deals very carefully— if they went sour it would hit me right in the pocketbook. That experience made me one of the best credit men in Detroit, and I still am."

Today, his organization processes the credit application all the way through and delivers the car before it sends the papers to the bank or the finance company. "Many times we agree, but once in a while they don't see it our way. They call up and say, 'We don't want to finance this one.'

"I say, 'Well, it's too late, I've already delivered his car to him.'

"Because they value the business relationship with us, they will say, 'Well, okay, but you'd better watch the next one more carefully.'

"Then I say, 'Well, you watch *this* one, and if it goes bad you be sure and let me know.' And that's the last I hear of it. Our credit experience is very good—maybe one out of every 200 cars we sell will develop into a problem."

Davis found it very difficult to arrange installment credit for his customers in the 1930s. In the 1970s, things have changed, but as the French say, the more things change the more they remain the same. Some automobile-finance companies "red-line" certain areas; they circle an area on a map and determine not to make an auto loan to anyone living there, no matter how good his credit rating or salary.

Davis thinks that "white people could understand that they are like a man in a room with a bumblebee. He is much more powerful than the bee, but still the bee can hurt him. If he backs that bee into the corner it will sting him—he will be hurt, and the bee will die. But all he has to do is open the window, stand back and let the bee go free. The bumblebee will be happy and he won't get stung.

"Why don't they turn loose the poor people that have cooked their food and cleaned their homes and have been loyal to them? Why don't they give these poor people a chance . . . ?"

Despite discrimination and the Depression, Davis's used-car operation was a success from the start. He was soon doing a thriving business handling almost every make of car. One day, he had a visit from a Studebaker representative who asked why he didn't handle Studebakers. Davis replied that he wasn't especially interested in them.

"Suppose we made you a Studebaker dealer?"

Davis answered, "Now I just might be able to develop some interest in that." He became a franchised Studebaker dealer in 1940; he also added a service department and continued his used-car business.

No new cars were manufactured from early 1942 until early 1946 because of World War II. During that time, Davis again concentrated on used cars, which were in great demand, and on service. Cars that otherwise would have been junked were kept running, and they needed frequent repairs.

The U.S. Army had a number of Studebaker automobiles and trucks and maintained a large depot near Davis's place of business. Because of the convenient location and the good service he provided, he was soon handling all the maintenance of the Army cars. This business was so substantial that it earned him a draft deferment on the ground that his work was essential to the war effort.

After the war it took several years to meet the pent-up demand for new cars. Then in 1950, because of the Korean War, cars were in short supply again for about two years. During this period, when customers were clamoring to buy cars, the salesmen didn't have to sell, they were able to allocate. All cars were sold at manufacturers' list prices or higher—many salesmen and dealers took cash payments under the table for fast delivery.

"I think we were one of the few dealers in the country that gave customers a fair shake during those years," Davis says. "We had a big board right out in the showroom where everybody could see it, and we posted every customer's name and the date that he had put down his deposit. We took them exactly in order. Even if it was the salesman's brother—or my brother—his name went up there, and he waited his turn like everybody else. And we never charged five dollars over list price. We were smart to handle it that way, because some of those customers are still coming back to us."

When Studebaker shut down in 1957, Davis continued to operate his used-car and service business. For a time he was also vice-president of a Ford dealership.

In the summer of 1963, he happened to be at a cocktail party that was also attended by Lynn Townsend, who had become President of Chrysler Corporation the previous year. Townsend was telling a small group that finding good dealers was one of the company's biggest problems. Somebody asked him, "Have you ever considered a Negro dealer?" At that time there were no black new-car dealers; Davis's Studebaker dealership had been the only one.

"We don't care what color they are, we just need good dealers," replied Townsend.

The other man said, "I know a Negro who would make an excellent dealer for you."

"Well," Townsend said, "I'd like to meet him." Davis was standing a few feet away at the time; he was introduced to Townsend. He called Townsend the next day to make an appointment for serious discussion.

Getting approved for a new-car franchise is a very elaborate process, involving extensive discussion, detailed character and credit checks and a great deal of planning. Under the best circumstances it can take a year or more. That first meeting was in July, and Edward Davis had his franchise by the middle of November.

It takes several hundred thousand dollars to open a new-car dealership in a big city, and most new dealers have to borrow from the manufacturer. Some borrow as much as 75 per cent of their total capital. Davis used his own savings plus what he could borrow on his own. Chrysler didn't have to lend him a dime.

He sold his building downtown and moved to 11825 Dexter Boulevard, where Ed Davis Chrysler-Plymouth opened for business early in 1964, selling Plymouths, Chryslers and Imperials. Most of the customers finance their cars through Chrysler Credit, which produces additional profit for Davis.

As far as his own credit is concerned, he is able to "pick up the phone right now and get more credit than I could ever use. I've been in business in this town for over thirty years and a lot of people know me, and they all know I keep my word. There were times when I couldn't pay a bill on time, but I would always call the man and tell him so. I'd say, 'I can't pay you now,' or 'I can't pay all of it now, but I'll get it to you as soon as I can.' And I always did.

"Every morning I open up the mail first thing, check the bills and if they're okay I get them right over to my controller for payment. We have an understanding with a number of people that we get a 5 per cent discount if we pay the bill within forty-eight hours. That little item earned us $11,000 last year. And you know, that covers one-tenth of my salary." He smiles when he says it. And yet . . .

A substantial percentage of Davis's new-car customers are white, and the proportion increases every year. ("Sometimes I walk through that sales room and every customer there is white.") He has forty-eight employees, most of whom are black.

One of the biggest setbacks in Davis's business career resulted from the civil-rights movement. In the mid-1960s, the trend of the times together with legislation and government pressure led large and small businesses to open up their hiring—slightly. Every company wanted to hire one or two blacks to place near the front door or window. They pirated away men that Davis had trained at his expense. "They all wanted ready-made Negroes in a big hurry," he said, "and they raided me. They took my salesmen, they took my mechanics, they took my supervisors." The first black General Motors dealer in the Detroit area is a man who learned the business as controller for Ed Davis Chrysler-Plymouth, Inc.

Several years ago, he began a calculated effort to hire people with unusual handicaps in addition to being black. He now has seven trainees—some are high-school dropouts, one can read a little but can't write at all, one is deaf and dumb, and one is paralyzed and cannot leave his wheel chair. These men are grateful for the opportunity and they show it by working hard. "I had to go a little carefully at first. I told one of my men, 'Now, I'm going to bring in a trainee and put him with you, but there's a little problem. . . .' They worked out so well that every one of the good production men now has one of these trainees with him. And two of them have graduated to running their own repair stalls in the shop and have men working under them. Eventually, these men will be my best employees, and I'm pretty sure they'll stay with me. . . ."

By the end of 1970, Davis was selling over 1,500 new and used cars every year. Including income from service and

parts, his total gross revenues for the year were close to
$10 million. After expenses there was a substantial amount
left for Edward Davis, the sole owner of the business.

Davis was born in Shreveport, Louisiana, in 1913, one of
five children. He lost his mother in the nationwide influenza
epidemic of 1918. His father was a small businessman, a
resourceful and energetic organizer who turned his hand
to various things. "I remember when I was little he had the
food concession for a big crew that was laying pipeline.
They would set up a camp of tents and start laying pipe, and
after they had progressed ten miles or so they would pick
up the camp and move it. My dad had the contract to feed
the laborers for a dollar a day. He also used to put on
carnivals and fairs."

When he was twelve, Edward Davis was sent to Detroit
to live with an uncle, and he has been there ever since. He
now lives about a mile from his place of business. He was
married in 1941; he and his wife have no children.

"I did not have an easy time building this up," Davis recalled. "Things have been very rough along the way. But
I've had a lot of fun, too. I've learned a lot and gotten a lot
out of it. I enjoy this business—what I do is part of me.
And I still learn something new every day.

"Nowadays I have some things going for me that other
dealers don't have. A lot of people have consciences that
bother them—they want to do something for black people.
For instance, the loan officer that gave me such a hard
time when I wanted to rent that building and later when
I wanted to buy it is now chairman of the board of that
bank. He and I sit together on the executive committee of
the Economic Club of Detroit, and I think it's still bothering
him that he wouldn't let me have a $6,000 first mortgage
over thirty years ago."

Davis has been a member of the Human Relations Commission of Detroit and, as would be expected of a prominent
black man, he belongs to the NAACP and many other organizations that work for civil rights. But he also belongs
to the organizations of the Detroit business establishment

—and there are no other black faces at those meetings. At the prestigious Economic Club of Detroit, he is a vice-president, member of the board of directors and member of the executive committee. And he is a member of the board of directors of the Detroit Chamber of Commerce.

Davis is outwardly genial and relaxed, like any good salesman, and many people don't realize that he is an impatient man with a quick mind and abundant nervous energy that he keeps carefully controlled. He is easy to underestimate, as those who do business with him have found, to their sorrow. He will sit quietly, smiling and nodding and seeming to go along with everything. In fact, he is listening, observing, taking in everything, and is usually six steps ahead of the other fellow.

He gets along on five hours of sleep and puts in long hours in his business. In his spare time he reads and plays golf, sometimes alone—he finds that a good way to get away from the telephone. Very often he returns from the course with several new ideas. "There's nothing," he says, "like a good idea whose time is right. Of course, it isn't enough just to have the idea. You have to follow through on it and put it to good use.

"Another thing is you have to work with people. Many good men go wrong because, even though they're smart, all of their thinking is aimed at taking advantage of somebody. This is something I never do. . . .

"The most important element in business is p-e-o-p-l-e. I think the big companies forget that. They treat their employees like numbers and they respond accordingly. As soon as sales fall off a little bit, the workingman gets a printed slip telling him he's out in the street—they don't even bother to tell him they're sorry. So a man on the assembly line doesn't worry too much if a screw isn't tightened properly—he isn't sure that he'll even be there next week, he may be at the unemployment compensation office. Maybe that's one reason the cars aren't put together as well as they might be. . . .

"We have had some success here, and I've been happy. But there is still more we can do, more prospects we can call on. I have a good sales force, and I push them hard, but I'm always looking for another good salesman. If I find one, I can make room for him. If he's really good, he can take over my job. . . ."

Davis revealed the secret of selling cars successfully. "Anybody can sell. If you want to sell, learn about your product, learn what people want, and then find a way to put together what they want and what you want them to do, and you'll end up having a lot of fun, too. You don't fight with the customer, you don't prove you're smarter than he is. Sometimes the answer is, No, we can't do it that way. But don't take up a lot of time arguing about it. . . . Some people get up in the morning fighting and they fight all day, and nobody makes a sale.

"The alarm clock goes off in the morning, and the wife looks out and says, 'It sure is dreary this morning with all that rain,' and her husband says, 'Yes, but our grass needs the water.' She thinks, '*Our grass* . . . why, isn't that nice . . . *our* grass!' Usually he goes off to work hungry, but first thing you know, she's up fixing his breakfast. So now he's fed and on the way to work. He's happy and she's happy. . . . He's made a sale."

Many years ago, Edward Davis was traveling through the South, and he stopped at a large Studebaker dealership to have some work done on his car. When he was told that the work would take some time because they had only one mechanic and several other cars waiting, Davis decided to stop in and see the owner.

He spoke to the secretary, who delivered his card and said, "There's a Studebaker dealer from Detroit here who wants to say hello."

The man said, "Fine. Send him in."

Davis walked into the office and saw the dealer sitting with his feet on the desk, his hat on his head and Davis's card in his hand. The dealer looked at him and said, "Who are you?"

"Name's Davis."

"What do you want?"

"Nothing."

"Well, then, what are you doing in my office?"

"I just came by to get my car fixed, and I thought we might talk about Studebaker cars."

The dealer's mouth fell open. He looked down at the card in his hand. "You mean *you're* a Studebaker dealer . . .?"

"We started talking about cars," Davis said, "and after a while he took his feet off the desk. We talked some more and then he took his hat off. We kept on talking—by then I had been standing there half an hour—and finally he invited me to sit down. We talked some more, and then he called the girl in and said, 'Call the shop and tell them to take care of Davis's car right away.' He didn't, of course, say Mr. Davis. . . .

"We ended up talking for four hours. As I was leaving, he said, 'Davis, if all the Nigras was like you, we wouldn't have no trouble in this country at all.'

"I said, 'You know, you didn't feel that way when I came in here, and you only changed your mind because you got to know me. Did it ever occur to you that if you got to know some more Negroes, you might find that they are very different from what you always thought . . .?' "

———

This chapter was based upon an interview conducted in the summer of 1970. Unfortunately, the recession of 1970–71 was particularly severe in Detroit, hitting that city harder and lasting longer than Edward Davis expected when we talked with him. In February 1971, as this book was entering its final production stages, Mr. Davis made the business decision to close his new-car dealership. A spokesman for the Chrysler Corporation told the authors that at the time of closing, relations between Mr. Davis and Chrysler were entirely cordial and that the dealership was still making a profit, although not enough, in Mr. Davis's view, to justify continued operation in the face of high interest rates and a static local economy. We are confident that we have not heard the last of this remarkable businessman.

8

A. Otis Smith:
Gas Station Proprietor

"When I get to the station, the first thing I do is go to the bank to make a deposit. Then I change my clothes and put my head under a hood."

Although Albert Otis Smith dropped out of high school twenty years ago, he now owns one of the most successful gasoline stations in New York City and regularly reports income of more than $20,000 a year.

His Shell station at the triangular intersection of 122nd Street, Eighth Avenue and Saint Nicholas Avenue in New York is a sizable business, employing sixteen men full time plus part-time help. Open twenty-four hours a day seven days a week, it grosses $750,000 a year, or over $2,000 every day.

Based on an analysis of the flow of traffic and competing stations in the area, the Shell experts who selected the location projected that after two years of operation the station should reach its maximum potential volume, which they estimated to be not more than 50,000 gallons of gasoline per month. The station opened in April 1966 and reached 50,000 that year. By the end of the two-year period it was doing 90,000; at the end of the fourth year of operation it was selling between 105,000 and 120,000 gallons per month.

Smith has come a long way. He was born on a farm near Oxford, North Carolina, in 1931, the eighth child in a family of nine, seven boys and two girls. His father was a logging contractor as well as a farmer. He made deals with sawmills in the area whereby he would cut and haul to them and quote a single overall price for the entire job. If he miscalculated and set the price too low, he took the loss; on the other hand, anything he could save on time and labor meant more profit for him. He employed as many as thirteen men and had his own tractors, trucks and horses.

"My dad used to bring home $200 a week right through the Depression," Otis recalled "and that was a lot of money in rural North Carolina in those days. Of course, he knew what hard work was. As far back as I can remember, he would leave the house at five o'clock in the morning and usually not come back until seven or eight o'clock at night. I think I learned something from that."

Young Smith always liked to take things apart and put them back together, particularly cars. By the age of ten he had learned how to use tools and make simple auto repairs, and at fourteen he was working in his brother's garage. He could start at 7:00 A.M., take an automobile engine apart, grind the valves, groove the pistons, replace the cylinder sleeves, rebuild the engine and have the car ready to drive away by 6:00 P.M. the same day.

In 1950, having finished the tenth grade, he decided to leave North Carolina to have a look at the rest of the world. He went to Boston and got a job washing cars. The pay was only $45 a week, but he averaged $8 to $10 a day in tips.

"I should have known better," he said "but I didn't even mention that I was a mechanic. They said they wanted a man to wash cars, so I went to work washing cars. After I had been there three or four months, the regular mechanic got into trouble one day. He took the distributor off a car that was almost new and couldn't put it back on. The owner was really mad and was about to go and get his lawyer. The manager asked me whether I knew anything about cars. I said, 'I sure do,' and I got it working in about five minutes. After that I did all the mechanical work at that station."

Smith was drafted in 1952 and served a little over two years as a medical corpsman in Europe. Much of his time was spent driving ambulances and also repairing them, since he did a much better job than the motor pool.

After his military service he spent a few months with his family in North Carolina. "I needed some spending money, so I went to work unloading trucks at a factory there. They had 300-pound bales of tobacco that three or four of us had to throw around. After one week I was promoted to truck driver, and after two months they put me in charge of the fleet of trucks. The boss used to give me the keys, and I'd go down there on Saturday and do all the repairs."

Smith then spent a couple of years at his old job in Boston. In 1956, he married a girl he had met a month before in North Carolina, and they moved to Los Angeles ("I heard somebody say it was nice out there"). He managed a gas station for about a year and then decided to try New York.

"When I came to New York I didn't know anybody and, you know, people don't just hire you off the street. But it happened that I passed a Gulf station at 116th Street and Eighth Avenue and saw that they were flooded with repair work. I asked if they needed any help. The manager said, 'What can you do?' I told him I could do most anything around a gas station. He asked me if I could do tune-ups and I said, 'Sure.'

"He had three tune-ups going, and one of them was all taken apart with bolts all over the floor. I asked him where the tools were. In about an hour and a half I had all three of those cars done. They gave me a permanent job. As soon as the work came in I'd knock it out.

"The boss watched me for a few days and then said to

his manager, 'I thought you told me he's a good worker—but every time I look he's sitting down smoking a cigarette.' I was sitting around because I had finished everything. I couldn't stay busy."

After about a year there, Smith became the manager of the station; two years later, in 1960, he bought it for $6,000, all of which he had saved. In 1963, not satisfied with the small station at 116th Street, he moved to a Mobil station that had been standing unused at 151st Street and Saint Nicholas Avenue. After another year, he decided to move again—this time to a Shell station at Fifth Avenue and 110th Street.

Smith has remained with Shell ever since. He feels they have treated him fairly; they, in turn, are extremely pleased with him. When he started, they asked him to take a course in station management. He found it helpful even though he had been in the business for ten years.

When Shell realized what a valuable man they had they began thinking of moving him to a larger station. A piece of land at 122nd Street and Saint Nicholas Avenue proved to be just right, and after demolishing the old garage on it, Shell built a station at a cost of about $170,000. Smith's monthly rent was to be determined by the amount of gas he sold. The formula is 2¢ a gallon up to 50,000 gallons; 1.5¢ between 50,000 and 70,000 gallons and 1¢ from 70,000 to 90,000. No rent is charged on sales over 90,000 gallons. In a little more than two years, Smith was beating Shell on the rent, so to speak, by selling more than 90,000 a month. In 1968, and again in 1969, the Harlem Service Center had higher gross revenues than any other Shell station in the Brooklyn district, which comprises Manhattan, Brooklyn, Queens and Long Island. This is no small achievement since Smith, operating on a crowded corner in Harlem, competes for first place with huge stations on heavily traveled highways in suburban Nassau County.

In addition to selling gas, oil, tires, batteries and accessories, the station handles minor repairs and replacement of generators, starters, brakes and the like—work that takes an hour or less. Smith would like to do major repairs but he doesn't have the space to handle work that takes a day or two. He is interested in buying a three-story parking garage next door for use as a car wash and complete repair garage, but the asking price is prohibitive.

In four years of operation, his station has never been robbed. Smith thinks this is because there are almost always at least three people working there, even at 3:00 or 4:00 A.M. "I've seen some of them coming by to look us over, and I know what they are thinking. But they change their minds when they see how many people we have around the place."

Smith credits his success to the way he deals with people. "If you're sincere with people and try to gain their confidence, whether it's in business or socially, and if you live up to your obligations, it's almost impossible to fail. And you never back off from a problem. The harder it gets, the harder you push. As much opportunity as there is to learn things in New York, you learn almost anything you want to; and you can do almost what you want to do, what you've built in your mind to do."

Smith usually gets to the station shortly after noon and stays until the midnight shift comes on and gets settled. That is his schedule six days a week. On Sunday he relaxes with his wife and daughter. It does not even occur to him to mention those long hours as contributive to his success, until he is reminded of it. "Well, that's true, I never have been a clock watcher. I never know what time it is; I just want to finish the job. I can't leave a thing until it's finished. Most people—ten minutes before quitting time they've already quit and they're washing their hands. I could never see that, because I can't find out where you're going when you leave. What difference does an hour make?"

Smith is well known throughout Harlem. He says that some of his customers "will drive past six or seven stations to come in here, because they know I will give them a fair shake. I remember one time two city building inspectors came in and said they wanted a battery charge, the starter wasn't working right. Well, we charged the battery, but that didn't do any good because they had starter trouble.

I called several parts stores, but we couldn't find a starter for that particular car—it was a six-cylinder Le Mans with overhead cams. They said, 'What can we do?' It was starting to get dark, and you know these government people get very uncomfortable in Harlem after the sun goes down.

"I said, 'Just give me about thirty minutes and we'll see.' I had one of the fellows take the starter off and throw it in the vise. The brushes were worn down to the plastic and the armature had big gashes in it. I put in some new brushes and sanded that armature down and re-grooved it. Then I put it together and back on the car. And one of them was watching me the whole time. I told him, 'Now you understand this is not a rebuilt starter. It might last you a year but it might last you only a week.'

"He said, 'That's all right, you did the job.' I charged them $15, and they were very happy. They come back regularly now, both of them. Once you get a satisfied customer, he'll drive twenty miles to get to you. I've made a lot of good customers that way, just by helping them out of a spot."

Smith is a strong booster of the Shell Oil Company and its products. He refuses to sell any of the heavily advertised oil and gasoline additives. If a customer asks for them, he says, "What do you want to put that stuff in your car for? Shell spends millions of dollars on research, they are constantly improving the formula for their products, and all the additives you need are right in their oil and their gasoline."

He has seen two businesses "ruined by taking advantage of people or by overselling. At one place where I used to work, all the employees were on commission for every can of additive they sold. When they pulled the oil stick out to check the oil, they made sure to scrape it on the motor to pick up some dirt. Then they'd tell the customer, 'Look how dirty your oil is!' Sometimes they'd sell a can of oil additive to a customer every time he came in for gas—three or four times in one week. But one by one the customers drifted away, and that station closed down. People catch on sooner or later."

Smith's brother-in-law, William R. Jones, spends several hours a week at the station handling the bookkeeping and preparing the many reports that have to be filed with Shell and various city, state and federal agencies. (Paperwork is one of the heaviest burdens a small businessman has to bear). Jones, a college graduate, also works full time in American Airlines' data-processing center at Briarcliff Manor, New York.

On visits with his family in North Carolina, Smith learned about a new interstate highway that will pass near Oxford. He began to look around quietly for property near the interchange that would be suitable for a gas station, garage and truck facility. Like the good businessman he is, he didn't fall in love with any particular site—though several looked promising. When he found the asking prices too high, he kept looking. "Maybe they'll come down to something reasonable . . . if they don't, we'll just have to find something else."

As with many small businessmen, if Smith has a fault it is in his inability to delegate authority. Outwardly soft-spoken, he seems to have unlimited patience and never raises his voice, but he has very high standards of performance. He is, in fact, a demanding man who is almost never satisfied with the quality and speed of his employees' work.

"People say to me, 'Why do you stay here so late? You have men working for you—why aren't you home?' You know, I *can't* stay home and leave this place alone—it's just impossible. Once the employees find out you're relaxed, they'll be way more relaxed than you are. They're looking for a chance to sit.

"When I get to the station, the first thing I do is go to the bank to make the deposit. Then I change my clothes and put my head under a hood. I just don't like to see work stacked up. My guys look like they're working to the best of their ability, but they're not moving it fast enough to suit me.

"You have to put in the time on anything if you really want to do a job. Once it's going, the important thing is to keep it going. The better it goes, the more you have to stay with it, because every time the income goes up those expenses go up, too."

Smith has a standing offer from Shell for a second station, but he has firmly resisted. "I think we're doing about as much business here as we can handle, and if I had two stations I think I'd actually lose business by being absent from both places a good part of the time."

Smith does not feel that his color has held him back to any great degree in his business activities. The one time he needed a bank loan, he was fortunate in that a manager of a Chase Manhattan branch happened to be a regular customer of his station and knew him well. He now has what he describes as an excellent relationship with the Manufacturers Hanover Trust branch at 125th Street.

He does recall a certain amount of foot dragging in his early negotiations with Shell. He felt that he had filled out all the forms properly, but somehow nothing seemed to happen. He called and wrote repeatedly, but they never called back.

"Finally, one of the guys there was honest enough to tell me, 'We have had some bad experiences in this district with our colored station operators, and we don't think we want to take on any more. But we've checked you out with Dun and Bradstreet and everybody else we can think of, and your record is absolutely clean. *We can't find any reason not to let you have the station.*' "

A Shell Oil Company official who supervises dozens of Shell dealers in Manhattan, Brooklyn, Queens and Long Island was asked for his opinion of Albert Otis Smith. His answer was brief and to the point—"I wish we had a hundred like him."

9

John W. Winters:
Home-Building Contractor

"I built and sold three houses in 1957 and seven houses in 1958. Then in 1959 I bought twelve acres of land and subdivided it into forty-one lots and started building. That project required a great deal of supervision and a lot of my time, so I had to quit my job as a skycap at the airport. . . ."

When he tried to volunteer for military service during World War II, John W. Winters was disqualified because of a childhood ailment, which, although insignificant, left mysterious scars. And so during the war, he worked as a redcap at the Raleigh, North Carolina, railroad station. Noticing that troop trains frequently stopped there late at night, after the station restaurant was closed, John Winters saw opportunity.

"I went to the man who operated the restaurant, and proposed that we try an experiment. Before closing, he would make up sandwiches and pots of coffee and leave them for me. During the night I would board the trains and sell them during the stopover. He thought it over for a few days and decided he liked the idea. He suggested that I work on a 20 per cent commission. The understanding was that every morning I would turn in all the money I had taken in the night before, and that twice a month they would give me a check for my commission. Now, had we set it up so that I kept my 20 per cent every morning before turning in the money, we might never have had a problem. . . .

"Business was so good I kept running out of food to sell, and I had to ask him several times to leave me more sandwiches. My first check for half a month was over two hundred dollars. When the restaurant manager gave it to me, he said, 'You know, John, you're makin' more money than I am.' And the second check was much larger than the first."

"This went on for about two months, and then evidently somebody decided that 'this nigger's makin' too much money.' They told me that they were going to cut my commission from 20 per cent to 10 per cent. Well, that seemed very unfair to me—after all, the 20 per cent figure had been *their* idea, not mine—and I had other things to do anyway, so I gave it up. I told a friend about it, and he decided to take it over. After he got the feel of it he saw that he could do better by making his own sandwiches and coffee. He didn't need them any more. . . .

"These people didn't understand the fundamental basis of business, which is that if it's the right kind of deal, everybody benefits. They had made a fair and honorable proposal and I had agreed to it—if they had kept to it everybody would have prospered. They were making money that they had never made before . . . several hundred dollars a week of brand-new business came to them while they were home asleep. I was the one that brought it to them, but they were so blinded by bigotry, by resentment of what I was making, that they kicked away all of that profit. My friend made a good thing out of that business without them.

"The successful businessman is one who worries about how much risk he is taking and how much *he* makes. If he worries about the other fellow making too much, he will miss some fine opportunities. Many otherwise shrewd men have passed up fortunes because they wanted to hog all the profit and weren't willing to let anybody else have any."

John Winters was born in Raleigh in 1920. His father was then in his fifties, and he also had been born late in *his* father's life; thus three generations of the family cover a broad span of years. Winters's grandfather, Oscar, was born free when Andrew Jackson was President of the United States. Oscar Winters bought his bride's freedom, and several of their children were born free before Emancipation. John Winters's father was born in 1867 and lived to be ninety-two.

In 1852, Oscar Winters took possession of a tract of land—then outside the little town of Raleigh but now close to downtown—to which he eventually obtained title by squatter's rights. Parts of the land were sold or lost over the years, but Winters has reassembled it. He now owns the same tract of land shown on mid-nineteenth-century maps as that owned by "O. Winters," and has acquired adjacent land as well.

Winters's father was a bartender who saw his trade abolished by the Prohibition amendment when he was in his fifties. After that he worked at odd jobs in the state legislature and elsewhere. The family had a difficult time when Winters was a boy. "Because we owned some land, nobody thought we were poor, and we didn't think so either, but we were." Winters was the tenth of twelve children, the youngest of six boys. Several of his older brothers and sisters had moved North. Frequenty he wore cast-off clothing that his sisters were given in the houses where they worked as maids.

His mother was the entrepreneur of the family. "When the circus came to town, she was there with a stand selling hamburgers and fried chicken. And she'd do the same thing at the State Fair. She'd make enough in a few days to keep us going for months. She took in sewing and did almost anything to make an honest dollar. She was a real organizer—she really knew how to put things together.

"Dad and Mother had a difficult time holding onto that land. It seemed that there was always some crisis—it was about to be taken for unpaid taxes or something, but then they'd send an SOS to one of my older brothers up North. He'd send some money and they'd hold on. My mother somehow managed to get some structures put up to bring us some rent income. I don't know how she did it—it was a classic case of mother wit—and I think I inherited my ability to build things and to organize from her. I know I didn't learn it in school."

Winters attended grade school in Raleigh. When he was thirteen, his mother died and he went to New York to live with a sister. He attended Frederick Douglass Junior High in Harlem and Boody Junior High and Boys' High School in Brooklyn.

"Back home in Raleigh we had an antiquated hot-water heater with pipes running through a wood stove. It didn't work very well, and our idea of taking a bath was to run about two inches of water in the bottom of the tub and then do the best we could. I'll never forget the first time I took a bath at my sister's house in New York. She ran that tub full—I just couldn't believe it. The idea of having so much bath water that it covered me up was the most luxurious thing I could imagine."

Winters went to college on football scholarships, first at Long Island University, then at Virginia State and at Shaw University. He and his wife were married in 1941, and when their first child was born, a year later, he had to drop out of college and go to work. Thereafter followed a variety of hard-work jobs. At one time or another in his life, he has shined shoes, cleaned washrooms, scrubbed floors, carried bags, delivered milk, waited on tables and fed chickens. He has always been willing to work at anything that would provide an honest living.

Not long after the short-lived sandwich enterprise, he had saved enough to open a nightclub in Raleigh, and at about the same time he and his wife bought a poultry farm. "Let's say that I was young and inexperienced. After working as hard as I did to save money, I began spending it unwisely, and I made some other mistakes, too."

He lost both the club and the farm in 1948; his fortunes declined to the point where he had to fix up the attic of his father's house and move his family into it. "I decided that if God gave me another opportunity, I would behave in a responsible way and take full advantage of it."

The lack of job opportunities in Raleigh was discouraging. He had applied for a job as a milkman, but since the company had never hired a black he didn't think his chances were very good, so he went to New York and worked as a waiter at Lundy's Restaurant in the Sheepshead Bay section of Brooklyn. While he was there the milk company notified him that the job was his, and he returned to North Carolina.

The dairy was owned by the two brothers of W. Kerr Scott, who was to become the next Governor of North Carolina. (One of the next generation of Scotts became governor in 1968.) When the company decided to hire its first black milkman, its two most experienced route men gave notice. One of the owners called them in and said, "I am sorry to hear you are thinking of leaving. You are my best men and I would hate to lose you. However, I have hired this man who happens to be black, and I have already told him to report to work. If you choose to leave, there is nothing I can do." They backed down and decided to stay, but they told him that they wanted Winters to stick to his own route and mind his own business—they wanted nothing to do with him.

Scott told Winters what these men had said and suggested that he stay away from them. "But I decided I'd make these fellows like me. The first couple of days I rode with a supervisor, and then I was assigned my own route and truck. The next morning I reported at 5:00 A.M. to load my truck and had to wait while the older drivers with seniority loaded first. So I just walked over to one of those two and said, 'Do you mind if I help you load your truck?' He looked surprised and didn't know what to say, but he got into the truck and I started handing crates of milk to him.

"When we finished his truck, I helped the other man load up. And I did that every morning. One morning the second week, they both moved their trucks away from the loading platform, parked them and came back to help me load mine. Eventually we struck up a pretty good rapport. Later when I was made a supervisor, both of those men asked to work for me."

Winters worked as a milkman for several years, starting at $40 a week. Soon the sales on his route had doubled, then tripled, and by 1951 he had been promoted to supervisor at a salary of $65 a week. But he had a wife and six children. (There are now eight children, three boys and five girls.) The attic in his father's house was getting crowded. He found a lot and made a down payment on it. Then he approached his boss and persuaded him to co-sign a note to finance the construction of a house for his family.

It went up quickly, and in 1950 he moved his family out of the attic and into 1309 North Hargett Street. Thus, while earning $65 a week at the dairy, Winters had bought land, arranged financing, designed and built his own home. Even for the postwar era, this was a remarkable achievement in North Carolina.

Next he decided to take advantage of the fact that his job at the dairy kept him busy only from 5:00 A.M. until about noon, and he began to look for ways to earn extra money. He answered an ad for a porter at the Raleigh-Durham airport. They wanted a man to work for a very modest wage cleaning the lobby and halls, running errands, waxing floors and cleaning the rest rooms. Blacks understand that when an ad says "porter," it means somebody who will clean washrooms. When Winters went out to the airport to talk about the job, he again sensed opportunity.

"I asked a few questions, sized up the situation and realized that they didn't have anybody there to help people with their baggage. So we worked out a somewhat different deal than they had had in mind. I didn't want to give up my milk job until I had tried this for a while; but I told them I would come to work at noon, clean the washrooms and sweep the lobby every day, and mop and wax the floors once a week, and for this they wouldn't have to pay me at all if I could also carry bags and keep any tips I made.

"The first week I made over $150, more than twice as

much as I was making as a supervisor at the dairy. And after that I did even better. Many travelers had been complaining to the airlines about the fact that there were no skycaps there. If an elderly person or a woman with a number of heavy suitcases came through, she had to ask the ticket clerk or the limousine driver to carry them. She thought it was part of the service and didn't tip them, so they were unhappy too. Everybody was glad to have me there—it worked out well all around.

"Now, looking back I can see that maybe I could have been smarter. They needed a skycap so badly that they would have been pleased to have me on better terms—they might even have paid me something and let me keep the tips besides, and I wouldn't have had to do all that cleaning. Well, everybody's a millionaire by hindsight, and I don't spend my time worrying about what might have been, or how I only made $99 when I might have made $102. That want ad led me to an opportunity I hadn't been aware of, and I took it and built it into a much greater opportunity.

"There's another thing. A lot of people will sneer at somebody who carries bags or waits on tables or cleans washrooms—they feel that kind of work is degrading. Well, I don't apologize to anybody for doing an honest job of service in order to support my family. The job is what you make it. You don't have to bow down, you don't have to humiliate yourself, you don't have to shuffle and grin.

"And yet there's nothing wrong with being nice to people. A man can smile and still be a man. It doesn't demean me to be pleasant to people. In service jobs you make money according to how you provide the service. If you are friendly and serve people intelligently, and especially if you give them extra service that they don't expect, they will pay you well for it—very well. That skycap job started me on the road to where I am today. It generated both the money to support my family and the capital that started a successful business."

Raleigh, the capital of North Carolina, has a population of about 115,000. Durham is slightly smaller and twenty-three miles away. The airport is roughly midway between, serving both cities and Chapel Hill as well. This tri-city area is the home of Duke and Shaw universities, several campuses of the University of North Carolina, sizable banks and insurance companies, including North Carolina Mutual, and a number of tobacco plants and offices. Thus the airport traffic is heavy and includes many prominent people—governors, legislators, tobacco-company executives, judges, educators. And the cities are small enough that people know each other by name.

Winters made it his business to know by sight the wealthy and busy men who passed through the airport. As he saw one drive into the parking lot, he would hurry over and say "Good morning, Mr. ———. I can see you're in a rush, but the plane to New York is running a few minutes late today so you have plenty of time. Why don't you give me your ticket and go on in and have some breakfast and make your phone calls that you need to make. I'll take your bags and check you in and bring your ticket back to you in the restaurant."

When college started and he would see a group of students obviously bound for the same destination, he would get their baggage checks, put all the bags on a big cart and bring it around to the front door for them. "Sometimes, if somebody was in a real hurry, I'd get out there and grab the bag out of the airplane before they had time to unload it. People are glad to pay for this kind of extra service."

Not long after he started at the airport, Eastern Airlines hired him to do their cleaning, and later United (then Capital) did the same. This enabled Winters to participate in medical plans and other fringe benefits provided for airline employees. As travel continued to expand, he brought a friend out to work with him. Later his oldest son, a teenager, came along too and operated a shoeshine stand. Working hard at the airport, Winters made very good money, enough to pay all of his debts and accumulate some savings. Now, he was ready to take his biggest step.

"Through the grace of God I have always had the ability to build. I can't tell you how it came to me. I never had a day's instruction in mechanical drawing or anything relating to construction or architecture, and yet I found I could read blueprints and understand them perfectly.

"As the years went by, more and more of my friends who came to visit us said, 'John, this is a beautiful house, why don't you build one for me?' It began to dawn on me that there was a tremendous opportunity to build homes for black people, because nobody was doing it. The white home-building contractors had so much business in those years they couldn't be bothered with the black market. They assumed that black people would have serious problems working out mortgage financing, which was true, and that all black people were poor, which wasn't true at all. In Raleigh we have college professors, schoolteachers, civil servants, and also quite a number of people who, although they aren't rich, have good steady jobs in stores, factories and offices."

When a black man wanted a new house, he usually saved his money, bought a piece of land and then found a black carpenter. The carpenter would work until the money ran out—as often as not, the house wouldn't be finished and the man would have to save up some more. With mortgage financing completely unavailable, very few black people were building houses.

Winters began to talk to some of the carpenters who were doing the little building for blacks that was going on, but he didn't find much support. In fact, they laughed. One said, "How can you talk about hiring me, when you know less about building houses than I do?"

"I finally realized," said Winters, "that we were talking two different languages. They understood carpentry, but I was talking about setting up as a general contractor in the home-building field. That involved fitting together all of the pieces—buying land, preparing plans, hiring subcontractors, building the house, doing the landscaping and then selling the finished product."

A large lumber and building-supply company in Raleigh was owned by Cliff Benson, who later became state highway commissioner. Winters had got to know Benson when he carried his bags at the airport, and later he bought lumber and materials from him when he built his own house.

"There were times when I was late in paying him, and once or twice when I didn't have cash, I paid by doing work around his house. But sooner or later, one way or another, I paid him in full, and he remembered that. My record with him was pretty good. He had seen that I could build and he seemed impressed by my determination, so I approached him about providing materials for another house on credit."

Benson agreed that if Winters could pay for the land and get title to it free and clear, he would advance the building materials and take back a first mortgage on the house. He also helped Winters put together a work force, since he knew of a contractor who had just failed and whose experienced, white crew was at liberty. "Those men were pretty skeptical of me," Winters recalled, "but I worked on them the same way I worked on those first two milkmen. . . ."

The house was built on speculation—that is, Winters started it without a buyer. As it happened, he found one fairly rapidly, a man who was moving to Raleigh to become a high-school principal. But the nagging financing problem remained.

Winters and his customer tried the Raleigh branch of the black-owned Mechanics and Farmers Bank. The manager there was firm, holding out no chance whatever of a mortgage loan. Winters decided to approach the bank's president, John Wheeler, whom he had frequently served at the airport; they had also worked together during a controversy involving segregated airport facilities. Winters had fought vigorously against them at considerable risk to his livelihood.

As a result of a trip to the bank's headquarters in Durham and a talk with Wheeler, Mechanics and Farmers made the mortgage loan. When the transaction was closed, the bank paid Winters in full, which meant that he could pay everything he owed for materials and still have enough to buy land and start work on his second house. The same bank took that mortgage, too. The third house was sold to a man who was able to arrange his own mortgage through a local savings and loan association.

Winters says he is going to write a book someday about

the problems black people have in getting mortgage financing to buy homes. "There were cases where I had to go personally to the Federal Housing Administration in Greensboro, after they had refused to insure a mortgage loan for my buyer, and give them written documentation of how he had been slandered and falsely downgraded by the credit bureau. In one case, a small furniture store had reported that a man was a bad credit risk because they were afraid he would go to one of the big department stores, where he would get better values. They wanted to keep him as a customer.

"In another case, the credit-bureau file showed that a small loan company had reported that the man was unreliable and didn't make his payments. I asked them why they had sent in that report, which made it impossible for this man to buy a home.

"They said, 'He came in here and signed an agreement to make his payments on the first of the month, and sometimes he didn't get them in until the twentieth.'

" 'But you kept on making new loans to him, didn't you?'

" 'Oh, yes, *we knew he was good for it, we knew he'd pay it back!*' "

And so, after building a house for his own family in 1950, Winters had built and sold three homes by the end of 1957. The following year he built and sold seven more. He was still working at the airport, although by this time his son and another man were carrying part of that load. He would get out on the job with the building crew at 7:00 A.M. because he had to supervise the work closely. After putting in one full day there, he would get to the airport about 4:30 P.M. and put in another full day until midnight. "I didn't sleep very much, but when you're really enthusiastic about what you're doing, when you can see that you are building something that will grow, you can miss a little sleep."

In 1959, John Winters made an agreement to buy twelve acres of vacant land about a mile from downtown Raleigh. It was owned by a black family. The asking price was high —about twice what it was worth at that time—but they were willing to accept 10 per cent down and take back a first mortgage for the rest. They also agreed that when the utilities were in and he started completing houses, they would release the lots from their lien. This was extremely important—no bank or savings and loan association will make a home-mortgage loan unless they have a first lien on the property.

Winters next managed to get a contractor to put in the streets and sewers on credit and take back a second mortgage. Cliff Benson of the building-supply company helped him arrange this. Of course, by this time John W. Winters and Company had become a very large buyer of building materials.

Winters named the development Madonna Acres. After dividing the land into forty-one building plots, he began building homes to sell in the $20,000 to $30,000 range. He feels that he overpaid for the land by about $2,000 an acre, or about $600 per building plot. But it is always hard to get credit on unimproved land, especially when you need additional credit for utilities and building materials. It was only the extremely liberal financing terms offered by the seller that made it possible for him to put the project together at all. And in real estate, as in any other large business deal, the price and the terms are part of a package—what you lose on one you make up on the other.

Like all state capitals, Raleigh hums with political activity. A combination of circumstances operated to get Winters involved in politics and keep him involved. Shortly after he started work at the dairy, the brother of the two owners ran for governor. Winters was asked to help the successful campaign for W. Kerr Scott, and he was glad to do so. Later his materials supplier, Cliff Benson, became closely associated with Terry Sanford, who in turn was close to John and Robert Kennedy. In 1960, Winters was active in supporting the campaigns of John F. Kennedy for President and Terry Sanford for Governor of North Carolina. A year or so later, when a controversy arose concerning segregated movie theaters in North Carolina, Governor Sanford asked

John Winters to go to Washington to represent him at a meeting with the owners of a large national theater chain. Winters participated in a lengthy and heated discussion in the office of Attorney General Robert F. Kennedy that led to a resolution of the matter.

Raleigh has a seven-man city council, its members elected from the city at large rather than from individual districts. Since the Reconstruction era, all of the councilmen had been white, although several black men have run unsuccessfully. The leaders of Raleigh's black community were seeking a black man of sufficient stature and also sufficient acquaintance with and support from the white community to be elected; in 1961, they asked Winters to run. On election day, he was sixth in a field of fourteen. Raleigh is less than 25 per cent black by population, and among registered voters the proportion is considerably less.

"I gave a lot of thought to how I should behave in that Council," Winters recalled. "Our people had plenty of grievances—and still do. There was a great opportunity for speechmaking and demagoguery. But I felt that the important thing was to get something done. After all, I was one councilman out of seven, and this was still North Carolina. I didn't see any point in making a speech or getting my name in the papers unless it had something to do with changing people's lives for the better.

"Some people don't understand this, and I'll admit I've been called an Uncle Tom. But results are what count. Just as I've always believed you can serve people without being servile, I also believe you can be militant without being a demagogue.

"Back when I started at the airport, they were using an old building that had been converted from an army barracks, and it had been done in such a hurry that they didn't get around to putting in segregated rest rooms. Then in the 1950s they were planning the present building, and they wanted to put in segregated facilities. I made such a row about that that the airport manager wanted to fire me. He thought I was a real troublemaker. He said, 'You're too aggressive, you're twenty-five years ahead of your time.'

"I was working for Eastern Air Lines, too, and Eastern's manager said, 'This man has as much right to protect himself as a man as he does to work. So long as he does his work as an Eastern employee he's staying right here—what he does to protect his personal integrity is his own business.'

"We lost that battle. They put up the 'Colored' signs, although they told black people that they could ignore them. In 1961, when President Kennedy came down to make a speech at Chapel Hill, they pulled those signs down the day before he arrived at the airport."

Councilman Winters decided to hold his temper, do his homework, listen and learn. He was determined not to speak up until he was sure of his ground. Sometimes another councilman would turn to him and say, "What is your view of this matter?" and he would say, "I'll reserve my comments at this time."

That is the way it went for most of his first year. At that time demonstrations and sit-ins were being held all over the South to force desegregation of restaurants and other public places. Everybody knew where Winters stood on the issue—he had privately encouraged and supported the demonstrators—but he had not used his position as councilman in that connection because he had not seen any effective way to do so.

One Sunday, a meeting was held to protest segregation at the Howard Johnson restaurant. One of the principal speakers was no particular friend of Winters, and may have felt that he would refuse to stand up and be counted on the issue. Perhaps with the intention of embarrassing him, this man said, "Let's go on out to Howard Johnson's right now and picket it, and let's ask Councilman Winters to lead us."

"And so I participated in the march and the picketing. The next day it was all over the newspapers, and a few white people petitioned the mayor and the council to have me impeached.

"When we councilmen next sat down together, I said, 'Gentlemen, I have tried to work with you and do my job here. But I cannot stomach segregated public facilities—that violates my integrity as a man. When we license someone to do business with the public, and he invites the public to come to his place and then bars some people because of the color of their skin, I think I have a right to protest—outside this council.

" 'Now, you should keep in mind that I have not invoked the power of government against this restaurant manager. I have not used this council table as a sounding board at this stage of the game. It may come to that someday, and when it does we will probably disagree, but that is not at issue today. I have made my protest as a man outside the council—it has nothing whatever to do with the performance of my duties.' And so of course they did nothing about impeachment—these men understood my actions even though they had not expected them."

After that incident the other councilmen saw their black colleague in a somewhat different light. They realized that his restraint did not indicate approval of the *status quo*. If there were any remaining doubts about this, they were removed when a group of black students went swimming at a segregated city-owned pool. The city manager immediately ordered the pool closed and drained—not until that order had been carried out did he inform the city council.

"Then we really had a battle. Then, for the first time, I did pound on the table. I said that this was a facility paid for by the taxpayers. I said that when the tax money comes in, we don't segregate it. I said that the action of the city manager could not be sustained or supported in any way, and I moved that the council order him to reopen the pool immediately. One white councilman seconded the motion. But he and I were the only two to vote for it.

"After the session was over they all came over to me, one after another, saying that there was nothing personal . . . 'John, you know this is no reflection on you as a man, you know I respect you,' and 'John, I sure hated to vote against you, and if it was just you usin' that pool you know I wouldn't mind,' and 'Now is not the time.'

"I said, 'Gentlemen, that really doesn't do any good. Let's go back where we started. Let's go back to the day when we put our hands on the Bible and swore to uphold the

Constitution of the United States of America. I think I upheld my oath today. I wonder if you feel that you did the same. For your sakes, I hope you do.' And with that I walked out.

"Well, there was a lot of conversation back and forth, and they kept telling me how sorry they were that we were in disagreement. They knew very well my arguments were sound, that a facility supported by the taxes of the people should be open to all the people. One day the mayor said to me, 'Councilman, I think we might reopen that pool if you will take the responsibility of seeing that your people use it in a reasonable way. . . .'

"What he meant was that only two or three black people should use it at a time, and it would be better if they weren't too dark, and of course they should be polite and deferential and not laugh or have too much of a good time. I wasn't about to promise anything like that, and of course if I had made the promise I couldn't have delivered on it. I told him that the pool should be open to the public—all the people—and that the police should ensure that there was no interference with anyone's right to use it." The pool stayed closed that season, but the following spring it was opened to all the public without any problems.

Having served as a city councilman for three terms, totaling six years, Winters feels that he was able to accomplish some important things. For example, black firemen were hired for the first time. And a great deal of groundwork was laid for other forward steps, which came to fruition after he left office.

Raleigh was a typical southern town in that very few streets in black neighborhoods were paved or lighted. As times began to change, white government officials admitted that this was unfair but that there was nothing they could do. The cost of paving a street is assessed against the property owners on that street, and it cannot be done without their consent. Because of home-financing problems, most black people could not buy their homes but rented them; the absentee white landlords would not consent to the assessment for paving. As chairman of the council's Public Works

Committee, Winters worked out and put through a plan for state money to be used for paving without consent of the property owners. During his last year on the council, 90 per cent of the money spent on city streets was used to provide new paving in black neighborhoods.

Winters is not a man to advertise his achievements, and many people in Raleigh do not realize how much he accomplished on the council. He feels that that is the nature of politics. If a man grabs all the headlines, others will not work with him; he will get very little done. There is practically no limit to what you can accomplish, as the saying goes, so long as you don't care who gets the credit.

Winters recalls a chat he once had with a friend who said that they were "finally paving my street after all these years. That sure is nice of the mayor to do that."

Winters said, "I guess you didn't know that I'm chairman of the Public Works Committee that has charge of all the work on the streets."

"Why, no, John, I knew you were on the council but I didn't know you handled that part of it. . . ."

In 1959, Winters was still carrying bags at the Raleigh-Durham airport. He was thirty-nine years old. Before he reached fifty he was a millionaire, having built over 400 single-family homes and apartment-dwelling units. He and his wife own a number of apartment buildings, the steady income from which would survive a home-building slump.

Winters, a devout Catholic, feels that he owes his success to the grace of God. "I am deeply grateful for the many things that have come to me through God's grace. I know very well that I haven't accomplished these things alone. Many things have been bestowed upon me, many opportunities have come to me that have passed by others who were just as well equipped to receive them. . . .

"It is true that I have prospered, but I feel that others have also benefited from what I have built. I believe that if we share with others, our own abundance will grow. If it was meant for a man to have everything himself, then he would be the only person on earth."

Like every other successful entrepreneur, John Winters

puts in long hours. "A lot of people talk about going into business for themselves, but they'd better not do it unless they realize that it won't be 9:00 to 5:00. Many a time I had to get up in the middle of the night because of some crisis at one of my projects. Once a pipe broke and water flooded through a house under construction. Of course, you can't find the subcontractor in the middle of the night, so I had to go out myself and crawl around under that house looking for the cutoff valve.

"Another time I spent all of Sunday morning bailing out a man's basement. My crew had forgotten to leave an opening for a footing drain. There was a very heavy rainstorm, and he ended up with six inches of water in his basement. He had already bought the house and moved in, but my people had slipped up and so it was my responsibility.

"When these things happen I have to go myself. The subcontractor and the men on the job are smarter than I am—they can't be found at midnight or on weekends. They disappear. But if you're going to have the satisfaction of owning a business and being successful, you have to accept the responsibilities that go with it."

In the course of developing his home-building business, Winters became a financial wizard. Any contractor must do this, but he has to be especially ingenious if he is building and selling homes to black people in the South. One imaginative idea that provided an immediate solution to a common problem later produced some unexpected difficulties. Every home builder has had the experience of working out a sale, including the mortgage financing, and then finding that the buyer doesn't have quite enough money, or says he doesn't, to cover the down payment. One solution is to cut the price of the house.

"That's an obvious solution," said Winters, "but it's a very unsatisfactory one. Let's take an actual case. One of the first houses I sold in the Madonna Acres development was priced at $22,000. The buyer was agreeable but could put up only $2,000 in cash. The bank agreed to write a first mortgage for $18,000. So we were $2,000 short. Now that $2,000 represented practically all of my profit on a $22,000 house—if I cut the price to $20,000 to make a fast deal I would wipe out my profit."

Since the bank was willing to lend $18,000 on the house, Winters suggested they write the mortgage for $20,000 but only pay him $18,000. The other $2,000 would be entered and remain as a deposit in a savings account for three or four years, until the buyer had made mortgage payments to reduce the principal of the loan to $18,000. Then the passbook and the $2,000, together with the accumulated interest, would be released to Winters.

The effect of this ingenious arrangement was that the $2,000 profit on the house was tied up and unavailable to Winters but was drawing interest. The bank was happy because it was risking only $18,000—it was in effect borrowing the other $2,000 from Winters at 4 per cent and lending it to the home buyer at 6½ per cent with no risk at all, and even a banker will admit that that's a pretty good deal.

The idea was so successful that it provided the means for Winters to sell a number of homes to buyers who couldn't quite make the down payment. By the middle of the 1960s he had accounts of more than $50,000 pledged to the banks that held them. But there was considerable uncertainty about how to treat the arrangement for income-tax purposes.

"Here's the problem," said Winters. "I sold that $22,000 house in 1959 for a $2,000 profit. Now profit is income, and I have to pay income taxes on it. But I didn't actually *get* that $2,000 until 1963, when the buyer had paid his mortgage down to $18,000 and the passbook was released to me. There was never any doubt about my reporting the $2,000 on my tax return. The question was *when* should I report it—in 1959, in 1963, or some time in between?"

Winters's accountant stated firmly that it isn't income untl you have access to it; since the money in the pledged accounts was not available to Winters, it didn't constitute income until the passbook was released to him. "We did more and more of these things, and it began to get into big money," recalled Winters. "I kept asking this man, 'Are you sure we shouldn't report this?' He seemed confident that we were on sound ground. But I was still worrying. And then a friend of mine pointed out that accountants tend to specialize like everyone else. This man was a good accountant for a restaurant but perhaps didn't have enough experience in the contracting field."

Though Winters could not get a positive answer from his lawyer, he did recommend that another accountant analyze the situation. This man pored over his books for eight months and came to the conclusion that there was a sizable element of doubt. He suggested a voluntary disclosure of all the facts to the Internal Revenue Service with a request for their interpretation. Unfortunately, Winters encountered a bigoted tax agent who arbitrarily decreed that the income should have been reported when the houses were sold. He ordered all of Winters's books and records seized and demanded that the taxes be paid immediately, together with interest and substantial penalties. Not only that, he threatened to have Winters criminally indicted for tax fraud.

It should be noted at this point that the internal-revenue agent was completely off base on all counts. In the first place, the original accountant was right. It is a settled principle of tax law that income is reportable when money is received or becomes available. It is true that there is such a thing as constructive income—you don't actually receive the money but you have access to it *at your option*—but this was not Winters's situation. He did not have access to the money in the pledged accounts until several years later.

In the second place, fraud involves *intent* to cheat the government. When a man conducts all of his business in a proper manner, with all aspects fully documented, no attempts to conceal information, no dealing in cash instead of checks; when he consults qualified accountants and attornies and relies upon their advice; and especially when he *voluntarily discloses* his problem to the Internal Revenue Service, there can be no possible question of fraudulent intent.

The agent knew very well that Winters was a city councilman and that a fraud indictment would certainly destroy his political career—and might well destroy his business, too. Fortunately, the director of the district office vetoed the idea of criminal prosecution, but he supported the agent's ruling that the taxes should have been paid earlier and also the assessment of penalties.

Almost certainly, Winters could have won if he had taken the matter to tax court. But court action would have involved a substantial legal bill, serious diversion of time and energy from more constructive activity, and probably some bad publicity. When a tax matter is litigated, most people assume that the taxpayer has been trying to cheat the government. They don't realize that in many cases, it is simply a matter of differing points of view about a technical accounting matter.

Winters settled the matter by paying $32,000, one of the costs—only one—of his being a successful black entrepreneur in the state of North Carolina in the last half of the twentieth century.

10

Henry G. Parks, Jr.: Sausage Manufacturer

"Some people are self-starters, and I am one of them."

One of the largest black manufacturers, and the first black businessman to go public,* is Henry G. Parks, Jr. On

---

* Well, yes and no. When Wall Street talks about a company "going public," they usually mean that a company whose stock is owned by a handful of people sells a large block of it all at once by mean of a public offering registered with the SEC and distributed by investment bankers to hundreds of new purchasers. In this sense, Parks was first.

However, it sometimes happens that a stock drifts onto the public market over a period of time. At the beginning, it has a few stockholders, most of whom know each other. At time passes, one will sell a few shares to a friend who will give them to his wife. Another will die and leave the shares to his children or in an estate for which a bank is executor. The banker will call a broker and say, "What is this stock worth?" Someone else may call the broker and say, "I hear so-and-so is growing and doing well. What does their stock sell for? Can you buy some for me?" A few more calls like that and the broker decides he can make money by "making a market" in the stock; in other words, he starts to keep track of those who own it

January 22, 1969, 274,000 shares of the common stock of H. G. Parks, Inc. were offered and sold to the public at $8 per share by the wealthy Wall Street investment firm of Allen & Company. The company's accountants were the large national firm of Lybrand, Ross Brothers and Montgomery. Legal details of the offering were handled by Breed, Abbott and Morgan, a prominent Wall Street law firm. Their seventeen-page prospectus on the offering gives complete factual and financial data about the company, but it carries not even a hint that Parks is black. Some of the brokers who sold the issue probably knew that, but most of the customers who bought it probably didn't. Parks sold some of his own shares in the offering and realized about $400,000 in cash, after underwriting commissions and before capital-gains taxes. The shares he still holds are worth over a million dollars.

Parks was born in Atlanta in 1918, and grew up in Dayton. His father was a wine steward, his mother a domestic. He worked his way through Ohio State, majoring in marketing, graduated with honors in 1939, and decided to ignore the advice of a college counselor who told him, "Go to South America, where you will have a real chance."

Shortly after graduation he went to work for Pabst Brewing. If they were enthusiastic about hiring him, he recalled, they managed to keep their enthusiasm under careful control. But he persisted, pointing out to them that most black people are poor and that poor people, if they drink, buy a lot of beer because they can't afford whisky. Somewhat gingerly, they took him on, making clear that of course he was to confine his activities to his own people.

---

and those who are interested in buying it. He lists the issue in the security traders' offering sheets. Occasionally, he puts buyer and seller together and makes a trade. All of this is done without SEC registration.

The stock of Supreme Life Insurance Company of Chicago drifted onto the market in just this way. It has been traded "over the counter" for many years, but it never "went public" through a registered public offering such as Parks had.

Also there have been several small offerings made entirely within one state or under the SEC's Regulation A, which covers offerings totaling less than $300,000.

He did so well that Pabst soon put him in charge of developing the "ethnic market" throughout the country. The company had no other black salesmen, so he hired and trained them himself. Among his strategies was to stand in the parking lot of a supermarket in, say, Beverly Hills and give a sales spiel for Pabst to every Negro chauffeur and cook who came to shop for their white employers. It didn't do much for the brand in Beverly Hills, but within a short time Pabst, until then virtually unknown on the West Coast, was selling briskly in stores and taverns in the black neighborhoods of downtown Los Angeles.

A good salesman can get rich pretty fast if he wants to work hard and save his money. Before he was thirty, Henry Parks had saved enough to become an entrepreneur. His first venture was Joe Louis Punch, a soft drink. It was an interesting idea for the 1940s, but regrettably it changed color when it came into contact with sunlight and changed its flavor when confronted by ice cubes.

Parks first ventured into the sausage business in 1947 when he became part owner and star salesman for Crayton's Southern Sausage Company in Cleveland. (Leroy Crayton had come to Ohio from Alabama as a boy, sold shoes to pay his way through Ohio State, sold sporting goods, started a grocery business, and then founded his sausage-packing company in the Depression year of 1937. Crayton's is still in business throughout Ohio; Leroy Crayton died in 1963, and was succeeded as President by Mrs. Nancy Stovall.)

In 1951, settled in Baltimore and possessing another nest egg, Parks started his own sausage company. He had two employees, rented space in an old dairy and began by selling in a few black stores. His salesmen visited every barbershop, made their pitch to the customers and left free samples with the barbers. Saleswomen did the same thing in beauty parlors. A pitchman dressed as "Parky the Pig" handed out free samples on busy shopping streets in black communities. It was a concentrated, intensive and expensive effort to sell Parks Sausages and establish the name as a known premium brand among black people. But he had no intention of confining himself to the ghettos. In twelve years of selling to black people, he had learned a lot about their buying habits and how they spread. From this knowledge and experience he developed a unique strategy of "reverse marketing."

Poor neighborhoods are dumping grounds for shoddy goods at high prices. Poor people know this and resent it. The result is that they have strong loyalty to prominent brands—even when they cost more, as they almost always do—and they will travel to middle-class neighborhoods to shop if they can, because they know they will get more for their money.

The reverse-marketing twist appeared when these pre-sold customers began asking for Parks products at white stores. Less than two years after he started, Parks signed up a white-owned chain with stores in white neighborhoods in Baltimore and Washington, D.C. The second chain was easier to sign up, the third and fourth easier still, and he was on his way. Once the product was displayed in a significant number of retail outlets in the Baltimore and Washington area, it became economically feasible to begin radio advertising. And so "More Parks Sausages, Mom!" was born.

Strict adherence to quality standards enables Parks to command a premium of as much as 10¢ or even 15¢ a pound above competing products at retail-store counters. The price differential enables him to afford a heavy advertising campaign, which of course reinforces brand loyalty and makes people more willing to pay the higher price. Parks has customarily plowed back at least 7¢ of every sales dollar into advertising, a very high figure for the food business.

Parks Sausages are now sold in some 12,000 retail stores from Virginia to Massachusetts, including most of the stores of the major supermarket chains in that area. Sales were close to $10 million in 1970.

"Some people are self-starters," said Parks, "and I am one of them. I've gotten used to getting thrown out of places and then going back. One meat buyer told me he wasn't interested in a nigger product. I told him I wasn't trying to sell him one, and then we began talking business."

11

Frederick E. Barrett:
Electronic Equipment
Manufacturer

"Look at the Pyramids. They are awesome in size, but the way they built them was to put one stone on top of another stone."

On February 14, 1952, Frederick E. Barrett arrived in the United States from the island of Jamaica. He had $85 in his pocket and high hopes but no definite plans. He was eighteen years old.

On August 4, 1969, bids were opened in Philadelphia for 57,000 telephone sets for purchase by the U.S. Army at $55 each. The total amount of the contract was over $3,000,000, with an option for the Army to increase it to more than $6,000,000. Several of America's large electronics companies competed, but the winning bid was that of Barrett Intercommunication Products Corporation of Brooklyn which had been in business for less than six months. Its bid was low by 12¢ per unit. Barrett was then thirty-four years old.

"We were lucky to win by only 12¢," said Barrett, "but everything else about that bid was a matter of hard work. And if it was hard to win the bid, it was even harder to hang onto it. They looked at each other that day in Philadelphia and said, 'Who the hell is this Barrett? Where did he come from? Has anybody ever heard of him?'

"When I went to Philadelphia to talk about it, their attitude was, 'Barrett? In business for six months? Does he understand the complexity and size of this job? Does he realize how much financing is required? His bid will be thrown out, he'll be disqualified, there's no reason to waste time with him.'

"And when they came to inspect our facilities, to determine whether we were capable of producing the item, they walked in with a certain amount of disdain. But they found we had the equipment well laid out and a good blueprint and plan for manufacturing the item. They gave us approval as a manufacturer based on our engineering and our production facilities.

"Still, the U.S. government tried every maneuver possible to get us off their backs, to disqualify us on the basis of financial incapability. They used unusual delaying tactics; the matter dragged on for eight months after the bids were opened. In fact, at one point they notified us that we were disqualified and the next bidder would get the contract.

"We immediately protested to the General Accounting Office and the Small Business Administration. For every move they made we made a countermove. We brought up some reinforcements—we had a U.S. Senator and a very vocal Congresswoman write them a letter and say that they were interested in the Barrett matter and would like to be kept informed as to how it was going. That's all they said, but that's all they had to say, because then the Army knew they were watching.

"We had studied the law and the armed forces procurement regulations. They are bound by these regulations, and whether they like the particular company or not, if it fulfills all of the requirements and is the low bidder, the regulations say it has to get the contract." Finally, in Feb-

Edward Davis of Detroit, Michigan, the first black automobile dealer in the United States

Benyas-Kaufman Photographers

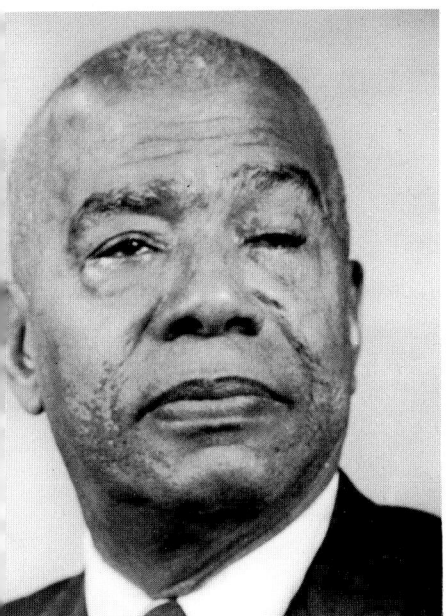

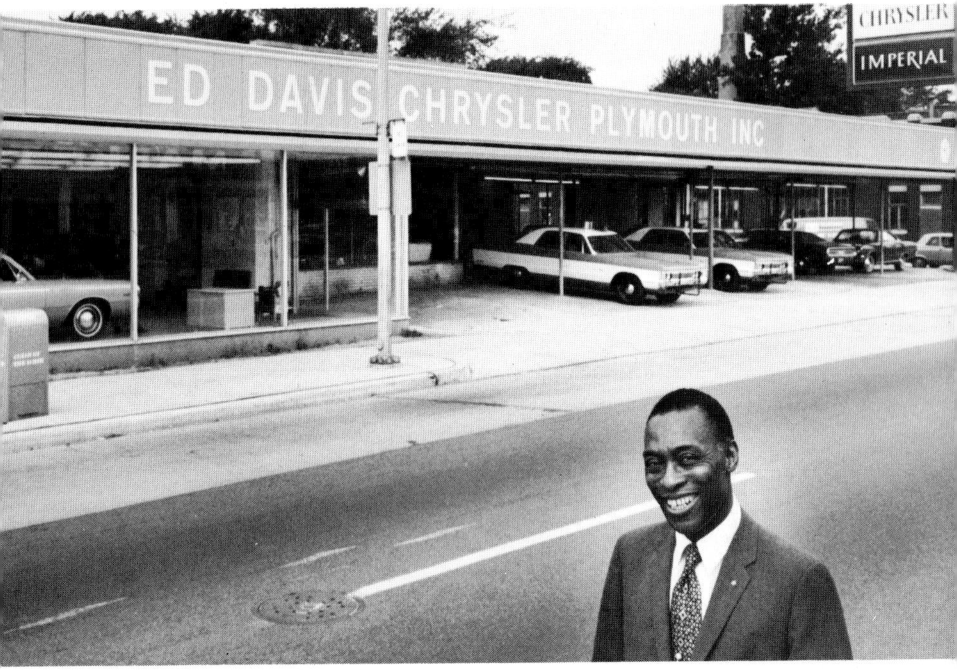

Count Jackson

Jesse B. Blayton, the first black certified public accountant in the United States

G. Michael Gunason

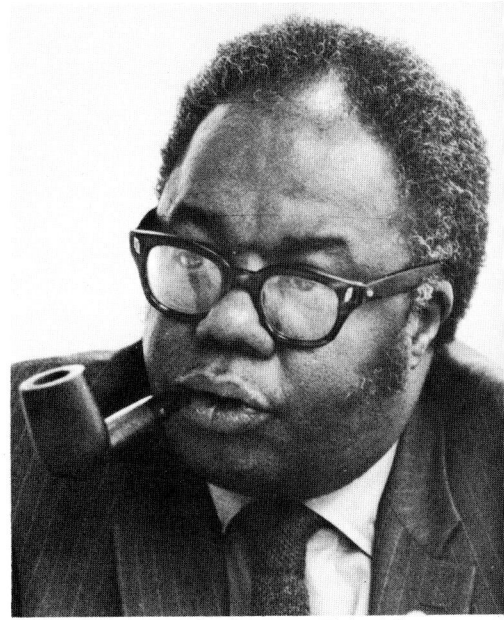

Indianapolis architect David F. Snyder

Building contractor and developer John W. Winters

Ken Co

Ken Coo

A Winters housing development near Raleigh,
North Carolina

Jesse A. Terry oversees a sleeve cutter in the Terry Manufacturing Company plant, Roanoke, Alabama

Terry Manufacturing Co.

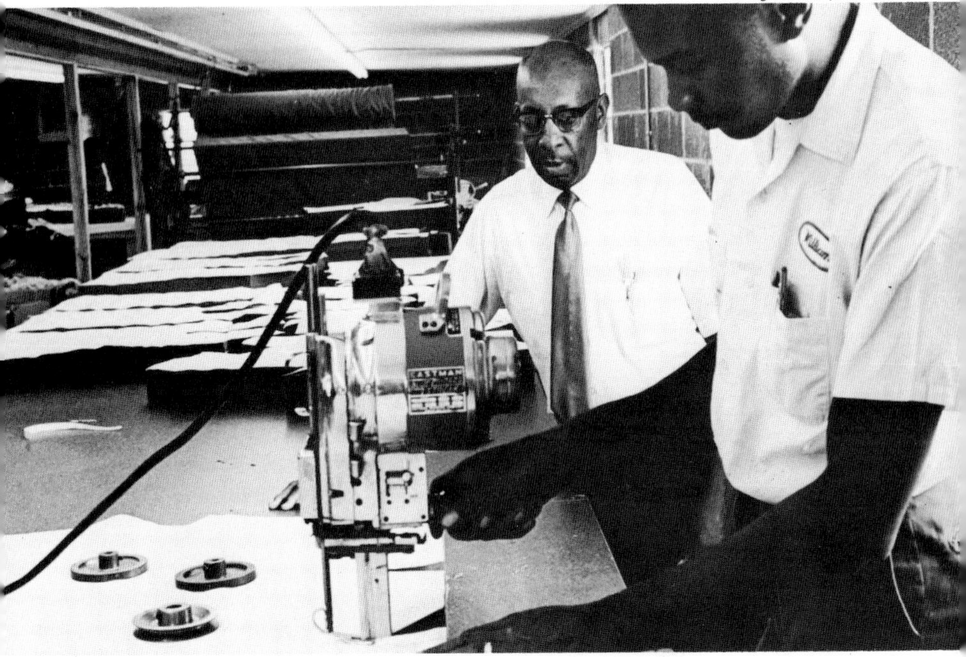

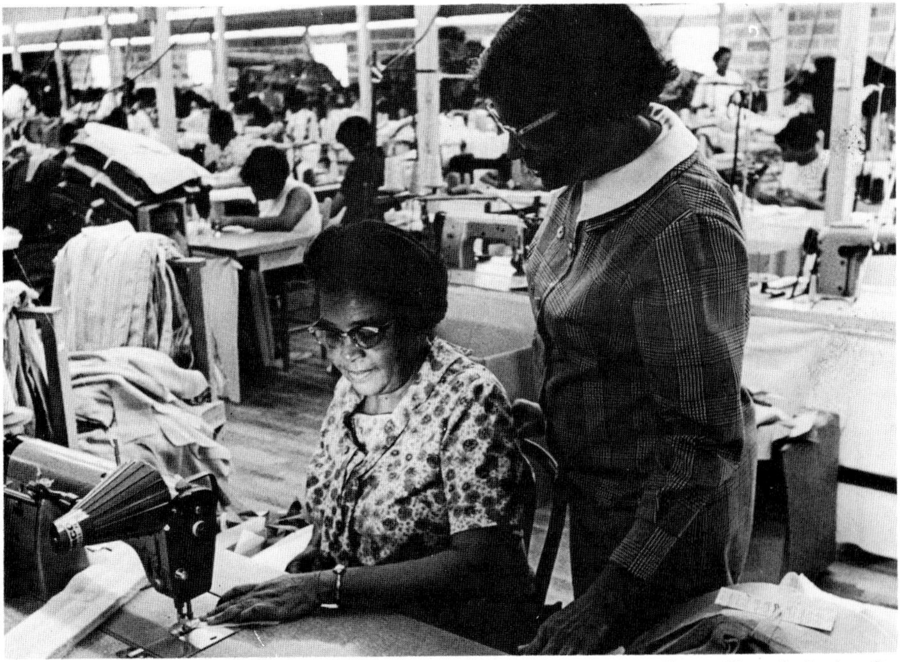

Terry Manufacturing Co.

Mrs. Terry checks the quality of workmanship on the ladies dresses assembly line

Architect's drawing of a
new Travis Realty Company
apartment house at Sixty-
third Street and Michigan
Avenue in Chicago, completed
in 1971

Dempsey J. Travis
William Grant

One of the ten banks of
duplicating machines at
American Tape Duplicators,
Inc., Los Angeles, California

Walter Metzler

Richard Allen, founder and
president of the company

Walter Metzler

Home office of the North
Carolina Mutual Life
Insurance Company in
Durham, North Carolina
Charles Cooper

Asa T. Spaulding, long-time
president of the company
Charles Cooper

Dallas businessman Joe W. Kirven and his family meet
President Richard Nixon

Frederick E. Barrett
supervising work on a
government contract at the
Brooklyn assembly plant of
Barrett Intercommunication
Products
Jim Theologos

Frederick E. Barrett
Jim Theologos

ruary 1970, the contract was awarded to Barrett Inter-comunication Products.

Frederick E. Barrett was born in Jamaica, West Indies, on December 15, 1934, the youngest of four children, three boys and one girl. His father was headmaster at an elementary school, and his mother was a teacher there. The Barretts were not rich, but neither were they poor. They had the security of income and the status that is associated with the professional civil service. In addition, Barrett remembers certain creature comforts from his childhood. Servants were available in the British West Indies at very low rates of pay and there were no household chores for the children.

By 1951 Barrett had completed high school and was already starting a premedical course in college. Then his father died suddenly, and the shock to his mother was so great that she stopped teaching, unable to bear the familiar surroundings where they had spent many happy years. Her small pension was not enough to support more than one college student. Since Barrett's older sister was further along in her medical education, it was decided that she would continue and he would drop out.

He heard from a friend that it was possible to work one's way through college in the United States, and his mother encouraged him to come here. However, a new medical school had just been opened in Jamaica and the authorities wanted to keep future doctors rather than export them. In order to get around this difficulty, Barrett stated in his visa application that he intended to study engineering. He enrolled as a freshman at Northeastern University in Boston, where he was one of only two or three blacks.

Northeastern operated on a co-operative plan in which the students spent about half of each year studying and the other half working full time. The University's guidance and counseling office was supposed to help them find jobs. Naturally, Barrett was interested in a job with some relevance to his career objectives, but during all of his years at Northeastern, the guidance office never found him a single position that had any relation to science or engineering. As it happened, he had several jobs that gave him valuable engineering experience, but he found them on his own, without any help from the office.

Because he could not depend on money from home, Barrett had to work during the study cycle, too. During those early years, he worked at "almost every menial job in the city of Boston. The guidance office was very helpful in finding this type of work." At one time or another, he was a garbage collector, a bellboy, a carpenter, a truck driver, a dishwasher and busboy. "Those restaurant jobs were good, because even if you worked only three or four hours you could usually get a meal and maybe something to take with you for breakfast or lunch the next day." For a while he worked washing and polishing cars at 65¢ an hour, not knowing that the minimum wage at that time was 75¢.

His first year in this country was a rocky one. His studies were not particularly difficult, although he did have to adjust to the American idiom and the American view of history. Even more troublesome than orienting himself to a new country and a different way of life was the heavy schedule of combined study and work, together with taking care of meals, laundry and so on—matters that had been handled by servants at home. The pressure was eased somewhat when he took a job as a taxi driver. He was able to drive with his books on the seat beside him and to study while parked at a stand or waiting in line at airports.

At first he continued to feel that medicine was his ultimate objective. However, since most of his courses were in mathematics and the physical sciences, he gradually began to develop an interest in engineering and to see the possibilities in the use of advanced electronics in medical applications, such as monitoring, testing and diagnosis.

Barrett finds it hard to recall any "flagrant displays" of discrimination during his years at Northeastern. "It was more a case of subtle situations, little embarrassments and little cruelties. These things were not done maliciously— they were simply a part of American life. For example, there might be twenty-five students browsing in the bookstore, each of us carrying a bag or briefcase, but every time I glanced down the aisle I saw the guard watching *me*. I'm sure he didn't realize how insulting his behavior was, but he had clearly singled me out as the only one likely to steal a book.

"One of the most important aspects of college is group study. Students get together and discuss the assignment, and the instructor, and you get a lot of educational therapy out of it, you *heal* each other's problems. Well, I never had any of this. I was never invited by other students so I did everything alone.

"In lab, we would work on a team basis, and this involved a lot of getting together outside of class, meeting at someone's apartment or having lunch together. The assignments were made alphabetically, and at the beginning of one class I heard Roger B. say, 'Oh, no! Don't tell me I'm stuck with Barrett again!' After that I did my lab work alone. It taught me to survive, to be independent, to do the whole job and think through the entire problem myself, rather than relying on others. It didn't give me better grades, but it made me that much stronger.

"I think one of my strengths is that I respond positively to rebuffs. I see them as challenges. I found myself in this new country, this new environment and, with the coolness of the other kids, I felt sort of misplaced. But my reaction was to strive that much harder to be better than they were.

"Coming, as I did, from a country that had no color prejudice, I had an inferiority complex pushed onto me in this country. The Negroes that I met here were quite subservient, it was clear that they had been made to feel inferior. . . . I didn't consciously feel inferior at all, but I think that deep down I was made to feel inferior . . . and that accounts for some of my drive to excel, to be better than my white counterparts."

Barrett graduated from Northeastern University in 1959 with a Bachelor of Science degree. It had taken seven years because of the combination work-study schedule. Although he was in the top quarter of his class, he feels that he would have done better but for the constant money problem.

"Still, it was a good experience. I had to learn to survive

at the same time I was studying because nothing was given to me. In some ways this was worth more than my whole formal education. It taught me to put the right priorities in front of me and to use my time effectively. I worked hard to earn a dollar, and then I squeezed the last penny out of it in spending it—this is an education in itself."

After graduating, Barrett found a position as an engineer with Ampex in Sunnyvale, Califonia. Within a few months he was promoted and reassigned to Opelika, Alabama. "That was another part of my education. I stuck it out for all of three weeks, and then I told them, 'Gentlemen, I'm going back up North. I don't know whether I'll be with Ampex or not, but I'm not staying here!' " Ampex transferred him to Bloomfield, New Jersey.

There he met and married a young lady of seventeen whom he describes as "just perfect for me. She was an unspoiled country girl who had an amazing ability to see things and was mature far beyond her years. She had known black doctors and Army officers, but she didn't know there was such a thing as a black electronics engineer." The Barretts now have four children.

While at Ampex he bought some of the company's stock under an employee-purchase plan. This proved to be a wise decision; he sold the stock a few years later for about six times what he had paid for it.

Barrett was earning $175 a week at Ampex, but he did not feel he was learning enough. One of several dozen engineers, he worked on only one part of a project and never saw what went before or came after. He did not have the responsibility —or the satisfaction—of starting a job and carrying it through to completion. At that time, he still expected to return eventually to Jamaica, and he felt that he needed broader experience before he could consider running an enterprise there.

In 1961, he and his wife moved to New York and he took a job at Arkay International, a small organization with thirty employees. The move involved a substantial cut in pay from $175 to $110 a week. But Arkay had only one other engineer, an older man who had grown up with vacuum-tube technology and had trouble adjusting to the new world of semiconductors. He left soon afterwards, which meant that Barrett was doing all of the company's engineering. Arkay was in the high-fidelity field, which interested him, but the most important thing was the chance to handle an entire project from start to finish.

"I was alone as an engineer, and I had to learn an awful lot in a hurry. They would hand me a project, and I'd start with a blank piece of paper on the drawing board and work it through to the finished product. Besides doing the designing and circuitry, I had to deal with the nuts and bolts, requisitioning material, shopping for the best possible prices for components and setting up the production line. I learned how to survive as an engineer and project director. I learned a lot of things they didn't teach in school!"

Arkay handled both commercial and defense work. At one time it made television sets, which were completely engineered by Barrett. Other projects included intercom systems, portable telephone sets for the military, transmitters and antenna systems.

Some of the items were extremely complex, such as a complete mobile radio-receiving shelter equipped with receiver, transmitter and Teletype equipment. "That one was so elaborate that it scares me when I look back on it, but for some reason it didn't scare me then. I figured if it could be done by another engineer, it could be done by me—after all, he's a human being, the same as I am. What I didn't know, I knew how to find out. It never occurred to me to say, 'I'm not that kind of engineer' or 'That is beyond my reach.' That is accepting defeat, and once you accept defeat, it completely immobilizes you—you can't function. And when I got into the project, I usually found that it was quite simple. . . .

"Sometimes if you look at a problem and try to get an overall perspective of it, it seems too big . . . insoluble. You have to deal with one step at a time. Look at the Pyramids. They are awesome in size, but the way they built them was to put one stone on top of another stone."

In 1963, Barrett saw a lucrative market for TV sets

about to open up in Jamaica, where the first TV station was under construction. At his request, Arkay sent him to investigate the possibility of opening a plant there. The population of the island is about 1,900,000, and there are over 400,000 households. However, the level of income is not high, and a marketing survey by a firm of experts predicted that no more than 25,000 TV sets would ever be in use on the island—not a large enough market to support a manufacturing plant.

On the basis of this pessimistic forecast the company asked Barrett to abandon the idea and return to New York. But he still believed in the project, so much so that he took a leave of absence to try to develop it on his own. "We actually got started, in a small way, and I ran through $7,000 of my own money. But I couldn't raise any more— I was a prophet without honor in my own country." After nine months he returned to New York and Arkay, sadder, wiser and poorer. But he had been right. The people of Jamaica have bought several times the 25,000-set projection, and are still buying. Not one but two assembly plants are now producing sets there.

During his years at Arkay International, which later changed its name to Comspace Corporation, Barrett had a number of memorable confrontations with military procurement officials. In each case, there was a sequence of correspondence and telephone calls to discuss the details of a bid or a production contract. The officer involved would get to know Barrett on a first-name basis—on the telephone —and develop a healthy respect for his engineering and managerial ability. Barrett speaks with the slight British accent and vocabulary that are characteristic of middle-class Jamaicans but can easily be mistaken for the speech of a Scotchman. "One contracting officer told me later that after talking to me on the phone, he visualized me as a forty-five-year-old Scotchman graying at the temples."

Sooner or later the transaction would require a face-to-face meeting. Usually Irving Becker, the owner of the company, would go to Washington with his chief engineer and another man considerably older than Barrett. Seeing this trio of two middle-aged white men and a slim, youthful-looking black of barely thirty, the Washington officials would wonder which of the white men was the Barrett whom they had learned to respect, and who was to dominate the meeting with his engineering expertise. They probably often wondered why Becker had brought a messenger along.

"It never failed," recalled Barrett. "That first meeting was a disaster from their point of view. When they found out who I was, they went into a state of shock. They could hardly open their mouths. While they were trying to recover, I would hammer away at all of the points Becker and I were trying to make, and we usually won most of them. Maybe it was sympathy, but we rarely lost our case. They were on the defensive, and whenever I get the other guy on the defensive, I will capitalize on it.

"It was a very effective tactic, and we used it to the fullest advantage. Sometimes when the negotiations by correspondence and telephone had reached an impasse, we would suggest a meeting that was not really necessary—we knew the shock would enable us to get the deal off dead center and moving again."

Comspace prospered during the years that Barrett did its engineering work. It had thirty employees when he started working there; by 1968 it had over 200 in three separate plants. In 1967, Barrett was made a vice-president, largely because Comspace had just bought another company, and he became the boss of four other engineers, who were white and older than he. Two of them had advanced degrees.

It was a bit tense at first, especially with one who was a Ph.D., "but with my B.S., some common sense and a lot of moxie, plus the solid support of Comspace, I won their respect. They saw that I knew how to get a project moving."

As the years went by, Barrett made some investments. "I wasn't earning very much, and I never could save money anyway, but I found that if I owed money to a bank I could always manage to pay it back. So I would go to the bank and borrow $1,500 or $3,000 for the down payment on a vacant lot or some other property. Then later on, I might sell it at a profit. I must have had ten or twelve of those loans during the 1960s." Barrett feels that the reason he was successful is that he never bought aggressively. He would sit back and wait until somebody had an emergency and had to sell in a hurry, and then he would pick up a bargain.

One particularly advantageous transaction involved a four-family house that he now owns and rents. Construction had been started on it in the Springfield Gardens section of Queens where Barrett lives by a builder from Westchester County. When he was unable to find a buyer at his asking price ($72,000) and let the house stand unfinished for almost two years, it suffered damage from vandals and the elements.

The builder told Barrett, "I can't travel over here to watch this place. Why don't you put up a little cash and buy it from me?"

Barrett did some calculating, and replied that he didn't like the terms. "I'd have to put in money to finish it and repair the damage, and in order to make a profit I'd have to sell it at the same price you're asking. If you can't sell it for that, what makes you think I can?"

The builder said, "The trouble with you is you're too smart!"

A few days later, the fellow came back again and said he'd like to make a deal, and asked Barrett to make him an offer. "I didn't have a dime or know where to get one, so I made him an offer that I thought was absolutely ridiculous. He didn't laugh, though, and shortly afterward we made a deal at a price a bit higher than my bid. It was so favorable that I was able to 'mortgage out'—I borrowed some money for a few months and when the work was finished arranged a first mortgage that covered the whole purchase price, including what I had borrowed. So I ended up owning the house without putting up any money at all. Now I have four good tenants who pay rent every month. That carries the mortgage and leaves me something over."

On another occasion he bought a licensed New York City taxicab, including its medallion, which was worth about $15,000 at the time, from the owner-driver and leased it back to him. He resold it within two years at a $2,000 profit. "If somebody needs money badly and has to sell something at a sacrifice, you can usually pick up a good value, hold it until you find the right buyer, and make a profit."

Barrett ultimately abandoned the idea of returning to Jamaica—during his trip in connection with the ill-fated TV venture he realized that life there was too slow-paced for him. He became a United States citizen in 1965.

He began to think in terms of staying at Comspace as a permanent career. He and Irving Becker worked well together and shared a mutual respect. "When I started there, I told him that broad experience was more important to me than money, and he really took me at my word. It took me almost four years to get back to the $175 a week that I had been making at Ampex. Later I found out what a chief engineer and vice-president ought to be paid in a company that size, and I wasn't getting anywhere near that figure."

After seven years at Comspace, he began to get restless. He felt that he had made an important contribution to the company's growth, but Becker did not offer him a share of the profits or of the ownership, or even a very good salary. Perhaps more important, he began to sense that Becker was slowing down and was satisfied with the company as it was. He seemed less willing to take the risk of developing new products that might pay off handsomely in the future.

Barrett had participated in every phase of the company's activities, including many of the management decisions, and he began to think seriously about starting a business of his own. "By this time I had done the complete engineering on more than twenty-five different projects, and I began to feel some confidence in myself." He enrolled in night courses at Fordham University in business management and contract administration.

In January 1968, he organized Barrett Intercommunication Products Corporation. He expected to remain at Comspace but planned to use his company as a vehicle to handle small items that Comspace didn't want to bother with. He also thought his company might work with Comspace on a joint-venture basis because of his "ethnic leverage." In addition, he saw the possibility of a locally owned enterprise that would employ black people in the neighborhood and be partly owned by them. (Barrett is acutely conscious of the movement of manufacturing operations to suburban and rural areas, leaving fewer job opportunities for people with limited skills in the central cities.) He offered Becker the opportunity to invest in his company, but Becker declined.

As time went on, Becker began to raise objections to Barrett's company, although he had given his approval at the beginning. "I think he began to feel that he was losing me, that I was going a little too fast." Finally, in July 1968, the Board of Directors of Comspace decided by formal resolution that Barrett's company put him in a position of conflict of interest and asked him to dissolve it.

"This was nonsense," said Barrett, "because I was continuing to do my work as well as I ever had, and I did absolutely nothing to undercut or compete with my employer. They knew everything that I was doing. The more they tried to discourage me the the more I concluded that maybe I was onto a good idea. Finally, I got a call one day from the company's attorney, who asked me whether I had dissolved my company yet. I told him I had not.

"He said, 'Well, I hope you'll do it soon, because I would hate to have to serve legal papers on you to force you to do it.'

"Just then something snapped in my mind. I said, 'You won't have to.'

"He assumed I meant that I would dissolve my company, and he said, 'I'm glad to hear that.' We went on to talk pleasantly about other things. But the ultimatum made a lot of things fall into place all at once for me. I realized that it was now or never. That was the right moment—if I didn't leave then I probably never would. I resigned on September 20, 1968."

The next morning Frederick Barrett set up a desk in the basement of his home and started his business. He obtained lists of government contracts put up for bidding and began to establish and renew acquaintances with purchasing officers. Within a month he submitted his first bid, on a voltage-frequency indicator that had previously been "sole source"—that is, it had been produced by only one company on negotiated contracts. "I went out and bought one, took it apart, and decided I could make it," says Barrett. "It has both military and industrial applications, and could be quite big over the years. In preparing my bid I allowed very little for overhead and profit; I looked on the first bid as sort of an investment."

The other company felt quite secure and actually raised its price. And so Barrett, without a plant or even an office, won the bid. The Navy complimented him on certain original design features that he introduced. Shortly afterward, he won a second bid to produce amplifiers, also for the Navy. He began to negotiate for rental of space and purchase of equipment. Although he had won the bids, the Navy would not award the contracts until it inspected his facilities and satisfied itself that he could produce.

One of his projects at Comspace had been a megaphone that he had designed for the Marine Corps. Comspace had produced it successfully and profitably for some time before being underbid by another company, which was behind schedule on deliveries. "I had a hunch they were running into engineering and production problems, so I took a chance and went to see them. Well, they welcomed me with open arms. They were having real problems with some of the engineering that I had worked out years before. They were very happy to subcontract that whole job to me."

By a stroke of luck, the two government contracts and the megaphone subcontract came through at about the same time. Together they totaled about $120,000 and were enough to get him off to a good start. The megaphone subcontract was especially helpful because it started fast; the engineering had been done and the prime contractor had already bought the components. Thus Barrett was actually making deliveries—and collecting payments—on the megaphone while planning and tooling up for the other two contracts. He opened his plant in an old building on Saint Marks Avenue in the Bedford Stuyvesant section of Brooklyn on February 27, 1969. Before the end of March he made his first shipment.

It would add to the drama of Barrett's success if he had started his company on a shoestring, but this was not the case. "Those little investments I made over the years had worked out fairly well. A house here, a lot there, all heavily mortgaged, but still my financial statement didn't look too bad when I put it together." He borrowed $12,000 from a bank against the security of his equity in real estate, and another $25,000 from the U.S. Small Business Administration.

Barrett has nothing but good things to say about the SBA. He found them very co-operative right from the beginning. His loan application was processed rapidly, and they have helped him with a number of matters since. For example, they issued him a certificate of competency on the $3,000,000 contract—which means in effect that the SBA guarantees the Pentagon that the contract will be fulfilled.

By the spring of 1969, he had been in business for a few months, and employed twenty-seven people (almost as many as Comspace had when he started there in 1960). Barrett decided to bid on the large Army telephone-set contract. "I guess at the beginning even I considered it more or less an exercise. As I made the rounds of the suppliers getting quotations for components, they said, 'You're not really serious about this, are you?'

"The more they tried to discourage me, the more determined I became. I knew something about the company that had been producing the item. I knew their people, and they don't walk on water. . . ."

To the consternation of his competitors and the Pentagon, Barrett Intercommunication Products Corporation was the winning bidder. He firmly resisted all of the efforts made to disqualify his bid. He moved rapidly to arrange over $350,000 of standby credit to finance the work. He has worked out a joint venture arrangement with Entron Corporation, which formerly produced the telephone set— Entron will do a substantial part of the work under subcontract from Barrett. Barrett will have access to components and equipment that he needs and that might otherwise be a total loss for the other company; so they both benefit from the partnership.

Barrett talked about the secret of his success. "It's nothing new for somebody to come to this country penniless and hungry and make himself a fortune in a couple of decades. It has been done before; it's more difficult today, but it can still be done. It won't be handed to you—you have to get off your backside and make it happen. There's only one way to get money legally, and that is to work for it. And when you've earned money, take it and let it work doubly hard for you.

"And if you get scared—forget it. You have to move fast and think fast, anticipate the situation if you can and grasp an opportunity when it comes along. If you're afraid you will hesitate, and then somebody else will move in front of you. I've never been afraid of failure—right now, for example, I might make one terrible mistake and lose my whole company. But if I start worrying about that, I'll never do anything.

"I have a lot of energy and drive. I think part of it comes from feeling out of place. When I was a kid, most of my friends were white, of English and Scottish ancestry. So I drove myself to excel and to be accepted by them. It was the same thing when I came to this country."

By the middle of its third year in business, Barrett Intercommunication had a backlog of work under contract or subcontract from the federal government totaling about $3,750,000. It employed over fifty people. Its president was just thirty-six; he had been in the U.S. for eighteen of those years.

If there is any doubt that Barrett is a successful American businessman, it should be resolved by the fact that he was hospitalized in 1968, at the age of thirty-four, with an ulcer. "But that was while I was another man's employee," he said, "and I think it was caused by some of the irritations and frustrations there. Since I've been my own boss, I've had no trouble with my stomach. . . ."

12

Jesse B. Blayton:
First Black CPA in the U.S.

"Now if he's that kind of man, who wants to have somebody always telling him what to do, then he should work for somebody else."

Jesse B. Blayton was born in 1899 in Indian territory that later became the state of Oklahoma. His paternal grandfather was a Creek Indian. "My father started out as an Indian medicine man and later became a Baptist preacher. He never learned to read or write well as long as he lived, but he had an excellent memory. My mother or my aunt would read chapters of the Bible to him, and he would remember what he heard and quote liberally from it when he was preaching.

"It was his custom to add certain embellishments to bring the Good Book closer to the lives of his congregation. He would say, 'Now it says right here in the Bible that when you get to heaven, and when you go over to Job's house for lunch, and they bring out the turkey sandwiches . . . .' He would be pointing to the Bible at the time. Sometimes he held it right side up and sometimes upside down.

"I found out later that we were poor when I was a child, but I didn't know it at the time." His mother became a schoolteacher, even though her own education had ended at the fourth grade of a segregated Mississippi school.

Young Blayton was acutely conscious of the difficulties experienced by his parents because they lacked education, and he was determined to get as much academic training as possible. He pursued his studies full time until his mid-twenties and part time until he was almost forty, although by then he was teaching, too.

He went to the local elementary and high schools in Oklahoma where almost all of his schoolmates were Indians. "They were fairly good schools because they received federal money under one of the Indian programs. Our teachers were well trained, and many of them came from the North." At Langston University in Oklahoma, he majored in the physical sciences. He received modest financial assistance from the federal government and also held a job while in college.

His education was interrupted when he volunteered for the Army during World War I. One of the officers in the One Hundred and Eighty-third Brigade suggested to him that he consider studying accounting. "I didn't really quite understand what it was, but somehow it had a nice sound to it. I told my mother about it and she said, 'What is accounting?'

"I said, 'Well, it's something like being cashier in a bank.' "

"She said, 'Lord God, my son's lost his mind!'

"She was almost right. In those days there were no Negro CPAs, no Negro accountants of any kind and I had never heard of a business run by Negroes. There were banks in other parts of the country, but I had never come into contact with them. There was nothing in my experience or the experience of anyone I knew to indicate that I could succeed in accounting or banking or business. There was absolutely nothing I could look forward to, but I went ahead anyway. I just decided that since I was an American, too, I ought to have the same chance as everybody else."

He studied accounting at the Walton School of Commerce in Chicago and after graduating took the three-day examination for certified public accountant given by the American Institute of Accountants. Although he was the first black man in history to take it, he did not notice any attempts to disqualify him or place obstacles in his path.

A careful survey taken in 1969 determined that 136 black men had succeeded in entering the accounting profession. (Only three of these—Jesse Blayton was one—were certified before 1940.) The total number of CPAs in the United States is over 100,000; therefore less than two-tenths of one per cent are black. Another survey confirmed the tiny black representation. In 1968 the New York State Commission for Human Rights sent questionnaires to the eight large national accounting firms. It found that these firms employed 3,629 professional staff members in New York City and that only eighteen of these were black.

One serious problem is the experience requirement. Most states will not permit a candidate to take the CPA examination until he has worked for a certified public accountant for a specified number of years. Until very recently it was almost impossible for a black man to find a job with an accounting firm in order to gain the necessary experience. Illinois does not require work experience, and more black CPAs have been able to qualify there than in any other state.

After passing the examination and becoming a CPA in 1928, Blayton established his own accounting practice. He also began teaching accountancy, first at Morehouse College and then at the graduate level at Atlanta University, which was established in 1930 as a graduate school to serve Morehouse and several other Atlanta colleges. Both Atlanta University and the colleges were all black then.

The Carnegie Foundation chair in accountancy at Atlanta University has been held by Blayton ever since its establishment in 1930. All of his students are working to become CPAs or to earn master's degrees. Blayton also has a degree in law but has never practiced. And he studied at the

University of Chicago Graduate School of Business, where he stopped just short of receiving a master's in business administration.

His accounting practice consisted primarily of small black businesses—restaurants, gas stations and the like. Once in a while a larger piece of work came his way. For example, when the Georgia insurance commissioner undertook an investigation of the actuarial soundness of a black-managed insurance company, he selected the only black CPA in the country to audit the books.

In 1925, Blayton and fourteen other men established the Mutual Savings and Loan Association of Atlanta. Each of the fifteen put up $100 of his own. That original, $1,500 grew to over $10 million by 1970.

(A mutual savings and loan association is not a business intended for profit. Its function is to receive the savings of individuals, pay interest on them, and invest the money almost entirely in home mortgages. Savings and loan associations are generally not permitted to handle checking accounts or make business or personal loans. As mutual institutions they are controlled and owned by their depositors, and any "profits" made are retained as reserves. Accordingly, those who organize a savings and loan association do so not out of a profit motive but because they are interested in the social and economic benefits that accrue to the community from controlling its own financial institution.)

Mutual Savings and Loan of Atlanta remained small for many years. It was not until the 1940s that it could even afford a full-time employee. Until then, Blayton and his associates handled all of the operations and bookkeeping, generally without fee.

During the Depression the association regularly credited interest in the depositors' passbooks, even though it didn't always have the cash. "Some of our homeowners got into trouble and were running late with their payments, but we usually tried to work with them and they paid us when they could. We were fortunate in that our depositors didn't come in and ask for their money all at once, because we would have had to ask them to wait."

By 1970, the Mutual Federal Savings and Loan Association of Atlanta had total assets of over $10,000,000 and reserves and surplus of over $1,000,000. And it had over $8,000,000 invested in mortgages, practically all of them on homes owned by black people in Georgia. It is the only black savings and loan association in the state.

It has a number of white depositors, a few of whom have rather sizable accounts. One of them told Blayton, "I don't want my account in my own community because I'm afraid the tellers talk."

Blayton replied, "I really don't think tellers talk that much. Tellers are pretty much like everybody else, they want to get the day's work done and then close up and go home. But let's suppose that you are right—don't you think black tellers talk, too?"

"Yes, but they don't move in my circle. . . ."

Blayton also has a number of white accountancy clients.

Throughout his business career, Blayton has worked closely with two good friends, Lorimer D. Milton and Clayton A. Yates, one of whose enterprises is the Yates and Milton Company, which owns and operates a chain of drugstores. Milton was for some time chairman of the board of trustees of Howard University. The three men were among the organizers of the savings and loan association; Yates is now chairman of the board and Blayton president.

In 1933, these three men bought Citizens Trust Company, a commercial bank with $189,000 in assets, almost half of which were uncollectable loans. It was surprising that they had the courage to take such a remarkable step when banks all over the country were failing and when, indeed, many people felt that the economic and financial structure of the country was rapidly heading toward total disintegration. Almost as noteworthy is the fact that they had the money to buy it when almost everyone else in the country was broke.

Blayton says, "We didn't buy it with money so much as with our fountain pens"—that is, with promissory notes. "The former owners didn't think it could be saved, but we thought so. And we managed it, although it took quite a while. All during the thirties I worked on the books at the bank in the evenings and never collected a fee." Today

Citizens Trust has assets totaling close to $30 million and is the second-largest black-owned commercial bank in the nation, after Freedom National of New York.

Blayton has invested in a variety of business enterprises over the years. One was a radio station in Atlanta, WERD,* which he bought in 1949 and sold at a profit twenty years later. We asked Blayton if he is a millionaire. He didn't say yes. But he didn't say no, either.

In addition to being a commercial banker, a savings banker, a CPA and an investor in a number of businesses, he has been involved in a wide variety of civic and community activities. He is a commissioner of the Atlanta Housing Authority, one of five appointed by the mayor and confirmed by the state senate. He is a trustee of the Ebenezer Baptist Church, where the Reverend Dr. Martin Luther King, Jr., was associate pastor. He has been for many years a member of the board of directors of the Atlanta Urban League, and was its chairman from 1956 to 1967. Not surprisingly, his listing in *Who's Who in America* covers thirty-one lines.

Blayton doesn't have too much spare time, but much of what he does have is devoted to reading. He has done extensive reading in the history of civilization and in philosophy. At the time of our interview he was working his way through Immanuel Kant. "I won't live long enough, of course, but I would like to know what the great thinkers have said about this world, and how they figured it out.

"When I was young, I thought I was very smart. But the longer you live, the more you find out you don't know. As I look back, I see that I didn't really know what I was doing a good part of the time. And yet somehow I managed to do pretty well and to build some things that lasted. . . ."

Would Blayton recommend to a young man that he go into business for himself?

"I don't think you can generalize about that—it depends

* The station had been named after Dr. Charles Drew, a black surgeon who invented the process by which blood plasma is separated and thus can be preserved, stored, shipped and made available for emergency transfusions.

on the man. I'd have to get to know him and observe him for a while to see whether he had the stuff it takes to be on his own. It takes a lot of independence, a lot of determination and long, long hours.

"An entrepreneur has to make a lot of decisions and make them alone. Some of his decisions will be wrong, and some of his wrong decisions will be expensive. And you know a lot of people—I would say most people—get scared when they have to make decisions. They are so afraid of making a mistake that they can't ever decide anything.

"Now, if he's that kind of man, who wants to have somebody always telling him what to do, then he should work for somebody else. People are different. . . ."

How does he feel about the changes he has seen in the South in his seventy years?

"There really isn't that much difference between the South and the North as far as treatment of black people is concerned. Slavery was an *economic* thing; if slavery had made economic sense in Massachusetts, they would have had slavery in Massachusetts. By the time of the Civil War, slavery no longer made sense in the state of Georgia, but they were so committed to it by then that they couldn't see the dollars and cents. The high people continued to have slaves because, well, it was like wearing your fraternity pin on your coat. . . .

"The Southern white man has always had the attitude that '*my* Negro can do whatever he wants to.' But I never let myself be *his* Negro. If I had, I could have gotten a lot further than I did.

"I think that life in America has changed considerably since the early 1950s. Some of that change came about as a result of legislation, but not all of it. I believe that there has been some change in the human mind. I think people, both black and white, understand a little more than they did before. A little more. . . ."

13

Earl A. Williams: Bindery Owner

"The place we lived in during the Depression was really out in the sticks. It had no running water, no electricity—kerosene lamps, and not too many of them. If you went into another room you carried the lamp with you. We ate a lot of steamboat molasses and stuff out of the garden. We ate what we grew—if we didn't grow it, we didn't eat it."

Earl Williams got off a bus in Chicago in 1943 with $20 in one of his shoes. He was fifteen years old and had been one of the fastest cotton pickers in east Tennessee. Five days later, he got a job at the I. S. Berlin Press in Chicago by claiming to be seventeen. With three years out for military service, he worked there almost every day except Sunday until 1961. He might have stayed there the rest of his life, but he found that many fine opportunities that were available to others were closed to him.

"One day," said Williams, "I was talking to one of the union members, and I said, 'You know, I must have more sense than you do. You're driving that old beat-up jalopy, and I just took delivery on a new car. You're paying rent to a landlord, while I'm making mortgage payments and building up equity in my own home. And I make a dollar an hour less than you do because you won't let me in the union. . . .' "

Williams almost never took a vacation, and he worked every Saturday to earn double time. "I didn't *want* to work Saturdays—I *had* to. One of the biggest problems the black man has is that since he is confined to low-paying jobs, he has to work very long hours to support his family, and he doesn't have time to give his kids the attention they should have. And that's one of the reasons some of them are out in the streets getting into trouble."

I. S. Berlin is a large printing and binding company producing books, magazines, catalogs and a variety of other printed matter. When he first went to work there, he was "fresh out of the cotton fields and full of energy, but I had a lot to learn. If they had told me to pick up the building and turn it over I think I would have tried it." He was sent to the bindery division and assigned to a large paper-cutting machine.

The chief operator of the machine, a man named Art Bleck, had four men working under him. Within a few weeks, Williams—alone—was doing the work of all four. Bleck liked the energetic young man and undertook to provide some fatherly guidance, which Williams needed just then.

"I had never had any money in my pocket before, and I didn't know how to manage it properly. A lot of people took advantage of me and sold me rings and watches that I thought were valuable but were really junk. Bleck took me over to the office one day and made arrangements for them to deduct $15 a week from my pay and deposit it in an account in the credit union. He stood right there while I filled out the forms to make sure I did it.

"And he taught me the importance of getting to work on time. It didn't matter if there was a flood or five inches of snow, Bleck himself always got there on time, and he instilled that in me." Williams had dropped out of high school to come North, and Bleck insisted that he attend night school to get his diploma.

"Bleck was a stern and demanding man, a hard task-master, but if you performed, if you did the job, he treated you more than fairly. He wasn't the most popular guy in the plant anyway, and there was a lot of grumbling about the way he treated me. They thought he was favoring me, which wasn't true at all. I just worked harder than most of the men did, and he knew he could depend on me."

The union local adamantly refused to allow Williams to join. As he worked harder and gained more responsibility, they were even more determined to keep him out, just because he was so conscientious. "A couple of them even told me that. They said that I was too ambitious, that I'd go right past them to the top." At one point the president of the company intervened with union officials on Williams's behalf, but to no avail.

A few years later, Bleck was promoted to foreman, and he made Williams his assistant. This allowed Williams to master the operation of the bindery, to learn the various machines and how to schedule work. "I would come in Saturdays and work with the maintenance department, greasing the machines and adjusting and repairing them. I learned how to improvise and keep them running so as to avoid expensive down time and expensive repair calls. That came in very handy after I had my own machines and my own bills to pay."

Eventually, Williams became *de facto* head of the department, such was Bleck's reliance upon him. "He turned more and more things over to me, and pretty soon it got so that he barely knew what was going on. Time and again I would schedule a vacation, but he would plead with me not to go because he depended on me so much.

"I was pleased by his confidence and his trust, and it was a beautiful opportunity, too. Among other things, I talked directly to the customers about the details of the jobs and when they would be shipped. I would hear their complaints and make adjustments, and that way I got to know a number of people who had business to give out, and they got to know me. A lot of them are my customers now."

After finishing high school at night, Williams took

courses in hatmaking, with the idea of possibly changing to that trade. He also studied bookkeeping and accounting. "I think that the company was genuinely embarrassed about the union problem. I had given them loyal service, and they felt they owed me something. Partly because of this, but also because I had taken courses and trained myself in accounting, they promoted me to the accounting department."

Williams was pleased to leave a blue-collar job for a white-collar one, but he was thinking further ahead. It had also pleased him to find that he could establish good relations with the bindery's customers, provide them with good service, calm them down when something went wrong and generally keep them satisfied.

He had always been ambitious to be a salesman, and he thought that he had the necessary ability and temperament. When he approached his superiors about it, "they were sympathetic, but they told me 'The world isn't ready for it.' I kept after them, and finally they said, 'Why don't you go and see X [a competitor] and apply for a position as salesman—if they offer it to you come back here and we'll match their offer.'

"Well, that wasn't much of a deal. If my own bosses, who knew my talents and abilities first hand, wouldn't hire me, why should someone who didn't know me take a chance? So of course nothing came of that."

Williams was frustrated and unhappy because he seemed to be bumping his head on ceilings everywhere he turned. He saw plant men that he had trained moving to highly paid supervisory positions, and the lucrative field of selling was also closed to him. "I like to be happy, and I just wasn't happy in that situation." A competitor who heard about his dissatisfaction offered him a 25 per cent increase in pay to come over and manage his bindery.

"I didn't really want to leave Berlin, but I couldn't afford to pass up that money. They offered me a small raise if I would stay—but they said, 'We can't go any higher. You're a good accountant but you're not a CPA.' "

Williams wanted both to make sure that the other man

would keep his promises and also to get a first-hand look at the other organization before burning his bridges; so he started work there while on vacation from Berlin. "They really rolled out the red carpet for me," he says. "It looked as though it would be a good place to work. The starting money was very good . . . I just didn't see how I could pass it by. Besides that, I also thought I might get further raises."

In 1961, after eighteen years, he left I. S. Berlin. "That plant is a block long, and I went through it from one end to the other shaking hands and saying good-by—and when I got to the end of the building, I was in tears. I felt no animosity or bitterness toward anybody there. In fact, they are customers of mine today."

He got along well at the new company and did indeed get a raise after less than a year. He was in full charge of all bindery operations. But after a couple of years, he began to sense that the company was losing ground and that its problems would get worse. (They did—eventually the company was sold.) He realized that he would have to make another change.

"By this time I was in my middle thirties, and I didn't think much of the idea of starting over again in a new job. A black man has to be overqualified—he is paid less than he is worth—and I knew it would take me a long time to gain recognition. I really didn't want to go through all that again. And I wanted to be a salesman . . . I felt I could sell. I began to give some serious thought to starting my own bindery."

Williams says he didn't discuss the idea with anybody except his wife. "It doesn't pay to tell people about your dreams, because they will just try to discourage you and tell you about all the problems you will have." It is probably just as well that he didn't. Almost anyone would have told him that the odds against him were tremendous.

The Fidelity Bindery Company opened for business in November 1964, on the fourth floor of an old building on Chicago's South Side. The space was not really satisfactory, but the rent was low. Williams was unable to get any financial help. He tried a number of banks. Some didn't even give him a hearing; others told him that his plans sounded very interesting and suggested that he "come back in a year or so and tell us how you're getting along." The only capital he had was what he had saved, a few thousand dollars. Most of it went for a down payment on a used paper-trimming machine. He soon found that he could not do an adequate job until he also had a folding machine. He ordered one and waited three months for delivery.

"By chance, I made contact with some people at the Simmons Company who had a large assembling and collating job. It didn't require any equipment, just a lot of human hands. It was a onetime job for them and they didn't want to hire temporary people, so they contracted it to us. It was a godsend. We interviewed over a hundred people and hired twenty-five, and we put them to work on three shifts assembling that catalogue. We didn't make much profit on it, but it gave us a chance to try out a number of people and find which ones were the best workers. It helped us pay the rent and keep the doors open. Then, just about the time it was finished, the folding machine was delivered."

Many of his first customers were people he had known while he was at Berlin. One of his earliest—and still one of his best—customers was Kukla Press, Schiller Park, Illinois. "They gave me a basic education in business; as a customer, they didn't really have to do that. They are fine people—I consider them not only good customers but also good friends." Another good customer is *Look* magazine.

Several dozen companies in Chicago did the same kind of work, and most had better equipment. All Williams could offer was quality and service, and he concentrated on these. In the printing and publishing business, where almost everything is done on a tight schedule, meeting deadlines is absolutely essential. Fidelity Bindery has always prided itself on its promptness.

"I try to keep to the schedule even if the other guy misses it. And he will appreciate that and remember it over the years. Sometimes he will send business to me even when my price is a little bit higher because he needs the assurance of meeting his deadline. That's the way you build a business." In the early days, he would often stay at the plant all night, catching a short nap on a mattress he kept in the back of his station wagon.

As the business grew, Williams constantly encountered financing problems. He was making profits, but in order to provide good service he needed expensive machinery. At the beginning, when nobody believed he would survive, it was practically impossible for him to get credit either from banks or from equipment manufacturers.

On one occasion, he placed an order for a $62,000 stitching machine. It had to be built especially to his specifications, and he saw that the salesman was skeptical about his ability to pay for it. Williams gave the salesman a $2,000 deposit and agreed to pay $1,000 a month, with the understanding that they would ship the machine to him after he had paid the $15,000 down payment.

"Somebody got their wires crossed, and the machine was delivered in three or four months. When the salesman saw it sitting on my floor, he was very much disturbed. 'Don't uncrate it,' he said.

"I got on the phone to the manufacturer in the East and talked to the treasurer. I said, 'Look, we acted in good faith here, and we didn't ask for any special favors. But since somebody made a mistake and shipped the machine, why don't you leave it here? It doesn't make sense to pay the freight bill for taking it out of here and then bringing it back later—if you leave it here, I'll put it to work and it will start to pay for itself.'

"Well, he agreed. I've found that if a man isn't prejudiced and will listen, I can usually sell myself to him. It's not that I'm a con man, it's just that I tell the truth and I don't give up."

Williams was eventually able to establish bank credit, but that too was a struggle. After repeated rebuffs, "I finally found one loan officer who said he believed in me, but that his superiors didn't. He said, 'Look, I'm going to lend you $500 for ninety days, and I want you to pay it back in eighty. Then, as soon as that's done, I'll lend you $1,000 for ninety days, and I want you to pay that back in eighty, too. Then we'll go to $1,500. . . .' "

That bank could easily see how well the business was doing, because all his deposits flowed into his checking account there. Even so, he had to go through the ninety-day exercises several times. "It took a year before they even bothered to take a half an hour to come out and look at the plant. After they saw it they offered me a big loan on a longer-term basis, but by then I didn't need it."

Now the banks are anxious to lend money to Fidelity Bindery. With his credit established, Williams can simply call and tell them to put $5,000 or $10,000 into his account, and they will do it that day.

Williams's faith in God has become a very important part of his life.

"I was always a God-fearing person. I went to church regularly and my wife did, too, and we always got the kids up and sent them to Sunday school. One day my wife started attending a Bible-study class given by Jehovah's Witnesses, and not too long after that she stopped going to church. We found that a great deal of what was said and preached in church wasn't in the Bible at all.

"For example, I had always been taught that unless I was good I would burn in hell, and I had always been afraid of that. But you can't find that anywhere in the Bible. God is the God of love, and we are his children—now if your children do something wrong, do you burn them up, do you put them in the oven?

"I still kept going to church, even after my wife stopped, but I started to ask the pastor some hard questions. He couldn't answer them—not only that, but he got very indignant about it. . . ."

Williams and his wife both became active Jehovah's Witnesses. "I pray every day. I pray for wisdom, knowledge, insight and thinking ability. I ask God to give me the knowledge to deal with the people I have to deal with. As to those who are plotting against me, and I have found quite a few, I pray that he will help me to deal with them, but not for revenge. I say let God's will be done."

As one of Jehovah's Witnesses, Williams engages actively

in the ministry. He is a congregation overseer and teaches Bible classes. "We don't go in for a lot of false doctrine. Jehovah's Witnesses follow what the Bible says, not what any man says. We follow the Scripture. A lot of people think that is old-fashioned, but the Bible is as modern as tomorrow."

Williams's faith has been put to some severe tests. Not once but several times he and his wife have suffered blows that would have destroyed and defeated people who do not possess their incredible inner strength. The cruelest blow of all came in 1965. A few months after Williams had taken the plunge into his own business, Mrs. Williams suddenly lost her sight. With seven children still at home, with the incredible emotional strain of launching a risky new venture, with no money coming in until the business prospered, the family was unexpectedly hit with this misfortune.

Mrs. Williams has adjusted to her blindness with equanimity, patience and good humor. As soon as she could, she started attending school to learn braille. She insists on doing her share of the cooking and kitchen work, even though the older daughters and a housekeeper could easily handle it. She is involved in a busy schedule of meetings and activities and has continued to practice the piano regularly. She also knits and crochets.

"My wife is a very intelligent and wonderful woman, and she has been an immeasurable help to me. She went to college and I didn't, but she never held that over my head. She helped educate me. If it were not for her blindness, she would have an important part in the business. . . ."

The Williamses have seven children, four boys and three girls. The oldest daughter is married and raising a family. Oldest son Larry and second daughter Pat both work at Fidelity, and the other four children will probably do the same.

Williams was born in Waterproof, Louisiana, in 1928. His parents separated when he was an infant, and his mother and grandmother took him to live in the cotton fields near Memphis. They were very, very poor. Williams earned a few pennies a day picking cotton before he was ten, and he had to work regularly after his mother died when he was twelve. He finished grammar school in Tennessee, but after less than a year of high school he decided to go to Chicago.

"I volunteered for the Air Force as soon as I was old enough because I was patriotic. I went to cooking and baking school and also typing school, but I ended up spending most of my time as a mechanic. I had always wanted to travel and to fly, and I got a chance to do a lot of flying. I was with a top-notch organization, the Ninety-ninth Fighter Squadron, and it had a lot of good pilots. The commanding officer was Colonel Benjamin O. Davis, Jr., who later became the second black general in American history; his father had been the first."

Fidelity Bindery is now a well-established success. Its sales are running at the rate of over half a million dollars a year. All of the company's business is printed advertising matter of one kind or another. Among other things, it cuts and folds coupon inserts for national magazines, assembles and binds catalogues and folds and assembles direct-mail advertising pieces for mail-order houses. Most of its business comes from regular customers who send work several times a year, sometimes every month.

The company has moved four times, always to larger quarters. Since January 1970, it has occupied a 15,000 square-foot plant, built to Fidelity's specifications, in an industrial park in Broadview, Illinois, a western suburb of Chicago.

The company started with one cutting machine and, a few months later, one folding machine. It now has nine folding machines, two cutters and an elaborate stitching machine. It has recently taken delivery of a high-speed, heavy-duty folding machine, which is the only one of its kind in the Chicago area. "All of our machines are the best in the industry, and we are very careful to keep them adjusted and in good repair at all times."

Fidelity has twenty-three employees, a few of whom are white and most of whom are young. All were unskilled when they started, and were trained on the job. Although Williams and his wife own all the stock of the company, several of his key people share in its success through bonuses.

"I try to give all my employees a fair shake and to treat them just as I do my customers. If anybody has a problem, we try to hear both sides of the story and work it out without animosity. I think we have good working relationships here, and a lot of the people who started with me are in key positions here now."

After an article about Williams appeared in *Ebony*, he received a flood of applications for jobs (as well as several for handouts), a number of them from prisons. One letter from a prisoner in Alabama was so touching and sincere that Williams agreed to hire the man sight unseen and so notified his parole board. "We're all imperfect, we all make mistakes. I may be disappointed in this man, but I don't think so. I have very rarely been disappointed in people I've tried to help.

"We have had some hard knocks along the way, but we have had some stretches of smooth road, too. We took quite a chance when we started, and a lot of people were looking for us to fail. We might have lost everything we have, including our home, and the nine Williamses would have had a rough time. My wife has been a wonderful support . . . she encouraged me to take the risk.

"Some people think that a black businessman has to really tuck his tail, but I can't say that. I talk to all kinds of people every day, and I talk to all of them the same way. I'm not superior to anybody and I'm not inferior to anybody. I think that being one of Jehovah's Witnesses has helped me to communicate.

"Of course, there are always problems. A few of our customers try to trip us up, try to get the job done for nothing. They try to get us to agree to a delivery schedule that they know is impossible and then try to charge us for their down time when we are late. Or they will pick through and find twenty bad pieces out of 2,000,000 and try to beat the price down because of a picayune thing like that."

Williams says he doesn't ever want to be a millionaire,

but he does want to stay active in the business. He would like to have a little more time to spend with his family, to take trips with them, and to play some golf. He almost never took a vacation at I. S. Berlin, and hasn't had one since starting his own company.

"I don't want to be a big shot. I keep a good suit and clean shirts here at the plant, because sometimes I have to go downtown and take customers to lunch at some of the finest restaurants in Chicago. But then I just come back here and change clothes, and if a machine needs greasing or adjusting I just go to work and take care of it.

"I have tried to make a contribution to society in my own small way, and I think I have succeeded. I suppose we could have opened a barbecue joint, but I wanted to do something more meaningful. I believe we have done something useful, but everything that has been accomplished in this business I owe to Almighty God.

"I don't really agree with a lot of the protest marches and so on that are going on. They have done some good, it's true, but I have never participated in them. The world is in a very mixed-up state—you hardly ever see any good news on TV or in the newspaper. I just don't feel that human creatures will ever be able to straighten out this world.

"There's too much delinquency, too much strife, too much hatred. The world can't go on the way it is now. In the past, God overlooked much, but now he is telling men that they must repent, because he has set a day when he proposes to judge the earth. Almighty God has got to bring this world to an end. . . ."

14

A Large Landowner
in the Southeast

"I think we have been able to make a contribution to this county and the people who live here, and to this state and this country, too. . . ."

Now in his sixties, he has spent many years out of doors in the wind and rain. Like men all over the world who work the land and wear hats against the fierce sun, his forehead is several shades lighter than his chin.

"I wouldn't say the neighbors were too crazy about it when I first took over this property," he said. "Back in the thirties they wouldn't give me the time of day. But then during World War II, when there were shortages of everything and it was especially hard to get help, we worked together a little better. One of them got into a spot one time, so I lent him a man for a day or two. Then after a while, he did the same for me, and pretty soon we were exchanging things and helping and—well, just getting along together. I thought maybe we were almost to the place where we could all live together like human beings, but I guess that was too much to expect. Most all of my neighbors voted for George Wallace last time. . . ."

His landholdings total several thousand acres in various locations. He farms some of them himself, and some are operated by white tenant farmers. He requires his tenants to provide permanent year-round jobs, not merely seasonal work, for black farm hands. In exchange for this, he charges them less rent than he otherwise would, less than the market would bear.

Some of the land is kept permanently in pasture; some of the cultivated land is also used for grazing in alternate years of the crop-rotation cycle. He has several hundred cattle and operates a commercial breeding herd, which means that he sells most of the calves to feeders, who raise them to maturity for market. He keeps only enough female calves to maintain the herd.

There are valuable mineral deposits on his property, and he derives a very regular and dependable additional income from this source. He takes pride in the fact that there are no liens or mortgages on any of the properties—they are all owned free and clear. Of course, it was not always that way.

We suggested that he might be the wealthiest black man in the U.S. "I'm not at all sure about that," he replied. "You have to remember that a number of them have gone behind the curtain and done very well indeed, and of course the value of things changes from year to year. Anyway, I'm not interested in any kind of contest—I think the important thing is that we were able to hold all of this together, and not only hold it together but build on it and develop it. This operation gives year-round employment to more than thirty people, and it pays a lot of taxes. I think we have been able to make a contribution to this county and the people who live here, and to this state and this country, too. . . ."

His grandfather bought the land he now owns for 25¢ an acre in the middle of the nineteenth century. His mother was born in slavery. She was a small child when Lincoln freed the slaves in 1863.

The youngest of five children, he was the only one born in the twentieth century; his oldest sister was born twenty-five years earlier. He also had two brothers and another sister. His parents insisted that all of their children get the best education, and as much of it as possible. Fortunately, they had the means to arrange this. He completed the local segregated school, which ended at sixth grade, and then he was sent to Chicago to live with an older sister so that he could go to school there. He was promptly put back to fourth grade, such was the difference in the level of instruction. Later he attended a well-known black preparatory school in the South. As a boarding student there, he always received money from home for incidental expenses and a liberal allowance.

All in all, he received the kind of upbringing that was typical of a propertied family at the turn of the century. The rules of behavior were those of the Victorian era. His father, kindly but stern, held his five children to high standards of performance and insisted that they work hard. He helped them with their studies and scolded them when they spent their allowances foolishly.

"Toward the end of his life, my father could barely walk, and he had a nurse caring for him all the time. He would have that nurse drive him over to my mother's house every day, and they would just sit and talk. . . ."

Remembering his father's final years still brings tears to his eyes. "One of the last things he said to me was to ask me to look after his nephew Ralph, one of my cousins, and to help him out if he ever got into trouble. And there were several times that I had to help Ralph out."

His father had been one of three children, and it had been understood that the land would be divided into three equal parts for the three families. When his father died, in 1933, the will left all of his one-third of the land to the five children, there being no half-brothers or half-sisters. The cousins went into court and tried to break the will, but the five black children fought back, and so carefully and thoroughly had the legal details been worked out that they were able to defend the will successfully and preserve their inheritance. That was in a rural Southern court in 1934.

After his two brothers died, he assumed charge of the family properties. Over the years, he strengthened and improved them, gradually whittled down the debts and eventually paid all of them, put his own five children through college and looked after his nieces and nephews.

This black man can be accurately and appropriately described as a man of means, a substantial citizen, a working farmer and a gentleman farmer. His exemplary and constructive life have done honor to his parents, his children and his country.

Thus did he respond to the unspeakable brutality of the society into which he was born and of the laws of his native state, which prohibited his black mother and his white father from living together legally under the same roof or ever being legally married.

15

James E. Hurt, Jr.: Housing Developer, Supermarket Operator and Volkswagen Dealer

"If anybody else in this country can do it, we can do it, too."

In April 1969, a new supermarket called Central City Foods opened for business at the corner of Grand and Delmar in Saint Louis, Missouri. It is a beautiful store—clean, orderly, tastefully designed, well lighted and maintained, with a large parking lot, wide aisles and attractively displayed merchandise. It is very much like other modern supermarkets that have been opened throughout the country in recent years, but this particular store has some features that most people would consider unusual.

All of the store's owners, all of its managers and supervisory personnel and almost all of its employees are black. It is located in a black neighborhood. About one of every five customers is white.

Five black subcontractors were involved in the construction of the store—they handled the excavating, bricklaying, roofing, electrical work and landscaping.

The First National Bank of Saint Louis advanced the construction money. The plot on which the store stands was bought, with money borrowed from one of America's large life-insurance companies, from the Land Clearance Authority of Saint Louis under a federal urban-renewal program. It was the first federal urban-renewal site ever to be sold to black purchasers anywhere in the United States.

Within a few months after opening, sales were over $50,000 a week, extremely good for a store with a 10,000 square-foot selling area. Before the seventh month of operation the store began making profits, which is not only good, it is phenomenal—America's large chains usually expect their new stores to run at a loss for at least two years. Yet a consumer-group survey of a number of Saint Louis food stores showed that Central City's prices are as low as those in any other store and lower for most items.

The store is owned by about 2,000 people, who bought stock at $10 a share. Some have only one share.

James E. Hurt, Jr., who organized Central City Foods, is an advocate—one might even say an evangelist—of the idea that black people must achieve economic power before they can bring about any meaningful change in their lives and join the American mainstream. In 1963, Hurt began holding meetings with a group of black ministers. "Since they speak to more black people than anybody else, I thought I would try to educate them in economics and how money makes things happen in America." The Wednesday Morning Breakfast Club has a total membership of about sixty ministers, and it meets every week, winter and summer, in Hurt's office.

Over the years, as the members got to know each other and began to look for projects they could work on together, the idea of Central City was born. Its purpose was to develop both ownership opportunities and jobs for black residents of Saint Louis. Hurt says, "We didn't really start it to make a profit," Hurt says. "Basically we wanted to prove to black people that if anybody else in this country can do it, we can do it too."

It was decided to raise money by selling shares of stock within the black community. The ministers held evening meetings at their churches to tell the story, and within a few months $200,000 had been pledged. "I would say that 80 per cent of the investors in Central City Foods never had any concept of what the word 'stock' meant. Maybe 70 per cent of them still don't. But the fact is that they have at home now, in a drawer somewhere, a stock certificate."

The largest stockholder has 500 shares. "This is a fellow that, if you saw him, you wouldn't believe he had $5,000 worth of stock. I've never seen him with a tie on, and he lives in a furnished room, but actually he's a businessman. He has five or six trucks that he hires out."

It probably would have been impossible to find the money anywhere else, but there was also an important fringe benefit to the stock sale. Central City's stockholders are among its best and most loyal customers, and they may account for as much as half of its sales.

Hurt also approached a number of white ministers and asked them to get pledges from members of their churches to shop at Central City once a year. They were not asked to change their shopping habits, but just to come once a year. "We realized that many white people want to do something to help black people but don't know how to go about it. We told them that this was their chance to do something. 'And by shopping at Central City,' we said, 'you will do something else—you will mingle with black people and find out that we don't all carry knives. Most important, you will leave something in the ghetto that you never left before—your money. But for your money you will get excellent value.' "

Central City buys much of its merchandise from General Grocers, a large white-owned Saint Louis wholesaling firm. Hurt made contact with General Grocers early in the discussion stage and asked for their help. Their specialists spent many hours meeting with him and discussing site selection, layout and design, hiring, merchandising and practically every phase of planning and operating the store. "We would never have attempted it without their help," says Hurt.

Central City Foods has a delicatessen with carry-out sandwiches and other foods. It has a complete drugstore, including a pharmacy, that is operated on a leased basis by an independent businessman who runs a separate cash register. In most supermarkets meat accounts for about 25 per cent of sales, but Central City takes in 38¢ of every sales dollar through its meat department—and meat is one of the most profitable items in the store.

The organization and financing of Central City would do credit to the most imaginative Wall Street investment banker. Since the land was an urban-renewal site, it had to be purchased by a redevelopment company. Hurt created Vanguard Redevelopment Corporation as a subsidiary of one of his other companies. Vanguard bought the land, built the building and rented it to Central City Foods, Inc. The U.S. Small Business Administration, through its lease-guarantee program, has ensured that Central City will pay its rent; this helped considerably in arranging the financing.

"We had a difficult time with the urban renewal people," Hurt said, "because we were all black men and they didn't feel we had the expertise to do the job. It took us eight months to convince them to let us have the site. We had to present plan after plan after plan. Of course what they wanted was an economic base, an organization that looked like it was strong enough to do the job. Fortunately, I have some housing and building experience and some good people in my organization, and we also had the strength of most of the black ministers in Saint Louis. Even so, I had the feeling that they thought they were taking a terrible chance to let us have it.

"After we got the okay from urban renewal and firmed up our plans for the store, we leased part of the site to Ralston Purina for a Jack in the Box restaurant. We took the Ralston Purina lease down to General American Life Insurance Company and borrowed enough money on it to buy the other part of the plot where the supermarket was built. But they only took a mortgage on the half of the land that Ralston Purina was using, so that gave us the other half free and clear. We used that land as a down payment on the third phase of the project. So we're doing it without putting a nickel of our own money into it.

"This is the economics that black people must be able to understand and become a part of, because this is something that white people have been doing for years. The name of the game is to borrow as much of other people's money as possible."

Before it had been in business a year, Central City was running its cash registers at the rate of over $3,000,000 a year, making it, in terms of sales, the largest black-owned business in Saint Louis County. Its forty employees, almost all of whom are black, are earning an *average* of $3.57 an hour. Its prices are the lowest in town, and it is making a profit.

Hurt was born in Saint Louis in 1923. His father was a businessman and a doctor, a general practitioner who came from a poor family and had a real struggle to get his medical education. He would go to school for a year, then work a year and save enough money to go back to school. During his alternate working years he operated a number of business ventures, including an automobile-repair shop and a newspaper in New Jersey. He continued throughout his life to run businesses even while practicing medicine full time.

"My father was the source of all of my philosophy and everything I say. This is one of the advantages I have over other black men. I'm one generation ahead of most of them, because I had a father who talked nothing but business. I was brought up in that background. His true success was in his medical practice, but he always had an interest in business. He had an extraordinary ability to turn a nickel into a dime."

Hurt wanted to go to college in Saint Louis, but it was "whites only" before the war, so he started at Ohio State in 1940, majoring in business administration. His education was interrupted by military service—three years in the China-Burma-India theater of operations. After the war, he was able to enter Saint Louis University, where he received his B.A. in 1948.

He then went to work for Employees Loan and Investment Company, a small firm that his father had started in 1938 with an investment of $2,000. Young Hurt watched his father build the loan company and learned many of the practices and habits that he follows today.

"We had a unique ability to trace bad accounts because we used every method known. If a man owed us money and we didn't know where he worked, we'd just go to his house at 5:30 in the morning and wait for him to come out. Then we'd follow him to work and come back and run a garnishment against him.

"I'll never forget one fellow that I waited for one morning. When he came out, I followed him, it must have been five miles, and finally he went into a plant. I walked right in behind him and watched him punch the clock. When I got back to the office and called up, they said he didn't work there. I couldn't figure it out because I had seen him punch in.

"Two years later, a fellow came in one day to make a loan, and when he gave his address a little bell rang in my head. I said, 'You live down there by my friend, Sam Jones.' He said, 'Oh, you're talking about Joe Smith, he changed his name.' So, two years later, I got him."

Employees Loan and Investment Company, like any finance company, had to borrow a lot of money in order to have something to lend, and in its early days that was very difficult. The company was able to do so only because the elder Hurt and some of the other directors were men of means—the borrowing was done on their personal credit. Employees Loan paid high rates and had to repay in monthly installments, just as its own small-loan customers did.

"One time my Dad and several other men went to the bank and offered to put up almost a million dollars worth of collateral to borrow $15,000. And the bank said no. Many people think that sort of thing hasn't happened since 1870, but this was Saint Louis, Missouri, U.S.A., in 1961!

"It happened that a few weeks later an item appeared in the newspaper mentioning me as a possible candidate for the Saint Louis Board of Education. That very day the bank *called me* and asked what had happened to our loan application.

"I said, 'You turned us down.' They said that there must have been some mistake, and would I please come down to see them. The end of the story is that I picked up a check that day, not for $15,000 but for $25,000, and they lent it to me on my signature with no security at all."

Hurt became a member of the board of education that year, and has served on it since. He was president for two years. He belongs to a number of other committees and civic groups, and he is a capable and impressive public speaker. As a result, he is one of the few black men in Saint Louis who has a large number of acquaintances among its bankers, businessmen and political leaders.

Today when Hurt wants to borrow from a bank or an insurance company, he first makes a phone call to its president, whom he inevitably knows because they have served together on some board or committee. "I get a good reception because they know me personally. But this has not been true throughout my business career, and it surely isn't true for other black men who aren't known. It shows what a black man has to do to get into the system."

As the years went by, Hurt, like his father, began to get involved in a variety of business ventures. He opened a retail-furniture store, which has been a continuing success in a small way, and during the 1950s he managed a public-housing project for two years. Although he then returned to the loan business, he continued to take an interest in housing.

Some years later, a public-housing project decided to contract out its management. Hurt saw an opportunity and moved swiftly to exploit it, organizing a company to bid on one of the management contracts. He called the woman (white) who had been his deputy as a project manager and asked her to work for him again, and she agreed.

Hurt's housing company—now called Vanguard Bond and Mortgage Company—is presently managing a public-housing project in the Kinloch section of Saint Louis and supervising the construction of two others. Another project involves sale, on a subsidized basis, of attached one-family houses to people of low income, and Vanguard has a contract to provide training and orientation to home ownership for the new owners and also for other neighborhood residents.

"We have a uniqueness in our organization that makes it possible for us to get these contracts. Other people are trying to get them, but there is no other organization, black or white, that is constituted like us, or that has our experience and know-how in public housing."

Hurt has been involved in housing-project planning and design as well. He has not yet functioned as a general contractor for the actual construction, but this is a step he hopes to take soon. He has filed with the federal urban-renewal authorities several proposals for housing projects that, if approved, will be built under his sponsorship.

Hurt was asked whether he makes an effort to employ blacks. "Of course we do, but we try to do more than that. Our whole philosophy is that, although building-trades employment is tremendously important, a quicker way of accomplishing something is through black entrepreneurship. When we were building the supermarket, we said to the contractor, 'If you want this contract, you must hire five black subcontractors—not employees, subcontractors.' He hemmed and hawed and jumped and shifted, but we had the economic leverage—it was our project. So he hired them— the bricklaying was black, the electrical work was black, the roofing, excavating and landscaping. When a contractor takes in a black subcontractor, you automatically have black workers brought in wholesale as opposed to a token situation.

"When we started to build West Side Community Gardens, a $1,600,000 project, we took those same black subcontractors and moved them over. Then we went further. I said to the contractor, 'If you want this contract, you're going to have to place your performance bond and all your insurance through a black insurance agency.' He went through the roof!

"I just let him think about it. We have over $33 million worth of construction either under way or planned, and I knew that this was the leverage I had on him. I'd ask him about it every once in a while, and then it got down to time to sign the contract, and finally he said, 'I can't do that.'

"I said, 'Why can't you do that?'

"He said, 'Well, I've been dealing with my bonding company all these years. They know me and my financial position, and they will do things for me.'

"I said, 'I'm not interested in the bonding company, I'm interested in the insurance agent that you place it with. We have black insurance men that can place insurance anywhere—they'll place it with your bonding company, don't worry about that. I'm interested in the commission, the profit.' These profits on projects in the black community have been going to white insurance agencies for years—I wanted that profit to stay in the black community.

"Two days before it was time to sign the contract, we talked again, and I said, 'Now is the time, my friend, because I'm not signing that contract unless you do this.'

" 'Well,' he said, 'you tell him to call me.'

"So a black insurance agent got the bond and all the insurance . . . not only that, he'll get the permanent insurance —that's the good stuff because that keeps going, the commissions come in every year.

"Every Friday, or every other Friday, the majority of black people get paid. By Monday morning, 95 per cent of the money that was paid to them is back in the hands of the white community. There's no way for the black community to become an economic force if it gives back everything it makes.

"The black guy who is making it has got to help the guy who is coming up. What we're doing we're doing for a profit, don't get me wrong, but we're doing it in such a manner as to help other blacks make it."

Hurt has become the first black new-automobile dealer in the Saint Louis area and the first black Volkswagen dealer in the world. The national distributing company for Volkswagen heard of him; they felt that he could do the job successfully even though he had no experience in anything related to selling cars. He didn't go to them, they came to him.

There are very few blacks living in suburban Saint Louis County, where the agency is located, and it is clear that most of his sales will be to white people. Hurt had to invest "well up in six figures" to start the agency, but he was able to borrow a good part of it.

"I would never have taken this on," said Hurt, "except that Volkswagen agreed to keep looking over our shoulder until we got established. We couldn't make it otherwise—this business is too complicated and too competitive. Black entrepreneurs will never make it unless there is an executive loan program so that they can get the advice and guidance they need. It's not enough to get a man's doors open and then walk away and leave him to flounder."

Early in 1968, Hurt and Howard B. Woods founded a weekly newspaper for the Negro community of Saint Louis. His Saint Louis *Sentinel* represented a brash challenge to the existing weekly, which had been in business for fifty-five years and was, as Hurt put it, "a real pillar of the community. But we thought that black people here had a vigor and vitality that was not being projected by the other paper. Woods came from over there, and he came with me because he had some new concepts that they weren't interested in."

Although the *Sentinel* is now making a slight profit, it has been a disappointment. It did not receive the support that Hurt had hoped for from white advertisers, most of whom seem to think that there is only one spokesman for black people.

Hurt is the kind of man some people would describe as a square. He doesn't drink or smoke; he schedules business meetings on Saturday mornings and Sunday nights—and even Saturday nights. He never goes to parties and very rarely gives them.

He has no real hobbies or recreation other than his wide variety of business and community activities. He tries to spend what little spare time he has with his wife Gloria and their three children, a ten-year-old girl and five-year-old twin boys. Mrs. Hurt frequently accompanies him on business trips. Hurt thinks she is "the most understanding person I have ever met."

A number of his largest current projects are connected with housing and urban-renewal programs that are financed with government money. He gives a good deal of his time to community meetings and discussions in the organizing stages, but once the project takes shape, Hurt will participate in it through one of his companies—which expects to make a profit. He offers no apologies for this.

"If you look at the history of this country, right from the beginning there were government programs for giving things away to people. The Homestead Act gave 160 acres of land to a man, and he could do anything he wanted with it. Later they gave the right of way to the railroads. And nowadays we have farm subsidies and airline subsidies and all kinds of subsidies. At no time has the government ever said, when it was subsidizing a segment of the population, that they couldn't make a buck on it—not until the time of black people. Now they have these poverty programs, and the first thing they say is you have to form a nonprofit corporation. Our own government has the black man in a bag. There's no way in the world for us to make it if all our programs are nonprofit.

"This is something that concerns me greatly. If we're not careful, black people are going to be the only race in the world led by the poor. A lot of knowledge and background and ability and motivation are needed to make a big housing project go. Now if you put people from the lower echelon of the ladder in charge of it, they normally don't have the know-how and the independence to make their own decisions. So you end up with somebody else making the decisions, and they rubber-stamp them.

"The greatest horror of it is that across this country today, many of the brightest black men are heading poverty programs. So our best brains are geared to a nonprofit society. We just don't have enough black people that think economically." Hurt is now working with several Senators and Congressmen on a proposed amendment to the OEO legislation to permit profit to be made in connection with the poverty programs.

Hurt and many others who are concerned with the development of leaders among black people are giving serious thought to a black mayor for Saint Louis. In the city proper

40 per cent of the population is black; the figure is likely to exceed 50 per cent within the next few years. Late in 1969, Hurt's Saint Louis *Sentinel* invited its readers to mail in a coupon that said, "I would like to see as black mayor of Saint Louis the following individuals: . . ." When the returns were in, they included practically all of the black-elected officials in the city and a number of other prominent leaders. The name James E. Hurt, Jr., appeared very high on the list. Hurt, however, denies that he has any interest in running for mayor. "I want to see us have a good mayor," he said, "but I am not the right man. I am a businessman, not a politician."

We asked Hurt for the secret of his success.

"Well, I would say that I'm a firm believer in doing . . . I don't want to waste too much time talking about it, I want to do it. And I'm never satisfied until its done. I guess one of the other things I'd say is I love to work. Time is not a factor, it's the job that's important—seven days a week, twenty-four hours a day, it doesn't make any difference.

"I learned a little something from my Dad, and it's been tremendously helpful to me. I do my best thinking at four or five o'clock in the morning when it is quiet. I sit down and write everything. I make a list of the things I want to do that day, and then everything that has to be done in the office that day, and then everything that has to be done next week. I write everything I can think of, and then I put somebody's name on it who is supposed to do it. So when everybody comes in, they'll have a list of things to do."

What advice would he give a young man who thinks he wants to run his own business?

"He'd better forget about the forty-hour week. The greatest detriment to a man going into business is his wife, because the women are used to forty hours. All her friends' husbands work forty hours a week, and she can't understand . . . she won't stand for you working until eight or ten o'clock at night. I've been fortunate, though, because my wife is one thousand per cent with me.

"I'd also give him some advice that was given to me by a

very successful black lawyer who lives in East Saint Louis, Illinois. He told me, 'I planned my life. The first part of my life, I went to school. I learned everything I could learn. The second part of my life, I went out and worked. I didn't care about how much I was paid, that wasn't the point, but I kept on learning everything I could learn. The third part of my life, I made everybody else pay for what I knew. And the fourth part of my life I'm living now, I'm enjoying the fruits.'

"A young man must first discipline himself to the fact that he's going into one of the toughest, one of the most competitive and yet one of the most rewarding careers that he could go into. But he must discipline himself to making the necessary sacrifices. He must recognize that he cannot operate the way his friends operate; this is the most difficult part of it. He must make the sacrifice of time and recognize the fact that his reward is a reward of the future, not of the present. And he must set goals, both long range and immediate. You don't just operate from day to day, you've got to have something that you're looking for next month and something you're looking for next year. And they have to sort of dovetail into one another.

"And there's more opportunity for success for black people in business than there is for white people. Any business a black man wants to go into is wide open."

16

Richard Allen:
Producer of Tape Recordings

*"I think we are going to see a repetition of what happened
after Reconstruction, when white militants drove us back
into the ghettos. This country is rapidly moving toward the
pattern of South Africa."*

Richard Allen was born in Indianapolis in 1932 of exceptional parents: both were energetic entrepreneurs who
ran a variety of businesses. Allen says, "If you look at
entrepreneurs—men who have the ability to organize, the
vision to imagine something big growing out of nothing and
the energy to put it together and make it happen—I think
you'll find that many of them picked it up at home. I know
I did.

"My father, whose name is German Allen, is in his sixties
but looks fifty and acts forty. His principal business now is
trucking; he has four big trucks that haul sand and gravel.
He almost always had some kind of trucking operation
going when I was young, although it was catch as catch
can during the Depression. For years he also ran the Top

Hat Cab Company, which was an irregular taxi operation of the kind that is so common in Northern cities, where authorities refuse to issue taxi permits to black men and licensed white drivers refuse to pick up black passengers.

"So, my father ran the trucking business and the taxi company out of one office, and my mother ran the Top Hat Restaurant next door. Besides serving people who came in, she would pack up hot meals and have them delivered. I notice that in recent years some restaurants have bragged about the delivery of hot meals, but my folks were doing it in the 1930s without thinking anything about it."

At one time or another the Allens also owned a hotel, a moving-van service, a chicken farm and a furnace installation and repair company. They were selling records out of the taxi office for a while. And they speculated in real estate. "There was really no limit to their enterprise. If somebody in the restaurant said, 'Damn, I got to go down to motor vehicle and pick up my license plates, but I don't know when I'll find time to stand in that line,' my mother would send somebody downtown to do it for him and charge an appropriate Depression-era fee, such as 75¢. Both my folks were always on the lookout for a way to make an honest dollar. I absorbed all of that . . . business was all around me, and I soaked it up."

Allen was working for his father before he was ten. He learned to drive before he was thirteen, and when he was fourteen, he had his own one-ton truck with a sign painted on the side: LIGHT HAULING—CALL HEMLOCK 3402. "I'd be out playing basketball, and when I got home my mother would say, 'You had a call.' It might have been somebody who had seen the sign on the truck and wanted some dirt hauled away, so I'd grab two guys and offer them $1.50 each for an hour or two of work. I'd charge maybe $15.00 for picking up that dirt—then if I could sell the dirt somewhere I would.

"I didn't know it at the time, but I was learning how to be a businessman—the raw stuff that they don't teach at Harvard Business School—contracting the job at a profitable price and utilizing people's talents for a profit. These are the basics of business. Later on, I learned all the sophisticated details about amortizing the equipment and so forth, but at the time I was just figuring what the market would bear and whether there would be a couple of bucks left over for me."

As a teen-ager, Allen worked a while for a man named Bloom in his pawnshop on West Washington Street in Indianapolis. "He used to say, 'When you're sweeping the floor, don't sweep toward the door, because you'll sweep customers away.' As I watched and listened to him, I saw another illustration of how business is learned and absorbed. Over many centuries as merchants, some Jewish families have developed and passed down some very effective techniques for running retail stores. I learned a great deal from him about business and negotiating with people.

"It's difficult to break away from things that are part of your childhood . . . and I was probably destined to end up running a business . . . but something made me try to evade it for a while." He started pre-law at Indiana University but switched to sociology. Then he moved to California and studied at Los Angeles City College, where he received a two-year degree in speech therapy.

"I never did get a four-year degree—I just bounced around from one college to another, a year here and a semester there. I think I got a greater diversity of education. It was more rewarding. I never would have learned as much about people if I had stayed in one school for four years." Allen says he has noticed that many of the most successful people he meets took their degrees in fields totally unrelated to the work that they finally settled on. He also feels that the educational system tends to restrict people and prepare them for a lifetime of working for others. "It locks you into that pattern—it doesn't encourage the kind of free thinking and creativity that you need if you are to be on your own."

Throughout his high school and college years, Allen held a variety of "nickel-and-dime jobs. I was willing to do almost any kind of honest work, except delivering newspapers and shining shoes." And he seized entrepreneurship opportunities whenever he saw them. While in college in Los Angeles, he operated a Hollywood health club on a lease arrangement from the owners, who didn't believe it could make money. Within less than a year, he had it running profitably, whereupon the owners promptly canceled the lease and took the business away from him.

Allen once took a college course in marriage and family planning, which caused a considerable degree of hilarity among his friends. But he feels that it was helpful and taught him many things that were valuable in the selection of his wife and in their seventeen years together. (In 1953, he married a native of New Orleans; their two sons were born in 1956 and 1958.)

While in college, Allen sensed that electronics was in the early stages of a period of enormous growth. He learned as much as he could through courses, self-instruction and work experience; for example, on one job he acquired a thorough understanding of the engineering of television sets. Then, although TV was still in its infancy, he shifted his interest to the even newer field of tape recording.

In 1953, Allen went to work for the Concertone Company in Los Angeles as a designer of tape recorders. After three years there, he moved to the Bel Canto Corporation, which was one of the first companies to pre-record musical tapes for retail sale. One of his reasons for moving was that he saw a much larger potential market for tapes than for tape recorders. "The razor manufacturers sell the razor at very little profit or even give it away, because what they are really interested in is continuing sales of blades. Similarly, a man will buy one tape recorder or stereo system, but then there is no limit to the number of prerecorded tapes you may be able to sell him."

Within a short time, Allen became involved in practically every aspect of the company except selling. "I was running the electronic gear, repairing it when it broke down, doing the purchasing, running the office, and I also typed and ran the duplicating machine. I was an all-around boy friday—you know, we are never really men in this society. I worked almost around the clock, and sometimes would sleep at the office. I was making close to $500 a week in the late 1950s.

"In those early days, there was only a handful of people in the company, and we were really overworked. I talked to a number of fellows I knew, who had jobs at the post office or something of the sort, and tried to get them to come to work for Bel Canto. Most of them wouldn't even consider it . . . they wanted to hang onto that civil-service security. But a bus driver named Warren Gray liked the idea, and he liked music, too, so he came over. After he got to know the business, Warren found that he was a natural-born salesman."

Bel Canto grew rapidly; by 1960 it had over fifty employees. In that year, the company was sold to Thompson Ramo Woolridge. Although the former owners stayed on, a number of new people were brought into management, and Allen was not pleased with the changes. He liked the situation even less when he was told, not asked, to transfer to Columbus, Ohio. He made the move alone and commuted to California on weekends to see his family.

About the time Allen was transferred, Warren Gray was promoted and made sales manager for eleven Western states. "I thought about it for a while and realized that Warren and I had things pretty well covered. Between the two of us, we were handling everything that was involved in production, administration and sales for Bel Canto. I decided that if we could do it for them, we ought to be able to do it for ourselves.

"One day I said, 'Listen, Warren, why don't we start something on our own? I think we could rustle up the money to buy some equipment, and if you can land the orders I think I can run the plant and the office—I'll be the inside man and you'll be the outside man.' And that was the beginning of American Tape Duplicators, Inc."

Allen resigned from his job in Columbus in June 1962 and returned to California to organize the new company. Gray joined him a few months later, and the company started operations early in 1963. Each contributed $500 and a large share of what Allen described as "eternal optimism that we would prevail." He demonstrated that optimism by buying a $40,000 house as soon as he returned to California, even though at the time he had no money coming in at all. The basic business of American Tape Duplicators was exactly what its name indicated. The company received a master tape from a customer on the other side of town— or the other side of the world—and produced one copy or 100 copies or 10,000 copies. Both partners worked hard, and the company was successful almost from the beginning. It did about $100,000 worth of business in its first year and showed an increase every year during the 1960s. By 1970 its volume was close to $1,500,000.

However, as the tape-recording industry continued to mushroom and its technology advanced, Allen and Gray began to fear for their company's future as a tape duplicator. Recording equipment was becoming more reliable and less expensive. Many small firms entered the field, and so did the giants of the recording industry. Vigorous competition forced prices down. "We noticed that some of our good steady customers were not coming back as often, and we realized that they were shopping around for lower prices. If some other guy offered to do the job for a few dollars less, he would get it." As in any business, when prices drop, profits drop even faster.

The company continues to do a considerable amount of profitable tape-duplicating business, but in 1969 it began to diversify into the production of its own proprietary line of prerecorded tapes. Allen realized that he could not compete directly with the giants of the entertainment industry, with their huge financial resources, established distribution systems and recording stars under contract. "We learned something about that ballgame a few years ago, when we tried to market one 45-r.p.m. record. We dumped about $18,000 into that and didn't even begin to get it moving.

"We had to find a piece of the market that they weren't covering and that we could get into without spending seven fortunes." One aspect of ATD's solution was to concentrate on what Allen calls "evergreen music"—music that continues to have an audience year after year and does not require star performers. Mood and background music,

Hawaiian music, country and western and gospel music are examples. Some of ATD's musical library is produced originally, but most of it is leased from other recording companies on a royalty basis.

Another part of the strategy was the launching of a tape priced at $2.99, which was considerably below the existing price structure. But perhaps Allen's most dramatic idea is a new approach to distribution. "Look what the drugstores did. They put in clothes, toys, hardware—they got bigger and bigger. Here in California, we have so-called drugstores that are open twenty-four hours a day, and will sell you everything from a bottle of aspirin to a garden tractor.

"The music industry is behind the times—it still confines itself to the distribution channels of a generation ago. One hundred per cent of the records and tapes are sold in only 12 per cent of the retail outlets in the country." Allen intends to go after those millions of retail outlets that make up the other 88 per cent. He wants to sell pre-recorded tapes in supermarkets, barbershops, restaurants, clothing stores —in fact, anyplace where people come and go regularly.

"Here's a piece of 1971 American life," says Allen. "Mother says to daughter, 'Are you going by the record store? I hear there's a new Andy Williams tape out, could you pick it up for me?' Daughter says, 'Oh, mother, you're so *square!*' Mother says, 'Oh, all right, forget about it . . . you young people are impossible!'

"Now that woman will never buy that tape. She won't make a special trip to the record store because she is afraid of being molested by a hippie. But suppose we had a rack of tapes in the supermarket—she's wheeling that shopping cart along past the frozen orange juice, and suddenly she finds herself looking at a picture of Andy Williams, or she sees some waltz music or something else she likes. The tape is only $2.99—not only that, her husband won't notice the three bucks because it is buried in the grocery bill. So she just picks up that tape and drops it in the cart. That's the business we're going after."

American Tape now has its own proprietary line of pre-recorded tapes under the ATD label, which it will distribute through all kinds of retail outlets. By early 1971, it had over 100 tapes on the market. In addition, it produces tapes for sale through the Radio Shack chain under their label. And it has a Tape Listeners Club, which operates along the lines of a book club. The company is also producing a variety of tapes outside the music field. For example, it sells a "reading acceleration" tape as an educational aid. It produces sales-aid tapes, and travelogue tapes for use when driving through the national parks or touring Paris.

"Everything we sell provides some kind of service or helps make people happy. You have to remember that at one time I was thinking about being a sociologist. I think I have compassion for people, and I feel that everything we're selling is something positive that is going to be a stimulating factor in somebody's life. You couldn't give me a company that produces hand grenades, no matter how much money it would make. Some people will think I'm a poor businessman for saying that . . . that a businessman should go after anything that offers a profit and isn't against the law. Well, I'm a pretty good businessman but I happen to be a human being, too.

"A lot of businessmen subordinate everything to profit. They will sell their souls and sacrifice their integrity, because they think that's what they have to do to survive in the free-enterprise jungle. Well, I don't see it that way. We try to keep some humanity around this place, and I will not compromise my integrity for profit—if it ever comes to that, I'll get rid of this business and get into something else.

"You don't have to compromise your integrity in business, but you have to be ready to make adjustments. For example, when somebody is mad because he thinks you short-changed him or failed to deliver what you promised, the first problem is to find a way to cool him off. Learning to deal with people is an essential part of business.

"And you have to be flexible—things are constantly changing. Every day in business you come up against at least one situation that is a little bit different from anything you have ever seen before. You can't look in a book for instructions on what to do. You just have to work it out by trial and error, and there is a lot of trial and a lot of error, but every bit of it teaches you something."

Describing the future that he sees and the problems that face his company, Allen combines enthusiastic optimism with deep discouragement. He says that his business should grow by 300 per cent a year. On the other hand, he said, "I'm realistic enough to know that I'd better not get so big that I start competing with RCA and Capitol and Columbia, because they will beat my brains out."

One of the exciting prospects on the horizon is the development of video-tape equipment for home use, so that a family can record a favorite television show or a ballgame, and play it over again on their own set. Allen would like to get involved in that field, but he thinks it is impossible because at this stage it would take millions of dollars of research-and-development money. Later on, when the equipment has been perfected and standardized and is much cheaper, the giants will dominate the field, and it will be too late for a small company to get in.

"There is no reason why this operation should not be doing $100 million a year if we had been able to get the kind of banking assistance that we wanted. But we fell into the category of second-class citizens. It's that simple. So we'll just plug along here, putting our little nickels and dimes together, until the big companies bring us to our knees, and then we'll have to move to something else.

"The big boys in this country know how to look out for each other—maybe one of our problems is that we haven't learned to do that." Perhaps the largest black-managed business in the country is Motown Records, and Allen feels that ATD and Motown could work together profitably in a number of areas . . . but he can't even get the president of Motown to return his calls.

Allen feels that his mother was a great influence on him. "She believed in astrology—or anyway she said she did. I was born under the sign of Leo, and she kept telling me how strong I was. It seemed as though she told me the things I wanted to hear and really built self-confidence into me. It's a funny thing, if people tell you often enough that you are strong you will begin to believe it—and then pretty soon you will be strong even if you are not.

"It makes a lot of difference what direction you are pointed in early on in life. If a boy is named "George Washington," he's going to try like hell to be President, but if he is named "Jesse James," he might end up as an outlaw. If you don't believe it, think about any kid you ever knew who was nicknamed "Rocky"—no matter how small he was, I think you'll find that he was trying to act like a tough guy. . . .

"I am an eternal optimist—with a very pessimistic outlook about the realities of life. Whether or not this company survives, I know I can survive in this jungle. But it's what's happening to other black people who have been less fortunate that depresses me. In this society there are limits for us . . . we can only go so far. The white immigrants who came here from Europe could tell their children that the sky was the limit, that they could go all the way. A black parent cannot say that to his children, at least not today.

"Throughout history we have always been allowed in too late. The game is almost over by the time they let the black man play. There could have been many wealthy black families in Los Angeles if they had had the opportunity years ago, when this city was young—they could have owned half of Wilshire Boulevard. But that chance is gone now. It can never be. Unless of course there is a basic redistribution of wealth, and I think we'll land on the sun before that happens. . . .

"We're going to have to find ways to solve these problems. Both President Kennedy and President Nixon have said that there is no problem this country can't handle if it has the commitment. I believe that—I believe that any problem made by men can be solved by men. *If we have the commitment. . . .*"

17

Joe W. Kirven:
Maintenance-Company Owner

*"Teaching school was about the only decent job available
to a black man, and I wasn't about to spend my life teaching
school at $380 a month, so after I graduated from college
I worked as a bellboy at the Adolphus Hotel."*

The world will never know how much it has lost because
men of brilliance, energy and creative imagination in the
South found all doors closed to them. Men who might have
been—and should have been—governors, research scientists,
millionaires or Supreme Court judges spent their lives teaching school instead. The pupils were richer for it, but the
larger society suffered a loss that can never be measured.
Joe Kirven has three uncles who taught school and later
became principals, and one of his brothers is a school principal, too. "I think," he said, "that the free-enterprise system is the best system that's ever been devised, but I also
think that all the citizens should have an equal opportunity
to share in it. I knew I could always teach school if I had to,
but I just decided I was going to find a way to share in the

fruits of this society. I wasn't sure how . . . so while I was thinking about it, I worked as a bellboy, saying 'Yes, sir' and 'Thank you, sir,' and making about $125 a week."

Kirven's grandfather owned a 1,000-acre farm as early as 1900. Although the family fortunes suffered after that, his father still owned a small farm seventy-five miles from Dallas where Joe Kirven was born in 1932. His parents separated when he was nine, and his mother took him to Dallas, where he attended the public schools.

Joe Kirven has more energy than most mortals, and has always used it fully. From the age of twelve until he finished school, he worked at one job or another, also finding time to excel in a number of high school sports.

"My high-school football coach was one of the most important influences on my life. His name was Raymond E. Holley. I remember him well, and I remember a whole lot of the things he drilled into us. We played hard-nosed football, but beyond that he had some maxims and sayings that always stayed with me. For instance, 'Hard work eliminates alibis,' 'We never ask more than a field that is fair and a chance that is equal to those we compete against,' 'Those who quit in football will also be quitters in life' and 'God in Heaven loves a fighter—not one who lies down like a lamb and dies but one who fights like hell to live.' Later on when I was doing cold call selling, these admonitions came in very handy."

Kirven went on an athletic scholarship to Wiley College in Marshall, Texas, where he starred in football and track and received a B.S. degree in 1954.

"A friend of mine named Lloyd Sharp thought he could make a go of it in office cleaning and maintenance, and he invited me to go into business with him. We talked it over, but I didn't know anything about the field, and somehow it didn't seem to be what I was looking for. Later on, he came to me again and said he wanted to spend two or three weeks in Philadelphia. He asked me to look after his business for him, and in the course of doing so I began to get interested and to see the potential here. . . .

"My friend's trouble was he was young and adventurous.

He liked to wear good clothes and drive a fine car and just generally enjoy his money. And he couldn't stay put. Now, if you're the sole proprietor of a business and you like to travel extensively, that business isn't likely to do very well. He would build the business up to where he was taking $1,500 a month out of it, and then he'd start to enjoy life and it would slip back again."

Finally, Sharp decided that the grass was greener in Philadelphia and offered to sell Kirven the business. So, for $500 down and $500 in monthly payments, Kirven became the president and proprietor of Abco Building Maintenance Company, Inc. (Incidentally, his friend did move to Philadelphia, then continued to wander, came back to Dallas and worked for Kirven for a time, and eventually ended up in Los Angeles, where he started a very successful building-maintenance company.)

The business consists principally of daily cleaning of office buildings after working hours; the company also handles a few warehouses and other buildings and does minor repair and maintenance work. Ordinarily, it works on a month-to-month basis.

When Kirven took over, the company had only five contracts and a handful of employees. It was much too small to be profitable, so he undertook a systematic campaign to attract new business. "I had been a salesman of industrial tile for a while and found that after I learned my product I could sell successfully. I was convinced that I could find new customers. I would get out every morning at a quarter to eight and just start knocking on doors. . . ."

Selling is hard work, and cold call selling is one of the hardest jobs in the world. Most people are too shy and timid to spend their days making aggressive overtures to strangers, who are usually skeptical, suspicious, impatient and often rude. Few people's egos can endure the steady stream of rebuffs and rejections that is part of making cold calls without previous introductions.

"Of course, I was turned down far more times than I made sales, but I was never really discouraged. I just had a lot of faith that I would succeed. Everybody I called on was already having his building cleaned by somebody. I simply explained that I felt we would be more reliable and dependable and do a better job. Better, not cheaper. I never tried to get a job by underpricing my competitor, and still don't. Our prices are probably the highest in town, but we think we deserve them because we do a better job. It's still true that you get what you pay for.

"When I went in to solicit a job, I didn't shuffle and grin and scratch my head the way some people expected. I just presented my program and explained it as intelligently as I could. I felt that if the man really needed service, he would hire us."

Kirven set himself the goal of landing two new accounts a week, which was somewhere between improbable and impossible. But he did manage to average two a month.

"One of the keys to success in this business is pricing. Every job is a little bit different. There are some rules of thumb—so much a square foot or so much per person working in the office—but those rules don't always work. I made some bad mistakes at the beginning . . . every one of them taught me something. After a year or so, I got to where I knew how to price a job pretty accurately. The object, of course, is to set the price low enough to land the business but not so low as to end up losing money on the job."

The other essential in the office-cleaning business is developing a reliable staff of employees. Even the best workers need supervision and Abco now has a number of excellent and reliable supervisors; but in the early days Kirven was the only one, and he did everything himself. He would start out early in the morning and spend most of the day making calls, soliciting new business and also keeping fences mended with customers. He would also buy all the materials and supplies and deliver them to the jobs. During the evening when the work was going on, he became a supervisor. "And then late at night, I'd go around and inspect every job to see that it had been done properly. Then back knocking on doors before 8:00 A.M. Those were long days.

"On the weekends, I'd go around and collect the trash that had accumulated during the week. For several years I never took a vacation or even a day off. Sundays, holidays, it didn't matter, the work had to be done. . . ."

Kirven didn't take a penny in salary out of the business for two years. In fact, he had to put money into it, investing in equipment such as vacuum cleaners and floor-polishing machines. But the biggest financial problem was waiting for the customers to pay their bills. "We would send a bill promptly at the end of every month, but by that time we'd have paid our employees for thirty days, and it was usually another two or three weeks, sometimes more, before we got the check. Every time I landed a new account, I would figure that to be safe I'd need enough to pay the people on that job for sixty days before any money came in. The more business I got, the more money I had to have."

Kirven reasoned that a satisfied customer would be the best possible reference and that the reference would be more valuable if the customer were substantial and well known. Accordingly, he called on large and prestigious companies. He was able to land contracts fairly early in the game with General Electric and a number of small banks in Dallas. "Some of our customers were so pleased with our work that they solicited other business for us."

His first big account was the Pollack Paper Company. At the time they were using the biggest maintenance company in the country, but Kirven talked them into giving him a chance. "That was when I finally knew I could make it. From then on there was no turning back." Pollack, which has since become a subsidiary of St. Regis Paper, has been with him ever since.

The biggest building serviced by Abco is the thirty-one-story Empire Life building in downtown Dallas. Some eighteen or twenty of its employees go into Empire Life every evening.

The company now has more than 100 active accounts, and is grossing almost $1,000,000 a year. It has upwards of 130 employees; slightly more than half are part time. Some of its best employees, including two supervisors, work at other building-service jobs during the early part of the day and then come to Abco in the late afternoon. One is a senior custodial official in the Dallas school system.

The company has found it harder to expand in the past few years because of the tight labor market in Dallas. Kirven will not take on a job unless he has the people to handle it properly. The recession of 1970–71 has made it easier to hire good people.

Abco has some problems, as any organization does. Sometimes people don't show up or fail to perform and have to be replaced. Kirven brings in business by offering to do a better job, but once in a while business is lost because "we don't do the job as well as we should." Occasionally, the company is underbid, and sometimes he loses business just because somebody wants to give it to a friend.

"One of the biggest headaches in this business is the paperwork. That is one part of it that I seriously underestimated when I started. When you have a large number of employees the forms really pile up—social security, withholding, unemployment compensation, Blue Cross, workmen's compensation—there is almost no end to them."

Kirven feels that one of the key factors in running the company smoothly is "my relationship with the people that work for me. I try to treat them the way I want to be treated, and I don't allow my supervisors to talk down to them or mistreat them in any way. Whenever anybody has an argument or a problem, I always try to listen to both sides. Once the supervisors found out we did things that way, they developed a much different and much better attitude." All of his supervisors originally started out as workers.

"After we succeed in landing the job, the key to keeping it is having the right relationships with your people. We think we have them. A number of people have left big companies to come with us." He is quite serious about this. As late as 1968, after thirteen years in business and with over 100 employees, he knew everyone on his payroll by sight and name. "I'm afraid I don't any more, though. In the last couple of years I've just been away from here too much."

He has been kept increasingly busy by his schedule of civic and political activities. In 1968, he ran for the Texas state legislature on the Republican ticket. He didn't win but ran strong in the Dallas County-at-large contest. There are well over 1,000,000 people in Dallas County, probably 80 per cent white. Yet Kirven led the Republican ticket with 150,000 votes, just below the low man on the winning Democratic slate, who received about 160,000.

That same year Kirven was elected president of the Dallas Negro Chamber of Commerce, which, although considerably younger than the National Business League, was the first local black chamber in the country, organized in 1926.

Kirven feels that the most basic need of black businessmen is capital, and he made the financing problem the top priority of the chamber. Under his leadership, a nonprofit funding agency called Venture Advisors, Inc., was organized. A large part of its original capital was contributed by the Sam Wyly Foundation, and in 1970 Venture received an $86,000 federal grant. In its first eighteen months it provided over $200,000 of capital to new and existing black businesses in Dallas.

Kirven knows how hard it is for a black businessman to borrow money; he tried when he was building his business in the late 1950s. "I have to say they listened politely," he says of bankers he approached, "but they wouldn't even consider lending me money without collateral. And, of course, if I had had collateral I probably wouldn't have needed a loan."

There has been a modest improvement in the racial climate, but since money has become very tight in recent years, credit for a black businessman is still very hard to come by. Kirven says, though, that the Small Business Administration in Dallas is treating black applicants better than it used to. "Nowadays they send most of them right over to us at Venture."

Kirven now spends a good deal of his time at the Venture Advisors office. He says he can do this because he has reliable people to handle business details for him at Abco.

"We really need a black bank here," he said, "and I hope we can get one going. Some of us tried to start one a few years ago with some white men, but somehow their share of the ownership increased and ours didn't, and pretty soon it wasn't a black bank any more."

In 1968, Kirven was chosen one of the five outstanding young Texans of the year by the Texas Junior Chamber of Commerce, the first black man ever selected. He is active on a number of committees and boards, including those of his church and the YMCA.

Mr. and Mrs. Kirven have a nine-year-old daughter who attends the exclusive Hockaday School, the first black student ever admitted there. In 1970, Kirven became a trustee of the school. Not long after that, he was also appointed to the Dallas Board of Education.

In addition to running Abco, Kirven has saved and invested money in real estate. He will not estimate the present value of his holdings, but the mortgages against them amount to over $100,000.

Asked for the secret of his success, Kirven said first that he was "not sure I've been all that successful. I'm no millionaire, I just make a living. Still, I've made more money working for myself than I could have made on any job available to me when I started . . . or now, for that matter. And I've had the freedom to do what I wanted, to be my own boss—that's pretty nice.

"I try to know as much as I possibly can about what I'm doing, and then I just do what has to be done. To make a business work you have to understand what it is and what has to be done and then spend the time. I have never minded putting in the hours. I don't really work that hard, except that I do spend the time. . . ."

Somehow, when Kirven describes what he has accomplished in only thirty-eight years, he makes it sound as if it had been easy. Starting with $500, this black man built a successful business by selling himself and his services to skeptical white strangers in a Southern city—first to businessmen who needed building maintenance and later to the voters of Dallas County.

He got into the business by accident, but all successful men seem to have a series of happy accidents. They are lucky, but they make their own luck. They seize opportunities when they come along and make the most of them. Characteristically, Kirven does not predict the future directions of his life, probably because he isn't sure himself. Opportunities can come along unexpectedly, and fate often takes surprising turns.

He probably can be a millionaire if he wants to. He probably can be elected to the city council, or the state legislature, if he wants to. Or to Congress . . . or . . .

18

David F. Snyder: Architect

"There must have been five hundred guys in that room. I figured if I were dropped in the middle of those hundreds of engineers, there was no way in the world I could rise to the top."

Of approximately 30,000 practicing architects in the United States, probably no more than 100 are black. "I guess," says David F. Snyder, "there just aren't enough of us for them to bother to discriminate." Snyder has a wry sense of humor.

Most architects work as employees, some for contractors, others for large businesses or government agencies, and many for architectural firms. In the last case, the more talented or more fortunate may rise from employee to the status of associate or junior partner. A very, very few become proprietors or senior partners in their own firms—that is, owners.

The first black architectural firm, McKissack and McKissack, was organized in Nashville in the early 1900s. Then

Paul Williams of Los Angeles struck out on his own and established a successful practice before World War II. The next was Hilliard Robinson of Washington, D.C. By 1970, there were at least ten architectural firms owned and run by black men. One of the larger and more successful of these is Snyder Blackburn Associates of Indianapolis, Indiana.

Snyder is its chief executive officer; he has been a registered architect in the state of Indiana since 1954, is a member of the American Institute of Architects and is one of the directors of the Indiana Society of Architects.

The secret of his success? Snyder's answer was incredible.

"I've just been lucky, really. I've had good friends looking after me. At several strategic points in my life, I happened to get some very good advice and guidance from some fine men. . . ."

As a student at Indianapolis's all-black Crispus Attucks High School in the early 1940s, Snyder found that he had a talent for mathematics and drafting. He easily got A's in mechanical drawing. The instructor, whose name was Ted Simpson, recognized his talent and encouraged him. "When I found out I could do the work easily, I began to let down, but he leaned on me and kept my nose to the grindstone. He would say, 'I'll have to give you a C if you don't get your assignments in on time.' He knew I could turn out more work than the average student and he made me do it."

Crispus Attucks High School had been founded in 1927. The purpose of starting it was, of course, to segregate black students who came to Attucks from every part of the city because they were not allowed to attend any other school. As it happened, the salary levels established initially for teachers were quite high, high enough to attract a number of black college professors, with the result that Attucks became, and has remained, an excellent school academically. For example, Snyder took four years of math, including college algebra and trigonometry; when he got to college, his knowledge was sufficient to exempt him from taking these courses.

"At first I thought I wanted to be an aeronautical engineer. I had always liked to put model airplanes together, and of course there was a lot of interest in aviation during World War II. But one day I was looking through a booklet called 'So You Want to Be an Engineer,' and I'll never forget one picture in it. It showed a drafting room at one of the airplane companies—a huge room that stretched as far as the eye could see, with rows and rows of men at drafting boards. There must have been 500 guys in that room. I figured if I were dropped in the middle of those hundreds of engineers, there was no way in the world I could rise to the top."

Meanwhile, Simpson planted a seed in the young man's mind by casually encouraging him to browse through architectural magazines. (Snyder remembers an item in one about a department store designed by black architect Paul Williams.) Simpson also gave him special projects, such as designing a roof or even a whole house.

"Even though Williams had been able to do it, it seemed like a wild dream. By the time I finished high school, though, I had just about decided to be an architect. I guess I was too young and too dumb to know how heavily the odds were against me."

Snyder was an enthusiastic football player in high school, and even though he weighed only 145 pounds, he played guard. (He says that during the two years he was on the team, it had the worst record—two games won in two years—of any period in the school's history, then or since.) In the 1940s, Attucks was not allowed to compete against the other Indianapolis high schools, so the team traveled long distances to play other black schools. "It was a ridiculous system, but we enjoyed the trips. We would play Dunbar High in Dayton, Central High in Louisville, Roosevelt in Gary and Sumner in Saint Louis—that Saint Louis trip was great because it was overnight. We still lost, but we had to travel long distances to get beaten."

Partly because of his interest in architecture and partly because of his interest in football, Snyder decided to attend the University of Illinois in Champaign-Urbana. At that time no state college in Indiana had an architectural school, and he could not afford the private schools.

"We disposed of the football part of it pretty fast. When I took a look at the 250- and 270-pound guys that came out to play line positions on that team, I decided I could get along without football. Before I graduated they set up a lightweight team, but by that time I realized that I just couldn't spare the time."

Architecture is a very demanding course. Because of the lab-type classes and the enormous amount of drawing that must be done, it requires at least twice as many classroom hours as most liberal-arts courses and just as much homework.

At Illinois in those days there were "meal jobs" at the fraternity and sorority houses. If a student put in a few hours washing dishes or waiting on table at lunch and dinner, he got his meals in exchange, seven days a week. And very often he could scrounge something to take away for breakfast the next morning. It was a barter system—no money changed hands either way.

"I'd save money working during the summer. Then I'd go over there and plunk down $80 for tuition, a little something for books, $90 for my room for the semester, and $15 for a season ticket to all the athletic events. And then my meal job almost eliminated the need for money altogether. There were free concerts, movies and other events. You could literally walk around campus with no money in your pocket at all—in fact, I did that quite a few times. I couldn't possibly have gotten by as cheaply at any other school."

Snyder was born in Mississippi in 1927. Before he was a year old, his parents moved to Indianapolis, where his two younger sisters were born. His father worked in a foundry during the Depression. In 1940, tiring of the hot, heavy work, he took a post-office job. He retired from that in 1965 and became a preacher.

"We had it pretty rough through the Depression, but I have to say I don't ever remember being absolutely hungry. It was what you might call a 'fun-type' deprived childhood. My Dad had me working at one thing or another while I was still in grade school. I had a paper route for a while, but I didn't do too good a job—he'd have to follow along behind me and collect the money. . . .

"When I was younger, I was what you might call 'financially disorganized.' I just couldn't save money. Expenses at Illinois were low, and I should have been able to earn enough every summer to get me through the following year. Well, I earned enough all right, but I couldn't hang on to it. I'd usually manage the first semester, but when February came around I had to get help from my folks."

At the end of his second year at Illinois, Snyder came very close to flunking out. "There was no reason for it—I could do the work, but I just wasn't applying myself. The dean gave me a break and passed me, though. That summer I worked as a laborer, but when September came, I just didn't have enough money to go back."

He stayed out a year, which he spent working as a draftsman in an architect's office.

How did a young black man in Indianapolis in 1947 find a job as an architectural draftsman?

"Once again I got lucky. There was a black engineer here in town who was trying to establish himself and who was doing consulting work for various architects. I went to see him and asked him if he knew of an architect that might hire me. He sent me to a man named Les Ayres, who had a one-man shop—just himself, a secretary and an occasional apprentice. He had hired another Illinois student for the summer and that man was ready to go back to school. So I moved in when he moved out.

"Ayres was a fine man. He paid me only $25 a week . . . but whenever he collected on a job, he would give me a bonus, and it was just the experience I needed. It's amazing how much you learn, and how fast you learn it, when you're spending eight hours a day on the drafting board and doing field work, too." Snyder worked there every summer until he graduated.

In the fall of 1948 he returned to Illinois and had no further trouble with his studies. He graduated in February 1951 with the degree of Bachelor of Science in Architectural Engineering. At that time, the state of Indiana required an architect to have one year of experience working for an architect, plus the degree, before he could apply for certification as a registered architect. Snyder already had his year of work experience and so he was ready to apply. However, there was an interruption.

In 1945, when he turned eighteen, Snyder had been called by the draft but rejected because of a heart murmur. The draft was reinstated during the Korean War, and shortly after graduating from Illinois he was called again. "I went to our family doctor to see if he thought I was fit for military service. He had me jumping up and down and running around the office to test my heart condition. When we got all through, he said, 'Man, there's nothing wrong with you—nothing at all!' When I heard that, I knew I was in the Army. Sure enough, the next week I passed the physical."

On the basis of his intelligence and college background, Snyder was assigned to the Corps of Engineers and sent to Fort Belvoir, Virginia. His official military designation was Architectural Engineering Research Assistant. "Some of the white guys in that classification did some drafting, but my job was to sharpen pencils and hand out drafting sets and erasers and so on." Eventually, Snyder ended up as an acting supply sergeant with the rank of private first class.

He was honorably discharged after two years. When he took his final physical exam, the doctor said, "Hmm, I believe you've got a slight heart murmur."

"I said, 'Doc, you are just exactly two years late with that information!'"

While at Fort Belvoir, Snyder had explored the idea of working for Hilliard Robinson, the black architect who has a firm in Washington. Robinson would have hired him, but he decided he would rather stay in Indianapolis. However, when he made the rounds there, he found the prospects very discouraging. Les Ayres had died. He heard about an architectural job with the Navy that was about to become vacant. When he applied, they listened politely, but it was very clear that they would not seriously consider a black architect.

"I was feeling pretty low then. I knew I had the ability to practice the architectural profession, I had the academic training and I also had some good practical experience. But it looked as though nobody in Indianapolis was even willing to give me a start." Finally, more or less in disgust, he applied for and was accepted for a clerk's job at the Army Finance Center at Fort Benjamin Harrison.

One of the turning points of his life, Snyder says, came while he was on a stepladder. He was supposed to report to the Finance Center the following Monday, so he spent a few days hanging around home and doing a little work. "I was washing a wall and thinking about one thing and another, and I happened to remember an architect named Ed James, who had been a friend of Les Ayres. On pure impulse I came down off that stepladder, changed my clothes and went to see him without an appointment. Luckily, I was able to see him right away. I told him my situation and showed him some of my drawings. He said, 'We'll let you know.' The next morning he called and asked me to report for work Monday. I called the Army and told them I wouldn't be there—that was one of the happiest phone calls I ever made."

Snyder stayed at Edward D. James and Associates, Inc., for twelve years, during which he did many different kinds of architectural work. Toward the end of his stay, he became the firm's specialist in structural engineering and did all of that work for the office. He worked on schools, churches, college buildings, factories, office buildings, and even built a dam.

Snyder says that James was "as fine a man as I could ever hope to meet. He was kind of a benevolent dictator. He gave us all the latitude and responsibility we could handle, but if one of us messed up the job, he really nailed us to the wall. I was job captain on one project, and it was running late because the engineers were holding things up. I didn't think it was my fault, but James made me understand very clearly that as job captain I had the responsibility for meeting the completion date. If things started to go wrong, he wanted to know soon enough to do something about it. Ed James only had to chew you out once—that was enough to get the point across."

In due course, Snyder became an associate of the firm,

which is roughly the same as junior partner. Although he and the other associates each had a small share in the ownership, James still owned more than half of the business and completely dominated it. At partners' meetings the associates reported on what they had been doing and how their projects were coming along, and then they approved whatever James decided to do.

"There wasn't very much decision making on our part, but it was good experience for me. It gave me an opportunity to sit in on the discussions and see all of the problems that came up. I learned how a successful professional architect's office should be run."

Snyder had always felt that sooner or later he wanted to be his own boss and build his own practice. He found his association with James valuable and pleasant, but he wanted to be on his own. James did not discourage him. He said, "We'll hate to lose you, but let me know when you make the decision and I'll do anything I can to help."

The final push toward starting his own firm came from Cleo Blackburn, one of the prominent black figures in the Midwest and a leader in many fields. Among his activities, Blackburn founded and runs the Board for Fundamental Education, which helps adults correct the deficiencies in their early education, and he is the director of Flanner House, a nonprofit social-service agency.

Blackburn was very much concerned about the shortage of housing in Indianapolis for poor and even for middle-income black people. There were and are a variety of federal financing programs available, but housing requires an enormous amount of organizing and preparation, even when the financing is there. Blackburn wanted to get both BFE and Flanner House involved in housing.

Blackburn's son Walter had just received his architectural degree. Snyder and Walter Blackburn began to discuss the idea of going into practice together, with their first job to be a high-rise middle-income apartment building to be sponsored by Flanner House and financed under the Federal Housing Administration's 221 (d) (3) program.

David F. Snyder and Associates opened for business on

July 2, 1964. (Later, when Walter Blackburn passed the state exam, the name was changed to Snyder Blackburn Associates.) "We knew that the FHA project would take time, because it was a new concept for Indianapolis, but we had a church, a small office building and two other jobs lined up to help us get moving and pay the rent.

"We had them lined up—but they never came through. We learned that a lot of people have big plans and small pocketbooks. Many a dream never gets beyond the dreaming stage. We projected $4,000 in fees for our first month, and in fact we collected exactly twenty-five bucks. And we gave away a lot of services that we should have been paid for. Well, live and learn. . . ."

The preparatory work on the FHA apartment project continued to move slowly. The firm managed to pick up a few small pieces of work, and then in 1965 Snyder had another of what he modestly refers to as his lucky breaks. A friend who was a member of the Indianapolis school board helped him land a job designing an addition to a school building. It began as a $600,000 project but, with modifications and inflation, ended up costing almost twice that.

Then, in 1966, the firm was selected to design a low-income housing project for the Indianapolis Housing Authority, and in 1967 the large FHA project finally came through. It is called River House, and it consists of two twelve-story buildings with a total of 300 apartments. The overall construction cost was about $4,000,000.

Since then one housing project has followed another. The majority of the firm's work is housing developments that are financed through one or another of the FHA mortgage-insurance programs. In 1970, Snyder Blackburn was chosen as associate architect on the Indianapolis Operation Breakthrough project, a nationwide program initiated by the U.S. Department of Housing and Urban Development that, it is hoped, will develop new methods of industrialized housing construction. The prime architectural contractor on that project is Skidmore, Owings and Merrill, one of the largest architectural firms in the country.

Not all of the firm's work is housing. They have also

designed school buildings, churches and warehouses, with an occasional single-family house, usually for a friend. "Single-family houses are not profitable—the architect can't possibly charge enough to compensate him for the time he has to spend, and yet they get us more publicity than anything else we do. As soon as we do one, everybody knows about it."

Snyder Blackburn Associates did most of the architectural work on a $3,500,000 bus-body factory built by the Divco Wayne Corporation in Richmond, Indiana. We asked Snyder how he brought that one in.

"When I was with Ed James, I had gotten to know a contractor over in Dayton who sold pre-fabricated houses and also was a developer of industrial buildings. We had worked together on several projects, and I guess he felt that I had some problem-solving ability. One day he called me and told me that he hoped to build this factory and that another architect was already involved in it, but it didn't seem to be moving along. My partner and I went over there to take a look.

"We made a few comments and suggestions, and they decided to retain us. We could see that it would take some time, so we just closed down the office and moved over there and stayed until it was finished. That building is almost half a mile long—it's the largest bus-body plant in the world."

The firm had some rough sledding, particularly at the beginning, but every year was an improvement over the previous one. By the end of 1970, Snyder Blackburn Associates, with fifteen people on its payroll, was almost as large as Snyder's previous employer had been when he started there in 1953. It occupied a brand-new office building of its own design. It was working on several million dollars' worth of construction annually, generating fees to the firm of several hundred thousand dollars a year.

Its largest projects have been the $4,000,000 River House apartments and the $3,500,000 factory. In all, by the end of 1970, Snyder Blackburn Associates had designed about $20 million worth of completed construction, with another

$10 million "in the pipeline"—that is, either under construction, in the contract-letting stage, or on the drawing boards.

"The practice of architecture has changed dramatically in the years since I started. Through the use of consultants and computers, we can work much more efficiently than we used to. Years ago, when Ed James took on a $7,000,000 Indiana University building, he moved three of us to another building to handle everything else in the office. All the rest of the staff, which was about the size that ours is now, spent full time for over a year on that one job.

"We operate on a team basis. Until recently we were lacking a construction supervisor and other partners had to handle that, but we have recently hired one. As a result we can work on five jobs in this office at the same time."

Snyder had been making a good living as an associate of a successful firm. His income dropped sharply the first year he was on his own—in fact, he drew no salary at all for six months—and it took him two or three more years to get back to his old income level. After that he passed it by a considerable margin.

Snyder has been active in the Indiana Society of Architects, and is now a member of its board of directors. He is also a member of the society's very important fee-study committee. Architectural fees have traditionally been based on a percentage of the total cost of construction, but there is considerable dissatisfaction with this formula in the profession. Some attempts are being made to move in the direction of hourly billing, perhaps with a maximum figure.

Architects as a group are also trying to find ways to increase their control over projects and to take a more active role in planning, developing and financing. In recent years some of the larger architectural firms have acted as sponsors as well as designers of housing projects. Snyder hopes to be able to join this trend and initiate and develop some projects of his own.

One of Snyder's employees is a young lady from the Philippines. Another is an American black named Blasco Andino, whom he met when they were in second grade together. He had taken a course in drafting but never used it, going to work in a meat-packing plant instead. After several years the packing plant closed, so Snyder Blackburn Associates offered him a job. "He was green as a gourd when he started, but now he is one of our most valuable employees.

"I have found that we really have to train people on the job. Maybe it's a slight exaggeration, but I think the drafting schools do more harm than good." Some time ago, he was a member of a committee of the American Institute of Architects that closely examined a number of the drafting schools in the Indianapolis area. With a few exceptions, such as the one at Purdue University, they found them wanting.

"Many of these schools do nothing but fill up two years of a man's life—he would be much better off spending those two years learning on the job. It's a shame to take the students' money and tell them they will earn $200 a week when they finish. In fact, with what they learn, they are barely worth $50."

Snyder and his wife live in what he calls a "golden ghetto" on the northeastern outskirts of the city. A black man once owned a farm there, and as the city grew, he began to subdivide it into building lots. It has now expanded into a sizable black middle-class residential area.

His principal recreation is listening to music. "I don't know why I picked such an expensive hobby. I collect records, and collect 'em and collect 'em. . . ." He is also involved in a variety of civic activities, including the community corporation that runs the Indianapolis poverty program. "There was one evening when I didn't have a meeting scheduled, but I can't remember whether it was this month or last month. . . ."

Snyder knows what discrimination is. Indiana was a Ku Klux Klan stronghold in the 1920s—perhaps its only important base outside the south—and some of that sentiment lingers there today. He says that when he took the state architectural exam, one member of the board made a blatant effort to disqualify him. He remembers the restaurants at and near the University of Illinois campus where he couldn't eat for two reasons—no money and no blacks allowed. And he remembers looking for a job as an architect in Indianapolis in the 1950s and not even getting the courtesy of a hearing.

This highly successful architect tends to accentuate the positive when he looks back over the early part of his life. He modestly gives credit for what he has accomplished to good luck and good friends. But there was a great deal more to it than that. He is a man of enormous drive and determination. When asked directly, he admits that "I used to work regularly until 9:00 or 10:00 at night when I was single. Now I usually get out of the office by 7:00 or 7:30. . . ."

19

Asa T. Spaulding:
Insurance Executive

*"When I told the President that I was to come to Durham
on this occasion, he said, 'You too? It appears that the
entire government is going down to North Carolina to the
dedication of the North Carolina Mutual Life Insurance
Company's building and to see Asa Spaulding. I doubt
that there's been such an assembly of federal officials in
one place since the last Cabinet meeting.' "*

—Vice President Hubert Humphrey, speaking in Durham, N.C., on April 2, 1966, the
first time in American history that a Vice
President has spoken at the dedication of a
privately owned building.

The North Carolina Mutual Life Insurance Company is
the largest business enterprise owned and managed by black
people in the United States . . . probably in the world.

It has assets of over $115 million. Its gross income is
over $30 million per year. It has insurance policies in force
totaling almost three-quarters of a billion dollars and insuring the lives of some 800,000 people in fifteen states and
the District of Columbia.

Its new fourteen-story office building stands on the
highest point in Durham, a site formerly occupied by the
mansion of B. N. Duke of the tobacco family. The building
permit was the largest ever issued by the city of Durham
for a private building. The structure cost over $5,000,000
and, although Durham is somewhat of a small town, it is

every bit as modern, efficient and attractive as the newest office buildings in our large cities. It was described by *Fortune* as one of the ten best buildings completed in the United States in 1966.

A tour through the headquarters office of North Carolina Mutual is a unique and unforgettable experience, for the visitor sees something that does not exist anywhere else in the U.S. The company has about 1,400 employees, about 260 in the home office, and almost all of them are black.

There are black men in the mail room, the cafeteria kitchen and the maintenance department, and black women in the clerical pool, just as there are in every large company. There are black men running the card punch and print-out machines in the computer department, but there are also black programmers, a black data-processing supervisor, black actuaries and black salesmen. The chief actuary and the sales manager are black . . . and the controller and the treasurer, the medical director, and the investment experts who place the company's reserve funds in mortgages and securities.

On each floor, in the spacious executive offices at the corners of the building, there is a black man at every desk. And on the top floor, with its plush reception area, its expensively furnished board room and its suite of executive offices, all of the faces are black, including all the vice presidents, the executive vice president and the president.

The company has a twelve-member board of directors. Eleven of these are black men, and the twelfth is a black woman.

North Carolina Mutual was organized on October 20, 1898. It proposed to build a business based on insuring the lives of people who were less than forty years out of slavery, people who were mostly dirt poor, illiterate, superstitious and suspicious. And their mortality rate was so high that some people were predicting that the Negro problem would soon solve itself by the black race dying out in America.

It was not unusual in those days, when a death occurred, to pass the hat at the cemetery to help the family with medical and burial expenses. Furthermore, prominent citizens in the community were solicited whether they were present at the funeral or not. Two men in Durham who were seldom missed were John Merrick, who operated a barbershop for whites, and Dr. A. M. Moore, a physician. Merrick and Moore felt that something more systematic should be worked out to meet this problem, and they, together with five others, organized the company with an initial investment of $247. The other five fell by the wayside in less than two years.

The early days were described by C. C. Spaulding, an older cousin of Asa Spaulding's:

> I was manager, agent, clerk and janitor and had to do local collecting as well as organize new fields in the adjacent counties. Mr. Merrick and Dr. Moore served without salaries while I took to the field on a commission basis. I learned to talk insurance on my first trip, for I had to depend upon my success in selling insurance for my traveling expenses.... I tried to hustle insurance but everywhere met with discouragement. My friends, and others whom I tried to interest, were sympathetic and appreciative of the effort to establish an insurance company, but they did not believe it could be done. They advised me on every hand not to waste my time....

In 1900, the first death claim—$40—created a crisis because there was no money in the treasury. Merrick and Moore reached into their pockets, as did General Manager Spaulding, who contributed his last 29¢, so that the claim might be paid and the faith of the deceased policyholder justified.

This triumvirate would not give up, and finally things began to improve. By 1904, the company was confident enough to cross a state border and start doing business in South Carolina.

The company had been in business for over nine years before the North Carolina Insurance Department knew it existed. When he made the discovery, the commissioner immediately moved to examine its books and records. He found everything in order. Fortunately, by that time the company had accumulated sufficient reserves and surplus funds to meet the requirements of the law.

By 1918, the company was large enough to subscribe for

$100,000 of Liberty Loan bonds and to receive a highly publicized personal acknowledgement from the Secretary of the Treasury. Later that year, it was hit with a flood of death claims totaling over $100,000 as a result of the flu epidemic. In 1920, the company reached $1,000,000 in assets.

The members of the original triumvirate managed the company for over fifty years. John Merrick was president from the beginning until his death in 1919. He was succeeded by Dr. Moore, who served until he died in 1923, and then by C. C. Spaulding, who was President from 1923 until 1952.

In its early days, all of the company's insurance was the type that insurance people call "industrial"—probably because it has nothing whatever to do with industry. Industrial-insurance premiums are collected monthly or even weekly by agents who go from door to door. This arrangement is suited for people so poor that they can never accumulate more than a few coins at any one time, but a large part of the premium goes to paying the collection agents. Industrial insurance is gradually disappearing. North Carolina Mutual's industrial business is now down to about 40 per cent of its life-insurance total, and continues to drop every year.

One of the early problems faced by the company was a legal requirement that most of its employees be bonded. The existing bonding companies simply refused to write bonds for Negroes, so North Carolina Mutual helped organize one that would. Similarly, when it faced difficulty buying fire insurance on its offices, it assisted a fire-insurance company in getting started. The company also participated in organizing and launching the Mechanics and Farmers Bank and the Mutual Savings and Loan Association, both of which now thrive independently.

A small percentage of the company's insurance policies are held by white people, but this group includes some very large policies written in North Carolina. Until recently, the company had no white employees at all because none applied. "After we moved into our new building and leased some surplus space to the federal government," says Spaulding, "that began to change. The majority of the federal employees are white, and we all eat together in the cafeteria. When the white people of Durham saw that their daughters were perfectly safe working in our building, we began to get some employment applications from whites, and we have hired some."

One problem that has developed in recent years is the energetic effort by white insurance companies to sell to Negro customers. They have also been aggressive in recruiting black salesmen to help them reach this market. Thus the company faces increased competition both in selling policies and in recruiting salesmen.

North Carolina Mutual has always attempted to invest its reserve funds to serve the needs of black people. Unlike some insurance companies, it makes loans to churches and black-owned small businesses. It also makes sizable investments in home mortgages.

In 1938, the company started doing business in Pennsylvania. At that time Negroes in Philadelphia were finding it almost impossible to get financing to buy homes. North Carolina Mutual announced that it would set aside $500,000 for home-mortgage loans in the Philadelphia area. This paid off in two ways. It became an entering wedge that led other lending institutions to liberalize their policies. And the effect was not lost upon black insurance buyers; only five years after it opened, the Philadelphia office was writing more insurance than any other district office in the company, including Durham.

North Carolina Mutual, now over seventy years old, is viewed by businessmen who have had dealings with the company as a highly professional organization with able and energetic management. It is by any measure a sound and prosperous business.* But the measure of the black man's position in America is that this largest black-owned institution of any kind ranks about 140th in size among American life-insurance companies.

---

* It is a typical American business enterprise in almost every way. For example, its house organ looks like that of any other large company, except that the faces are black, and one is reminded of Robert Townsend's description: "Reading a house organ is like going down in warm maple syrup for the third time."

Spaulding has been closely associated with North Carolina Mutual for over fifty years. He was a protégé of one of the founders and a younger cousin of another. The company loaned him the money to finance his education, and he has worked for it ever since his first summer job there in 1919. He has retired as president, but remains a member of the board of directors. His story has been told many times because of his prominence among black businessmen. His name is included on everyone's list of black millionaires.

What makes this interesting is that he is not a millionaire.

"Our balance sheet showed surplus and reserve funds of over $15 million when I retired," says Spaulding, "and many people seem to think that all of that money belonged to me. But we are a mutual company, not a stock company. Our company is owned by its policyholders, and the surplus and reserve funds belong to them. All I ever got from the company was a salary, plus the same dividends on my insurance policies that every other policyholder received. How can anybody become a millionaire when he has nothing but a salary, especially with the income-tax situation the way it is?"

He was born in 1902 on a farm in Columbus County, North Carolina, about forty miles from Wilmington. Spaulding says that his father "was a hard-working man, but he was also a businessman who knew how to work other people." In addition to operating a farm, the elder Spaulding ran a general store, cut timber and ran a still that produced turpentine and rosin.

For the first sixteen years of his life Asa Spaulding was not conscious of racial discrimination. His family lived in an all-black community consisting of farms and two small settlements that could barely be called villages. When white men came from distant places to hunt deer, they would often spend the night in the Spaulding home. He remembers the white visitors at the dinner table and staying in his home, and he does not recall any incidents of friction. All the adults were on a first-name basis—both ways.

The laws of North Carolina in those days did not require much education for black children. School did not start until the crops were harvested, usually around the middle of October, and ended late in February, when it was time to start plowing and preparing the ground for spring planting. The quality of the instruction in the all-black school was not high, but young Spaulding took his studies seriously and worked hard. He was always first in his class and usually had the highest grade average in the entire school.

He had a special talent for mathematics, and his father took pleasure in showing him off at his store. As early as the age of nine or ten, he could be asked the price of 4½ pounds of salt pork at 18½¢ a pound and come up with the answer in his head faster than the adults could do it on paper. When he was thirteen, his father put an acre of land in his charge, telling him to plow and plant it and keep any money he made.

Because of the abbreviated school year, he did not finish grade school until he was almost sixteen, when most of his friends ended their education since there was no black high school in the area. Because of his outstanding grades, he was invited by Dr. A. M. Moore of North Carolina Mutual to come to Durham to attend National Training School, a private institution. Dr. Moore helped him get a tuition scholarship the first year, and it was renewed every year thereafter based on his scholarship rating, which was the highest in the school.

So, at the age of sixteen, Spaulding left home and was on his own. He stayed with Dr. Moore and his family and did odd jobs for his room and board. He worked at the insurance company during the summers.

In Durham he encountered the white man's world of racism for the first time. The "Whites Only" signs were a new experience for him. In those days there didn't seem to be any choice but to go along with the system. In speaking today of those years, Spaulding shows no bitterness or anger. He is a man of peace—and a man at peace with himself. Not peace at any price, however.

Spaulding finished high school ranking number one in his class. He then returned to Columbus County to be school principal. After a year he had saved enough money to start college, and entered Howard University in Washington as a freshman at the age of twenty-two. When that school year was over, he went back to Durham to work at North Carolina Mutual and save up enough for his sophomore year. After that he was able to stay in college without interruption because the company lent him what he needed.

In 1927, he enrolled for his sophomore year at New York University. "They must have known I was a Negro," he recalls, "because my application showed that I had been at Howard, but there was quite a flap when I showed up at the dormitory to move in. They muttered that there must have been a mistake; they checked and double checked, but they had accepted my deposit and I had their letter of acceptance. Then I heard a long speech about how the presence of Southern students would make me uncomfortable and how it would be an 'unsatisfactory living situation.' But I would not withdraw voluntarily, and finally they simply refused to admit me." He found lodgings in the home of a relative.

Spaulding studied accounting at NYU, planning to become a certified public accountant. At that time there was only one black CPA in the entire country. (See Jesse Blayton's story, chapter 12.) Professor Saul Ackerman, who had taken a special interest in Spaulding's progress, suggested that he consider becoming an actuary; that is, a specialist in the calculations relating to mortality and life expectancy that a life-insurance company needs to determine its premiums and reserves. There was not a single black actuary anywhere in the U.S. In fact, North Carolina Mutual, although it was a well-established thirty-year-old business, was not equipped to do its own actuarial calculations and had to have this work done by a white consulting firm. Professor Ackerman was sufficiently interested in the idea to visit Durham with Spaulding and discuss the matter with officers of the company and with the state authorities.

The idea was received with enthusiasm. It was decided that, with his B.S. in accounting, Spaulding would attend graduate school at the University of Michigan, then the country's best school of actuarial science. He enrolled there in September 1930.

"I remember vividly my first day in one of the classes at

Michigan. By chance a student from Tuscaloosa, Alabama, was assigned the seat right across the aisle from mine. When I came in and took my seat, this fellow very conspicuously and noisily moved his chair around and turned his back on me. Now it happened that the instructor in that class liked to have three or four students work on the same problem at the blackboard at the same time. And it also happened that I usually finished my work at the blackboard first. It wasn't too long before he straightened his chair around, and in about six weeks he asked me if we could study together. We got to know each other fairly well, and one day—I think it was his way of apologizing for the original incident—he said he sure would love to have me come down to Tuscaloosa for a visit with his family. I told him I thought it was a fine idea. But I never went."

Spaulding received his master's degree in mathematics and actuarial science at Michigan in 1932. Then, fourteen years after taking his first summer job at North Carolina Mutual, he headed back to Durham to stay. His first job was to establish and staff the actuarial department, with himself as supervisor. Once this was accomplished, the company took great pleasure in dismissing its outside consultants.

Spaulding worked hard, as always, and was given additional responsibilities as the years went by. He became assistant secretary, controller and then, in the late 1940s, vice president. During his years at the company he worked in every one of its departments, including a number of field offices, although he spent very little time actually selling insurance. In 1959, he became president of North Carolina Mutual Life Insurance Company and served until his retirement, January 1, 1968.

Spaulding feels that the company has been and continues to be important, not only because of its financial success, but as a symbol of what can be accomplished by black people working together and establishing something mutually owned by all. "Its contributions have been inspirational and social as well as economic. It opened the door of hope to young Negro men and women of aspiration when other doors, now open, were closed to them. . . ." In an early summer job in the mail room, he remembers, his supervisor emphasized the importance of using "Mr." or "Mrs." or "Miss" on every address. "It might seem like a small thing, but to a Southern Negro who has never been called "mister" in his life, and who rarely got any mail, it was pretty important."

He is also proud of the absolute integrity and honesty that has characterized the operations of the company throughout its history. He feels that this was an important factor in the satisfactory relations with the various state insurance commissions. "From the very beginning we established a rule that the agents, when making their collections, would keep their own money in one pocket and the company's money in another. It was a simple and effective system, in fact sometimes I think it worked better than all of these elaborate computerized bookkeeping procedures that we have now."

Spaulding, always a deeply religious man, has taught Sunday school regularly for many years. The same spirit has pervaded North Carolina Mutual since its beginning. A retired employee recalls that Dr. Moore took a fatherly interest in everyone who worked for the company and frequently counseled them on all sorts of problems. When he wrote a prescription or gave medical advice to an employee and was asked for a bill, he would say, "Come to Sunday school Sunday."

Spaulding has been happily married for many years. The Spauldings have three sons and a daughter. Asa junior, after a brief period with North Carolina Mutual, has now established a data-processing business in Durham. Another son recently finished law school at the University of North Carolina and has opened the first interracial law firm in Durham. The third son is a lieutenant in the U.S. Navy. Their daughter is married to a physician.

Shortly before he retired, Spaulding sought advice from his doctor. "He told me that, with my physical condition and the life I had lived, the worst thing I could do would be to slow down. So I took him at his word."

He continues as a director of North Carolina Mutual and of other companies, one of which is a billion-dollar national merchandising firm. He is chairman of the board of trustees of Shaw University in Raleigh, serves as a trustee of Howard University and several other institutions, and is a member of a bewildering variety of boards, committees, commissions and study groups. He approaches each activity with the energy, enthusiasm and insatiable curiosity of a man of twenty.

Late in 1969, Spaulding participated in a people-to-people good-will tour behind the Iron Curtain, an experience he found moving and broadening. "I wish now that I had studied more history. In eastern Europe, I learned about an attitude toward war that we don't have in this country. When a country has experienced 125 wars in its history, when its capital has been destroyed and rebuilt forty-two times—how can a nation move ahead under such conditions?"

This prosperous and successful retired businessman has a rare and wonderful attribute—an open mind. He speaks in glowing terms of a thirty-one-day conference in New Delhi some years ago, which was planning a four-year program for UNESCO. "As we groped and fumbled, trying to communicate with each other across the barriers of language and differences in social customs, I developed many new insights into the problems of our country's foreign policy. But more than that, I learned things I had never imagined about men and how they live together. What a tragedy that we in the West have failed so completely to explore and attempt to understand the wisdom of the Far East!"

Practically all of Spaulding's retirement activities are unpaid, and in many cases he pays his travel expenses out of his own pocket. He feels strongly that a man's true worth, and what he is remembered for, is in what he contributes to society, not what he takes out of it. "He who will gain his life shall lose it, and he who will lose his life shall gain it."

Only a few months after retirement, this youthful man undertook a brand-new challenge—one that could have produced embarrassment and humiliation. He went into politics. The population of Durham County is something like 70 per cent white and 30 per cent black; the imbalance among registered voters is even greater. But Spaulding ran for one of the five seats on the County Commission. He not only won, he led the ticket—the first black in history to be elected to this position.

Spaulding paused and reflected for a moment or two when asked for the secret of his success, and then said, "I would have to say that I was always somewhat of a dreamer . . . always projecting and seeing myself somewhere other than where I was. I'd be following that mule on a hot day down on the farm, but I'd be thinking about the men I had seen grow up and leave and take jobs up in New York or New Jersey, and I'd wonder if I would ever have an opportunity like that. So when the opportunity came, I grabbed it.

"And when I was in school back in Columbus County— you know, it wasn't much of a school—I was industrious enough and had enough drive to try to do the best job I could. I always felt that one should not be satisfied with anything less than the best. There's a wide range between the minimum requirements for holding the job and the maximum possibilities of the job. There are too many people who are satisfied with a C grade.

"Any job will expand or shrink to the size of the man who holds it. We found with our best salesmen that they would build up so many [industrial] accounts we didn't think they could handle them all. So we'd take half of them away, and they'd go to work and before long have just as many as before. But if we took those accounts and gave them to one of the less energetic men, pretty soon he'd have lost half of them.

"The other thing I would say is that I tried never to say no to a worthwhile project. Many times I would accept a challenge even though I wasn't sure how I would handle it, and I found that this never failed to broaden me and teach me something. If you get into water over your head, you know you will have to tiptoe."

Spaulding has been criticized for not being militant

enough. Like any black man who grew up in the South at the beginning of this century, he had to learn to hold his tongue and endure humiliation. Although his manner is mild and his language polite, his feelings are firm and unmistakable, as demonstrated by the following comments, which he wrote a few years ago for the North Carolina Mutual house organ:

There is no more burning issue facing the public than that of civil rights. Let no one be misled into believing that this is a phony issue which will go away if ignored, or that Communists are solely responsible for the current racial unrest and activity in this country. The origin of the motivation is deep-seated in the Negro himself, in his determined desire to have the same freedom of movement, choice and opportunity as his fellow Americans of other races....

It has been abundantly clear to many for several years that the desire for freedom and a better way of life on the part of underprivileged people throughout the world is an ever-rising tide and the flow of it might be damned but could not be dammed, nor can this desire be crushed without destroying a major portion of the human race. The promissory note made to the Negro a hundred years ago, embodying the American promise and the American dream as set forth in the Declaration of Independence, the Constitution of the United States and the Bill of Rights and proclaimed through the Emancipation Proclamation, fell due long, long ago. The earlier Negro could not collect but was more patient and more long-suffering than the present-day Negro. The former was willing to accept interest only and to extend the maturity date over and over again. The present generation, however, considers the note in default and is demanding payment of the principal now and in full....

The young people are on the march. They will not be deterred by arrests, jail sentences, fire hoses, police dogs or death itself, for they feel that freedom and first-class citizenship are in the air and they are determined to collect the full amount of the promissory note at this time. I am convinced that the walls of segregation and barriers of discrimination based on race must go, and are certain to be washed away by the onrushing tide of history and change.

20

John H. Johnson: Publisher

*"I learned that there was no use in getting mad at
somebody like that—you had to outthink him."*

One of the best-known black entrepreneurs is John H.
Johnson. The cornerstone of his publishing empire is *Ebony,*
which now has a circulation in excess of 1,200,000 and is
grossing over $10 million a year in advertising revenue.
When Johnson founded *Ebony* in 1945, he clearly drew some
of his ideas from *Life,* which was then ten years old and
had transformed the magazine business with its phenomenal
success.

As this is written in 1971, *Ebony* is thriving and *Life* is
struggling. All-purpose mass-circulation general magazines
have slipped badly, and advertisers have largely shifted
either to TV or to more specialized publications that are
read more carefully by a smaller group of readers. The
average monthly issue of *Ebony* now carries about three

times as many pages of advertising as the average issue of *Life,* a weekly, or *Look,* a biweekly, and *Ebony's* advertising rates, measured in dollars-per-thousand-readers, are actually higher than those of either *Life* or *Look.*

Johnson was born in Arkansas in 1918; when he was six, his father was killed in an accident at the sawmill where he worked. Because there were no black high schools nearby, his mother took him to Chicago, where he attended Du Sable High School. He was an honor student, a member of the debating team, president of the student council and of his class, managing editor of the school paper, and business manager of the yearbook. Johnson was acutely embarrassed about the shabby, homemade clothes he had to wear in the early Chicago days. "The other kids used to laugh and make fun of me, and I decided I would show 'em. . . ."

As one of the outstanding black high-school seniors in the city, Johnson was invited in 1936 to speak at the annual Urban League banquet. The principal speaker was H. H. Pace, who had founded the black music-publishing firm of Pace and Handy in the twenties and was then president of Supreme Liberty Life Insurance Company, at that time probably the largest black business outside the South. Pace was impressed by the young man and offered him a part-time job at the company. He also helped him arrange a scholarship at the University of Chicago.

One of his assignments at Supreme Liberty Life was to help prepare the house organ, which reported various ac-tivities of the general black community as well as those of the company and its employees. Johnson scanned various publications for news items about blacks, then digested them and presented them to Pace, who made the selections for publication. This work gave Johnson a vivid awareness of the shabby treatment blacks received in the white press and of the need for a voice of their own. He conceived the idea of putting together the articles in a monthly magazine to be called *Negro Digest.*

In 1942, he borrowed $500 from a small loan company on the security of his mother's furniture and used it to mail out 20,000 letters to Supreme Liberty Life policyholders, offering them a charter subscription to *Negro Digest* for $2. "It was one of the most successful letters I ever wrote," Johnson recalled. It may well have been one of the most successful letters *anybody* ever wrote. Mass solicitations of this kind are usually considered outstanding if they bring checks from 1.5 or 2 per cent of the list. Fifteen per cent of those who received Johnson's letter mailed in $2, and that $6,000 started the magazine and the Johnson Publishing Company. Johnson was then twenty-four years old.

In November 1942, when the first issue was published, he found it almost impossible to get the news distributors to put it on the stands, even in black areas. So he enlisted all of his friends and had them make the rounds asking for the magazine. That got the copies on the newsstands . . . but they stayed there. Then he took most of his remaining money and sent his friends out again to buy up every copy. When the second issue of *Negro Digest* came out, the distributors were very happy to handle it.

The magazine started off successfully but slowly. A real surge was provided through an article by Eleanor Roosevelt, at that time First Lady, in its series, "If I Were a Negro." It pushed the circulation from 50,000 to 150,000 in one issue, and it stayed there. (It is interesting that Mrs. Roosevelt advised caution—"I would not do too much demanding. . . .")

This initial success was followed in 1945 by *Ebony,* based on the *Life* model. It had only been on the market a few months when Johnson announced that it would accept advertising, hoping to sell space, as *Life* did so successfully, to large manufacturers of brand-name consumer goods. The initial response was a deafening silence. After mulling over this problem for a while, Johnson realized that he was in fact trying to sell white advertising men on going into what they considered to be essentially a foreign market, even though blacks were buying their products every day. The concept was so revolutionary that it would have to be sold at the top.

Accordingly, he wrote letters to the presidents of dozens of major companies asking to see them. He used the interesting argument that if the chief of state of any foreign country, even the smallest, came to the United States, he would be entitled to an audience with the President, and that therefore he, Johnson, as president of a tiny company, was entitled to an appointment with Mr. Big. This dubious reasoning got him into the office of Commander Eugene McDonald, the late president of Zenith. McDonald called in his advertising director and asked why they were not using *Ebony*. "We're considering it, sir," was the response. The consideration, which had been going on for months and may or may not have been serious, was abruptly and affirmatively terminated by McDonald. Johnson walked out with his first big national advertising account, and Zenith has remained with *Ebony* ever since.

All of Johnson's publications are explicitly directed toward black people, with the sole purpose of giving expression to their feelings and attitudes and discussing subjects that they are interested in. For example, in covering national news events, such as the assassination of Senator Robert Kennedy, *Ebony* concentrated on the activities of blacks who were involved in the matter, and the reactions and comments of other blacks. It has some white readers—Johnson estimates 5 per cent.

To a white reader, perhaps one of the most memorable articles ever carried by *Ebony* was the one several years ago that told readers: "White people are just like everybody else. They have problems with their in-laws . . . husbands and wives argue about money . . . they worry about their son being drafted . . . should we buy a new car this year? . . . I hate the feeling of growing old. . . ."

In his pitch to advertisers, Johnson hammers away at three propositions. First, that the 23,000,000 blacks in this country have a lot more money to spend than they used to; second, that blacks are a special market, that they have different tastes and different preferences. Developing his third point, he says, "The black man has much more brand loyalty than the white man. We have been burned so many times by cheap, inferior merchandise that we stick to the tried and true, the names we can rely on. It's almost impossible to change a Negro's brand choice at the point of sale." The logical answer is advertising in *Ebony* to reach blacks and establish and sustain loyalty to a brand.

Ebony probably produces 80 per cent of the revenue of Johnson Publishing and an even higher proportion of its profit. The other magazines, *Jet* and *Tan,* are successful but small. In 1962, Johnson started publishing books, all on subjects of interest to black people, including some written or compiled in his own organization, such as *Negro Handbook.* A new literary quarterly, started in 1961, originally used the old name *Negro Digest,* but is now called *Black World.* Although a money loser, it gives black poets and authors a chance to be published. Johnson Publishing also owns a cosmetics company, Supreme Beauty Products.

In 1955, Earl Dickerson, who was then and still is president of Supreme Liberty Life Insurance Company, successfully urged Johnson to buy some stock in the company and take an interest in its affairs. In due course Johnson was elected to the board and, as he continued to buy stock, he became the largest single stockholder. Thus Johnson, following an old American tradition, started as an office boy and ended up being the boss.

Johnson sometimes draws severe criticism from militants and civil-rights activists, who accuse him of soft-pedaling the race problem. There may have been some truth in this charge in the early years, perhaps because Johnson was trying to land national advertisers and wanted to develop an image as a "responsible" publisher. But there have been decisive changes in the attitude of his magazines lately, although editorially they are still too mild to suit some readers. Johnson's comments on the change are those of the businessman that he is. "I wanted to protest. But the important thing is I had to. *Ebony* gets its lifeblood from advertising. It's no good carrying advertising unless we have the confidence of our readers. We won't have that confidence unless we publish the truth about controversial issues. We mirror our readers. Over the years, blacks have changed. *Ebony* had to do the same."

This comment gives an interesting insight into the Johnson personality. He clearly knows very well that black people haven't changed that much—what has changed is that they are no longer afraid to express what they feel. It could be argued that a leading spokesman for black people, rather than following his readers, might have taken the lead.

Johnson himself is no stranger to prejudice and discrimination. He enjoys telling the story of offering $60,000 in 1949 to buy a building, for use as the company's offices, in a changing neighborhood on Chicago's South Side. The owner refused to sell to him or any other black, but he did agree to sell to a white attorney, who was secretly representing Johnson, for $52,000. Johnson had never seen the inside of the building, so he had his lawyer ask permission to send in a maintenance man to look over the plumbing and heating system. And that was how the president of Johnson Publishing inspected his future headquarters—in overalls with a wrench sticking out of his pocket. Johnson's comment is characteristic. "I learned that there was no use in getting mad at somebody like that—you had to outthink him."

Asked whether he personally feels that he is accepted in the Chicago business world, he answered, "No, I don't think so. I get into these groups in the white world pretty much as a representative of the black community, even though I might not be identified as such. I don't think I am in there because I am a successful publisher, I think it's because I am a successful black publisher."

The ignorance of the white world about black businessmen was demonstrated unintentionally but very accurately in the New York *Daily News* of December 8, 1969. Half of its front page was taken up by a photograph of 100 famous men—black, mainland white and Puerto Rican—gathered together for an exercise arranged by the Urban Coalition, the filming of a TV spot. The caption read, "Star lineup mans benches at Manhattan studio as chorus, led by Mitch Miller, sings out 'What the World Needs Now Is Love.' In front row (l. to r.) : Urban Coalition's John Gardner, Urban League's Whitney Young, unidentified man, Johnny Carson and Bonanza's Dan Blocker. . . ." The unidentified man is America's number one black businessman—John H. Johnson.

21

After a Century of "Freedom"

Two-thirds of the way through the twentieth century, the rhetoric of politicians and the laws of the land assure the black man that he can now take his rightful place in American life. Once in a great while an effort is actually made to enforce these laws. By 1970, black men sat in both houses of Congress, on the Supreme Court and in city halls in Washington, Cleveland, Gary, Dayton and Newark. A black man ran for the second-highest office in the second-largest state. There is hope that someday black men may even be allowed to qualify as fully licensed principals in the New York City school system and as journeymen in the building trades—but of course these things will take time.

There are about 5,500,000 business enterprises in the

United States, excluding farms.* Black people, who constitute some 12 per cent of the population, probably own no more than 1 per cent of the businesses. And in the much more significant dollar measures—sales or profits or assets —their share is a very tiny fraction of 1 per cent.

The movement toward integration after World War II was a mortal blow to many black entrepreneurs whose businesses had been built in a segregated black economy. Customers who were not permitted to shop or eat "downtown" constituted a captive market for black store and restaurant owners; thus segregation protected the black businessman from white competition.

After desegregation of places of public accommodation, the captive customers had a chance to escape, and they did so without delay. Many owners of restaurants, hotels and night clubs were integrated right out of business. Once-fashionable black hotels—such as the Gotham in Detroit, the Theresa in New York and the Pershing in Chicago—became casualties of the integration push.

In the words of Johnson Publishing Company's *Negro Handbook:*

> As the barriers of race are hurdled, the Negro consumer who was once the private property of the Negro owner and operator of hotels, restaurants, night clubs and beauty and barber shops has turned with increasing alacrity to white establishments which offer, in many cases, extra services, luxury atmosphere and a degree of glamor for the same dollar. Even the long held monopoly of burying the dead is no longer an exclusive function of the Negro mortician....
>
> Eating and drinking establishments and other retail service businesses have experienced an absolute decline in numbers since 1950. The number of Negro-owned restaurants and other eating places, according to Department of Commerce statistics, declined

---

* It is very difficult to establish this figure authoritatively and precisely because of the problem of defining terms. What is a business? If a man owns seven apartment buildings, is that a business? A man operates a grocery store and a restaurant and also sells gas and makes auto repairs at a rural crossroads—is that one business or three? How about a supermarket run as a nonprofit membership co-operative? What of a law firm, an accounting firm, a medical practice—are these businesses?

by one-third between 1950 and 1960; other retail outlets declined by a slightly larger percentage. The number of funeral directors dropped by six per cent between 1950 and 1960, the number of barbers decreased by over 16 per cent, and while there has been an increase in the number of Negro-owned motels and hotels, they have obviously lost a sizeable portion of their most desirable clientele.

The U.S. Census reports that the number of "self-employed Negro businessmen" dropped from 59,820 in 1950 to 46,400 in 1960. Although the 1970 figure, when it is released, may show a further decline from 1960, the total has probably stopped dropping by now; but there is nothing on the horizon to indicate that any dramatic increase is about to occur.

The vast majority of black enterprises are still small retail and personal-service establishments—grocery stores, barbershops, luncheonettes, dry-cleaning stores, gas stations. Only a handful of black entrepreneurs have managed to make their way in finance, manufacturing, contracting or wholesaling. And even in the retail and service fields, there are very few establishments of any size. A study published in 1969 in New York City purported to show that more than half of the stores in Harlem were black-owned. However, the survey was taken on sections of Seventh and Eighth avenues, where only small stores are located. The important shopping areas in New York's black community are 116th Street, 125th Street and 135th Street in Harlem, and Fulton Street, Broadway and Nostrand and Pitkin avenues in Brooklyn. Practically all of the larger stores and theaters on these major shopping thoroughfares are white-owned.

Some of the oldest and largest black-managed enterprises are life-insurance companies. Among the more prominent, in addition to North Carolina Mutual, are Atlanta Life, Supreme Life Insurance Company of America, based in Chicago, Universal Life in Memphis, and Golden State Mutual in Los Angeles. About 3 per cent of the 1,800 life-insurance companies in the U.S. are black-owned; these fifty black companies have $2.5 billion of insurance in force and $450 million in assets. This is a fraction of 1 per cent of the total for the industry, which has $1.4 trillion ($1,400 billion) of insurance in force and over $200 billion in assets.

There are a number of black-managed savings and loan associations. One of the oldest is Illinois Federal Savings and Loan of Chicago. Others that have grown steadily over the years are Mutual Federal of Atlanta, Carver Federal in New York, Mutual in Durham, New Age Federal in Saint Louis and Citizens Federal in Birmingham.

There are twenty-six black commercial banks in existence today, according to the National Bankers Association. A number of others are in various stages of the organizational process. The association has recently hired a consultant to assist groups planning to organize minority banks. The largest black bank is also one of the newest—Freedom National Bank of New York, founded in 1965. The chairman of the board and one of the principal organizers of the bank is a former baseball player whose real name has seldom, if ever, appeared in the public prints—Jack R. Robinson. Freedom's assets are about $45 million; the Bank of America, largest in the world, has $26 billion.

In other areas of finance, black men have not been able to make much progress until quite recently. Mortgage banker Dempsey Travis was a rare exception for many years; a number of others have now joined him in that highly specialized field. Their combined financial leverage is growing rapidly but is still tiny in the nation's financial spectrum. A number of efforts have been made to organize stock-brokerage or -trading firms or mutual-fund sales firms; one or two have survived as marginal operations, but most have failed.

There are very few black-owned manufacturing companies. This is not surprising, for manufacturing usually requires a sizable amount of capital for buildings, machinery and equipment. At one time it was hard to find even one black manufacturer except those serving the captive cosmetics market.

Cosmetics has become big business in black America as well as white America. Among the oldest companies in the field are those founded by Madame C. J. Walker, Anthony

Overton, W. S. Cannon and S. B. Fuller. Chicago's Johnson Publishing Company owns Supreme Beauty Products. A cosmetics manufacturer selling to both black and white markets is fifty-eight-year-old Rose Laird Products, which was acquired by Carmen Murphy of Detroit from the heirs of the founder in 1968.

Another Johnson in Chicago—George E.—runs Johnson Products Company, which had sales of $13 million and net income after taxes of over $2,000,000 in its 1970 fiscal year. George Johnson is one of the wealthiest black men in the world. He owns over 1,600,000 shares of Johnson Products stock, which was trading on the American Stock Exchange at $33 per share in early 1971.

Other manufacturers include Glopak, Inc., which makes plastic packaging material in Passaic, New Jersey, Coles Wire Products of Los Angeles, Weco Tool and Engineering in Riverside, California, and Atlas Broom in Chicago. And there are a number of metal fabricators in the East. Among them are Acme Foundry in Harlem, L. & M. Products and B. & L. Metals in Brooklyn, Imperial Molds, Inc., in Newark, Smalltren Engineering in Rockland, Massachusetts, and American Steel Fabricating and Machinery and Hough Manufacturing Company in Cleveland. There are a number of clothing manufacturers, of which Terry Manufacturing is the largest.

One of the most promising areas of manufacturing is electronics, where very little heavy machinery is required and where technology is changing and advancing so fast that aggressive and energetic young men can make a place for themselves. Louis Roberts and Richard Walker have started Microwave Associates near Boston. In Chicago Jerry Jones has established Sonicraft Electronics. In Philadelphia, the Reverend Leon Sullivan has started Progress Aerospace, which has a $2,700,000 subcontract from General Electric. Barrett Intercommunication Products has been launched in Brooklyn.

In food processing, besides H. G. Parks, Inc., several other sausage companies have become established, three in Chicago: Dixie DeLuxe Sausage Company, Parker House

Sausage Company and Metropolitan Sausage Company. Uncle Walt's Sausage Company, formerly of Harlem, has recently moved to New Jersey. Argia Collins of Chicago has been struggling for years to get his Mumbo Barbecue Sauce on supermarket shelves. An unusual food processor is Evans and Sons Processing and Marketing Company, which "farms" and freezes catfish in Moscow, Arkansas. And a group of shrimp fishermen organized the Hilton Head Fishing Cooperative on Hilton Head Island, South Carolina. The co-op has its own processing plant, which provides over 100 jobs for impoverished black people during the June-through-December shrimp season.

The contracting business is one that has broken the hearts of strong black men all over the country. Many have tried it, most have failed; until very recently none was more than marginally successful. A number of them have managed to conquer the problems of capital, inexperience, hiring, and bidding and pricing, only to be defeated by their inability to purchase from an insurance company the performance bond that usually has to be posted before a job starts. Winston Burnett of New York struggled for twenty years before he finally broke through to big jobs in the late 1960s, partly with the help of the Boise Cascade Corporation, which now owns part of his company. Another Harlem contractor, Frederick Eversley, received similar financial assistance from American Standard, a large manufacturer of plumbing equipment. Other successful contractors include Bush and Smith, William Parker, and Cecil Carmickle in Chicago, Thomas Cook in Cleveland, Walker Brothers in Detroit, John W. Winters in Raleigh, and Jefferson and Sons Construction Company in—of all places—Fairbanks, Alaska.

Besides John Johnson, another Chicagoan, W. Leonard Evans, Jr., has become successful in publishing. After a career in advertising, which included the profitable operation for a time of his own advertising agency, Evans launched *Tuesday,* a Sunday newspaper supplement aimed at black readers. It is carried in the Sunday editions of such major newspapers as the Washington *Star,* Chicago *Sun-Times* and

Philadelphia *Bulletin,* primarily, although not entirely, in those copies sold in black neighborhoods. By 1970 circulation totaled over 2,100,000, a figure all the more remarkable in light of the fact that Evans built *Tuesday* into a successful and profitable advertising medium during a period when other Sunday supplements were losing ground or going out of business.

A number of black newspapers operate throughout the country. Two are dailies—the Chicago *Defender* and the Atlanta *World.* Largest in circulation, over 80,000, is New York's *Amsterdam News,* owned by Dr. Clilan B. Powell, who also owns the large and prosperous Unity Funeral Homes and other businesses.

One of the most unusual black businessmen, Berry Gordy, Jr., opened a record store in a black neighborhood in Detroit in 1953. It failed rather rapidly because he stocked distinguished jazz artists such as Thelonius Monk and Charlie Parker, while the customers kept asking for Fats Domino, whom he had never heard of. The experience provided a powerful demonstration of an old business axiom —don't try to dictate the tastes of your customers; rather, let them tell you what they like.

Gordy learned the lesson well. The secret of his success is that he combines an exceptional ear for the rapidly changing tastes of his record-buying public, mostly but not entirely adolescent, and both black and white, with enormous drive and organizing ability. His company, Motown Record Corporation, was started in 1959. It was successful from the beginning and had its first "gold platter" (record selling 1,000,000 copies) by early 1961. But it really hit the big time when the Supremes caught on around 1965.

Sales of phonograph records and tapes in the U.S. now amount to over a billion dollars a year. The three giants of the industry—RCA Victor, Columbia and Capitol—each have sales that may run as high as $150 million a year, including all types of music—classical, jazz, movie themes, ethnic, comedy and so forth. Motown, which covers a relatively narrow spectrum of rock and popular music, has sales that are probably well over $50 million and may approach

$75 million. (No record company will release exact figures or even estimates.) It is a fair guess that it ranks between fifth and ninth in sales among U.S. record companies, and perhaps higher than that in profits.

Over 100 radio stations beam their broadcasting to black people, but only about ten are understood to be under black ownership and management. Three—WRDW in Augusta, Georgia, WJBE in Knoxville and WEBB in Baltimore— are owned by soul singer James Brown. Brown within a few years has become one of the most successful entertainers of all time and a very wealthy man. Although his schedule of personal appearances across the country is very heavy, he finds time to participate in community activities and invest in a number of business ventures.

Another James Brown—the movie and TV actor and former Cleveland football player—has also concerned himself with black business development. Jim Brown organized the Black Economic Union, which has made loans to and otherwise assisted a number of black-owned companies.

Not surprisingly, other athletes and entertainers are increasingly associated with business ventures. Roy Campanella has a liquor store and Sugar Ray Robinson a restaurant. Joe Louis is a partner in a public-relations firm, Louis Rowe Enterprises. Lou Brock owns a number of businesses including a Dodge dealership in East Saint Louis, Illinois. Until recently, Ernie Banks was co-owner of Bob Nelson–Ernie Banks Ford in Chicago.

By 1971, there were at least thirty black-owned new-car dealerships. There are black dealers handling several foreign makes and every American make of car except Cadillac.

A prosperous and well-established businessman of an earlier time is A. G. Gaston. Gaston was born poor in Demopolis, Alabama, in 1892 and raised by his mother, who worked as a domestic after his father's early death. His first job at the Tennessee Coal, Iron and Steel Company in Birmingham paid him $3.10 a day. To supplement his income, he sold peanuts on the side and lent money to his fellow workers at an interest rate of 25¢ on the dollar.

He affiliated himself with the National Negro Business League and was inspired by the success stories its members told at the annual conventions. (He later became its president.) In 1921, Gaston and his father-in-law, with $35 between them, started the Booker T. Washington Burial Society, which grew into the Booker T. Washington Insurance Company. This was followed by the purchase of a funeral home. Then, because the insurance company found it difficult to recruit trained clerical help, Gaston organized the Booker T. Washington Business College.

Gaston invested and reinvested his profits in additional projects and enterprises that helped meet the needs of black people. Besides the insurance company and the business school, he now operates a chain of fourteen funeral homes, a group of motels, a housing development, a farm, a cemetery and a real-estate-development firm.

Percy L. Julian, a research chemist, was born in Montgomery, Alabama. Because of the inferior schools for black children, his mother took her three sons and three daughters to Indiana, while his father stayed behind and sent money. Julian and his two brothers eventually repaid this effort by earning doctorates; all three sisters have received master's degrees. After a distinguished academic career and seventeen years as director of research for a large food-processing company, Julian organized his own firm in 1954. Julian Laboratories produces hormones, drugs and fine chemicals. In due course, it was sold to a major drug company. Too energetic to retire, Percy Julian then established the Julian Research Institute.

There are several black-owned advertising agencies and public-relations firms. These include Charles Davis, Vincent Cullers, J. Cameron Wade and radio star Holmes "Daddy-O" Daylie of Chicago; D. Parke Gibson, Howard Sanders and Zebra Associates in New York; Anthony Davis of Dallas; Kenneth Wilson of Baltimore; Thomas Cleveland of Detroit and Dargan Burns of Cleveland. Executive-recruiting and employment agencies have been established by Richard Clarke and Ulrich Haynes, among others. There are many professional practitioners—doctors, lawyers, accountants and architects—but even the most successful of these operate on a much smaller scale than their leading white counterparts.

One of today's fastest-growing service industries is data processing. Those who work with computers need training, but they need little capital to start a "software" business providing data-processing services. A recent survey identified over two dozen black firms in this field. Most of them are relatively new, but two, Detroit's Data Processing Center and Telco Computer Systems, Inc. of Los Angeles, have been in business since the late 1950s.

A few of the tens of thousands of operators of retail and service establishments have managed to build sizable businesses. Among these are the Paschal brothers, motel and restaurant operators in Atlanta, Kenneth Sherwood, whose furniture company is probably the largest black-owned retail store in the New York area, and Samuel Berry of Chicago, who has built up the Star Paper Company and the Starlite Grocery chain.

Retail food marketing offers tremendous potential for black businessmen. A number of community-owned supermarkets have been organized either as co-operatives or as corporations selling shares to neighborhood people. Locally owned stores can provide better food value for their customers and also excellent training for supervisory and managerial positions. On a larger scale, a New York corporation controlled by Bruce Llewellyn with two partners, one Puerto Rican and one Jewish, acquired a chain of Fedco supermarkets, and has expanded it by building new stores. By early 1971, the chain had fourteen stores, over 400 employees and a sales volume of over $20 million a year. In Los Angeles, the Watts Labor Community Action Committee has acquired four Shop-Rite supermarkets that gross almost $10 million.

Many black entrepreneurs have been attracted to the booming franchise field, sometimes to their sorrow. Unfortunately, some of the franchising companies are considerably more interested in selling hamburger franchises, for example, than they are in helping the franchisee sell hamburgers. There is at least one black-owned franchising company, All-Pro Chicken, which is owned by former footballer

Brady Keys. Ex-basketball player Willie Naulls started with a Kentucky Fried Chicken store in Watts, California, and developed a shopping center around it. At the other end of the country, former teacher Preston L. Lambert hopes to do the same—he now has a Chicken Delight store and through Brooklyn Local Economic Development Company, of which he is executive director, he is planning a sizable shopping center and housing development in the Bedford-Stuyvesant section.

There are all kinds of ways to make a dollar. Two energetic black men own Arabesco Airlines, a freight carrier based on the West Coast J. J. Simmons of Muskogee, Oklahoma, made a fortune as an oil wildcatter, and Alonzo Wright of Cleveland did the same by building up a chain of gas stations and then selling it to a major oil company. One of the larger black employers is Dean's Protective Service of New York, which provides guards and watchmen and has a payroll of over 200. A number of black men own taxi fleets in various cities. And the Merchant Prince Corporation, which produces and distributes greeting cards, is publicly owned; its largest stockholder is a man named Berkeley G. Burrell.

Despite discrimination against their sex, as well as their race, a number of women have succeeded in becoming entrepreneurs. Rose Morgan in New York and Carmen Murphy in Detroit both own and operate chains of beauty shops under the name "House of Beauty." (Although the name is the same they are independent of each other.) Miss Murphy has also become a manufacturer of cosmetics.

A large Washington real-estate-brokerage firm is owned and operated by Flaxie Pinkett, and Mrs. Ernesta Procope owns a prosperous insurance-brokerage firm in Brooklyn. Ophelia DeVore founded the Grace Del Marco Model Agency over twenty years ago, and has built it into a successful business. Ruth Bowen runs Queen Booking Corporation, a successful talent agency that books theatrical and nightclub performers.

Anne Rodgers operates Village Maid International in Chicago and Washington; her employees do housework, but they earn $3 an hour for a forty-hour week. Miss Rodgers feels she provides an important service without subjecting her employees to the humiliation of the old-fashioned master-servant relationship.

No account of business development within the black community would be complete without mention of the Black Muslim movement. According to C. Eric Lincoln,* it was started in Detroit in 1930–31 by Farrad Muhammad, or F. Muhammad Ali, who is thought to have been an Arab. One of the earliest officers was Elijah Muhammad, born Elijah Poole in Georgia, who was named Minister of Islam in 1934 and moved the headquarters to Chicago, where he reshaped the movement under his leadership. He continues to dominate it today.

The movement stresses cultural and economic separation of blacks and whites. The Muslims advocate self-sufficiency and economic independence for the black community and enough enterprises to provide self-contained sources of employment for all blacks. The movement now operates a fine (though nonalcoholic) restaurant in Chicago, the newspaper *Muhammad Speaks,* a meat-processing plant, supermarkets in major cities, bakeries, used-car dealerships, repair garages, and laundries and dry-cleaning establishments. In addition, the Muslims have extensive holdings in both farms and urban real estate. No one outside the Muslim movement knows the extent or value of these holdings.

In 1958, the Reverend Leon Sullivan of Philadelphia organized a "selective buying" campaign ("Don't buy where you can't work") to pressure large Philadelphia companies to hire, and also promote, black men. He recognized that unemployed men sometimes lacked the education or training that industry wanted, and so he next organized Opportunities Industrialization Center, one of the nation's most successful job-training programs.

Then he raised money among the members of his church by a "10/36" plan ($10 a month for 36 months) to form

* *The Black Muslims in America* (Boston: Beacon Press, 1961).

Zion Investment Corporation, which has built an apartment project and a large shopping center and also started Progress Aerospace Corporation and a number of other business ventures. Zion Investment now has several thousand stockholders.

Early in 1971, the Reverend Sullivan was named to the board of directors of General Motors Corporation.

Dr. Thomas Matthew's National Economic Growth and Reconstruction Organization (NEGRO) raised money by selling bonds to set up a clothing factory and a construction company in New York City, as well as other projects. Dr. Matthew has also established a treatment center for heroin addicts.

A number of nonprofit programs are attempting to encourage black business development. Among these are PACT, Incorporated, in San Francisco, the Rochester Business Opportunities Corporation, the Chicago Economic Development Corporation and PRIDE, Inc., in Washington. One of the largest programs is that of the National Business League, which works closely with the U.S. Department of Commerce and the Small Business Administration.

Beginning in about 1965, there was widespread expression of interest in "black capitalism." A number of prominent white businessmen professed a deep commitment to programs to launch new businesses owned by blacks and members of other minority groups. Conferences, seminars and "workshops" on black capitalism were held all over the country, consuming thousands of man-hours of busy and talented people. Press releases and speeches were cranked out in substantial volume, until it was possible to believe that American businessmen were committed to decisive action. But holding a meeting or making a speech does not constitute action, and the private sector has not done much to help black entrepreneurs obtain the two things that any struggling business needs—capital and customers.

It is very, very difficult for a black man to find capital to start a new business or expand an existing one. But it is difficult for white men. Banks will rarely lend risk capital to any businessman, unless he has collateral to secure the loan, because that is not their proper function. They are fiduciary institutions—they have custody of other people's money—and their job is to lend and invest it with minimum risk. If a businessman starts with a basic stake, called "equity," they may make a loan that will then have a prior claim on the profits and assets, but they will rarely lend him the equity capital itself. Brooklyn businessman Preston L. Lambert has never forgotten a visit he made to a bank over twenty years ago. "I had always dreamed about owning my own business, and after I got out of the service I sent away for pamphlets to the Department of Commerce and the Veterans Administration and read lots of how-to books from the library. They all told me to seek advice from my banker. So one day, after carefully collecting my thoughts and putting down some income and expense projections and other figures on paper, I went to the bank where I had maintained both a savings and a checking account for many years. After some rudeness and delay, I managed to get to one of the officers, and sat down at his desk, laid out my papers and started to describe my plans for opening a restaurant. Just then somebody spoke to him from across the room, 'I wanted your okay on something, Ed, but I see you're busy.' 'Oh, no, that's all right,' replied this banker—this adviser to whom I was pouring out my soul, and whose counsel might change the course of my life —*I'm not doing anything.*' "

All business involves risk, and the equity money must come from someone who understands and accepts that risk. He invests his money and takes his chances, not knowing when—or whether—he will get it back. But as the business prospers, he may get it back many times over—that is his reward for risk-taking.

Where does a would-be entrepreneur find this "equity" or "risk" capital? The answer is that if he is to find it at all, it must be from wealthy relatives or friends. If he is very fortunate, his father or uncle will say, "Take the money and pay it back when you can." If he isn't quite so lucky, he will turn to a friend who wants a share in the ownership of the business, probably a large share, in return for investing in it. Most new businesses are financed this way—through relatives and friends.*

If the would-be entrepreneur doesn't know somebody who has money, he will probably never start a business and will spend his life working for somebody else, whether he is white or black. For there is no established mechanism in the American private-enterprise system that provides risk capital to would-be businessmen who do not have collateral or co-signers. The banks do not provide it, Wall Street does not provide it, nobody provides it—in the private sector.

There is one important source of this kind of start-up capital, and only one—the U.S. Small Business Administration. The SBA was created by Act of Congress in 1953; it makes loans to small businesses, sometimes by lending government funds but more often by guaranteeing loans made by commercial banks.

The Congressmen who fought for the establishment of the agency were principally concerned about small and medium-size businesses, which they believed were at a competitive disadvantage because they could not borrow from the banks as easily as big corporations. Thus the SBA's original objective was primarily to help existing small businesses borrow, for working capital or expansion, rather than to help people start new businesses. Indeed, it normally requires collateral for its loans, just like banks, and this effectively disqualifies most neophyte businessmen. And of course in the 1950s there was no interest in helping black men get started in business.

Over the years, however, the SBA has developed a number of new programs. In the early 1960s, under the leadership of Administrator Eugene Foley, it began offering unsecured loans up to $6,000 to those wanting to start businesses. Then in 1964 the Economic Opportunity Act, which was the original law that established the antipoverty programs, authorized it to make larger loans and also directed

---

* Some ambitious men, both black and white, who lacked a rich uncle have sought financial assistance for their businesses from a special kind of "friend" called a loan shark. This experience has provided them with new and exciting twentieth-century insights into the institution of slavery.

the agency to give special preference to those who had suffered racial discrimination.

The Economic Opportunity Loan program started slowly. But it moved a little faster under SBA Administrator Howard Samuels in 1968 and continued to increase its activity under his successor, Hilary Sandoval and black Assistant Administrator Arthur McZier. In the fiscal year ending June 30, 1969, the SBA reported that it made or guaranteed 4,654 loans totaling $105 million to minority businessmen—blacks, Puerto Ricans, Mexican-Americans and Indians. In fiscal 1970 the figure was considerably higher—6,262 loans totaling $160 million.

President Nixon has delegated to Secretary of Commerce Maurice Stans authority to coordinate all minority business development programs in the federal government. This is the first time in history that a Cabinet-level officer, with direct access to the Chief Executive, has had responsibility for this program. Secretary Stans has spent a considerable part of his time working in this area, and he has created the Office of Minority Business Enterprise, which is run by a black man named Abraham S. Venable.

The original SBA legislation was amended in 1958 to authorize a new venture-capital mechanism—the Small Business Investment Company. An SBIC is a private holding company that invests in small businesses, through either loans or the purchase of an equity interest. Such companies had been in existence for years without getting involved with the government, but the SBIC had three new features. First, it was to be licensed and supervised by the Small Business Administration. Second, it could borrow from the SBA. Third—and perhaps most important—if it lost money on a small-business investment, or if its own stockholders lost money on the stock of the SBIC, these losses could be charged against income as ordinary deductions for income-tax purposes, rather than being taken as capital losses. This feature was designed to encourage wealthy people to take the risk of investing in an SBIC.

Several hundred SBICs have been established throughout the country, and a number of them have sold shares on the public market. Their results, in terms of investment performance and profit, have been only fair at best, and a number have failed. As often happens with government programs intended to produce social benefits, a number of fast-buck operators moved in and misused SBICs in order to line their own pockets. At one point the SBA had to call a halt and review the status of all existing SBICs; it then canceled the licenses of over 100 of them.

At the beginning there was no thought of using the SBIC mechanism to meet the special needs of minority businessmen. Then in 1969, the Nixon Administration developed a new concept—the Minority Enterprise Small Business Investment Company. The idea was that large businesses or wealthy individuals would organize these MESBICs—which would operate under the regular SBA and SBIC procedures—and supplement private capital with borrowing from SBA, then lend money to minority entrepreneurs. By early 1971, the Administration had obtained commitments to establish more than 100 MESBICs and at least twenty-five had begun operations.

One of the tangible results of the interest in "black capitalism" in the late 1960s was the creation of several non-profit venture-capital pools. Among these are the Inner City Business Improvement Forum in Detroit, Venture Advisors in Dallas and the Coalition Venture Corporation in New York, established as a subsidiary of the New York Urban Coalition.

The Coalition is a very large committee. Its membership of over 100 includes businessmen, labor leaders, clergymen and foundation officials from the white establishment. It also includes businessmen, clergymen, block workers and leaders of poverty organizations in the black and Puerto Rican communities. The Coalition held its first meeting on December 1, 1967, at an elegant mansion in Tarrytown, New York. It was a memorable gathering at which presidents of billion-dollar corporations broke bread with Harlem block workers.

The businessmen and other representatives of the establishment agreed that the most urgent need in dealing with

the urban crisis was job training. The community representatives responded quite forcefully, both in private conversa-
tions and in an unscheduled address to the assemblage, that
job training was indeed important but that there was another
objective that was equally important, perhaps more so. We
want, they said, a piece of the action. We want a chance at
the profits as well as the wages. Why shouldn't a black man
be a boss, an owner? Why should the profits from all those
consumer dollars spent in Harlem move out of Harlem
before the sun sets that same day? For that matter, why
shouldn't a black man have a chance at the profits in the
white community, too?

This demand occasioned no little surprise, and perhaps
even some shock, among the businessmen. That surprise
is probably as good a measure as any of the unconscious
racism in America. It wasn't that anybody considered the
demand outrageous or even unreasonable; it was just that it
had never occurred to them before.

These busy and prosperous men had seen their sons go
off to Harvard Business School and then join large corporations and rise in the executive hierarchy. Or they had given
them money to start a business or buy a seat on the New
York Stock Exchange. Or they had entrusted to them the
management of several parcels of real estate. It seemed to
be a perfectly natural and normal sequence of events for
their sons and the sons of their friends. But, without really
thinking about it, they visualized the black man as more at
home as a high-school graduate who became a post-office
clerk or sheet-metal worker or subway motorman.

Other venture-capital programs have been established by
national organizations of the Episcopal, Methodist and
Presbyterian churches. And a handful of commercial banks,
notably the First Pennsylvania Banking and Trust Company
in Philadelphia and the Citizens and Southern Bank in
Atlanta, have made special efforts to develop equity-loan
programs for black businessmen.

These efforts by the private sector—MESBICs, nonprofit
capital pools, and special bank programs—probably had not
produced a total of as much as $20 million of venture cap-

ital through the end of 1970. This amount is insignificant by comparison with the estimated $350 million in loans to minority businessmen that were made or guaranteed by the Small Business Administration.

But even the SBA's effort is a small drop in a very large bucket. It is hard even to think about starting a business (other than something on the scale of a hot-dog or shoeshine stand) with less than $25,000. At this very minimal figure, the SBA's $350 million would be just about enough to replace the 13,000 black businessmen who fell by the wayside in the fifties, and would barely bring the black community up to 1 per cent of the business enterprises in the country.

Besides finding capital, another major problem that any business has is selling its product—in fact, with rare exceptions it is usually easier to make it than to sell it. The black businessman sometimes has an advantage in selling to black people, but he is almost certainly at a serious disadvantage when he tries to sell in the general marketplace.

He probably cannot afford a large sales organization or a big advertising budget. (Parks Sausages are advertised on radio and TV now, but it took the company over ten years to grow big enough to afford it.) The average black businessman does not have the friendship and contacts in the main business community that his white competitors may have, and a good deal of buying and selling is done in part on the basis of friendship and camaraderie. Some purchasing offices are simply closed to him because of his color. Also, much purchasing is based on reciprocity—you buy from me and I'll buy from you—and this puts any small businessman at a disadvantage.

One obvious answer to the black businessman's selling problems is for government agencies to make a special effort to direct purchase orders to him as a matter of public policy. There is nothing new about this approach—it has been used for years to assist American manufacturers in competition with overseas producers. Under the Buy American Act, U.S. companies are allowed a price differential in bidding on federal contracts—they still win the bid if their price is 20 per cent higher than the foreign company's. The original Small Business Administration legislation adopted this principle and authorized the SBA to direct that a certain portion of federal purchasing be allocated to small businesses, even though there is a price differential. This provision was a dead letter for many years, but the Nixon Administration has begun to use it. Robert L. Kunzig, who runs the General Services Administration, has worked especially hard in this area.

There is of course no good reason why private companies should not make a serious effort to direct purchase orders to black businessmen who can deliver the same quality and service at the same price. Indeed, during the flurry of interest in black capitalism during the late sixties, there was a good deal of discussion of this, but there was not much in the way of tangible results.

Bernard J. O'Keefe, the white president of E.G.G. Inc., a large electronics and nuclear-engineering firm, got a glimpse of what it is like to be black. His company bought a sheet-metal fabricating factory in Roxbury, Massachusetts, as a contribution to the economic development of that ghetto area, and put black men in charge of running it. "Everybody was hopped up over this thing two years ago," O'Keefe said in 1970. "Company presidents would say, 'Sure, we'll buy from you.' This would be passed down through vice-presidents to the purchasing agent. He'd give us $500 to $1,000 worth of business, which is worse than nothing at all. I guess I know what blacks mean when they talk about tokenism. . . ." E.G.G. Roxbury was closed a few months later.

Besides capital and customers, the struggling business-man also needs to have management ability—that rare and wonderful talent that involves keeping track of many small details, making decisions rapidly, judging people and know-ing how to take advantage of both their strengths and their weaknesses, making effective use of his time, negotiat-ing low prices when buying and high when selling, and understanding that some things are possible and some impossible—and knowing which is which. Probably not more than one man in 100—black or white—has what it takes to run a business. Even those who have it often fail because they need time to make mistakes and learn the lessons of experience; often they go into business on a shoestring and their capital runs out too soon. This is true of business generally, not just black business. The mortality rate is very high; it is estimated that half of all new businesses fail within eighteen months and 80 per cent within five years.

The struggling black businessman who needs management advice cannot afford to hire a management-consulting firm as the big companies do. Efforts have been made to develop management-assistance programs to counsel minority businessmen without charge. The Small Business Administration and the commerce departments of a number of states and cities have established programs that utilize the services of both active and retired white businessmen as counselors. The Interracial Council on Business Opportunity, established in 1963 by the New York chapters of the Urban League and the American Jewish Congress, has a similar program and now has offices in seven cities.

For some years the federal government has had a program of direct cash payments to companies who agree to train educationally disadvantaged, hard-core unemployed for permanent jobs. At this writing, consideration is being given to a program that would provide not direct cash payments, but tax credits to companies providing management training for persons who are "socially, economically and educationally disadvantaged." It has also been proposed that tax credits be given for investment in minority-owned businesses.

We do not contend that massive black-business development programs can solve this nation's urban problems, or even that they should receive first priority in the allocation of public funds. Capital investment requires huge amounts of money, and it seems clear that the feeding of malnourished children, for example, and more effective enforcement of the narcotics laws have a higher claim upon scarce tax dollars.

Some critics object in principle to the use of public money

for investment in or assistance to profit-making businesses, even those owned by minority groups. On principle, they have a point—the trouble is that the U.S. government has never followed that particular principle. The budget for minority-business assistance is infinitesimal in comparison with the aggregate of aircraft, airline, maritime, farm, highway and other subsidies that channel the taxpayers' money directly or indirectly into the pockets of owners of private businesses.

Furthermore, this nation has poured out billions of dollars to finance economic development in Africa, Asia and Latin America. Our taxpayers have extended help to practically every underdeveloped minority in the world—except those in the United States.

In this prosperous but troubled nation, and especially in its cities, there are millions of people with extraordinary and debilitating handicaps. Like poor people throughout human history, they face the normal and customary tendency of all societies to so arrange themselves that the rich get richer and the poor get children. But in addition, they bear the burden of 400 years of slavery and its aftermath. Even today, in 1971, black people must still live as helpless victims and targets of the scorn, ridicule, discrimination, prejudice and bigotry expressed daily and hourly in word and action by the overwhelming majority of the white population. No one whose skin is white can possibly imagine what it is like to live with a black skin in this country, even in its liberal and enlightened Northern cities, because he can never *feel* the frowns, the little rudenesses and the contempt. We are still, in fact, a racist country.

Therefore, anything and everything that can be done to enable blacks to enter the mainstream of American life must be done—immediately. Everything is necessary, everything is urgent, everything is top priority—housing, education, remedial education, jobs, job training, enforcement of anti-discrimination legislation in employment and housing, better police practices, better health and prenatal care. The list is almost endless. The encouragement and support of black businessmen is only one of many items on the list.

America has been a land of opportunity for many who have

inherited wealth and many more who have risen to it. The black man must have his chance at that wealth, too. Black people want a chance to go as high and as far as anyone else— or higher and farther. They want the right to follow every trail, but also the right to blaze new trails. There can be no limits, no boundaries, no closed doors.

The doors that lead to business enterprise have been closed, but the men we have written about managed to force them open. Many more will do so—indeed, they are doing so already. And their objective is the same as that of all entrepreneurs everywhere—to get their businesses and keep them . . . *in the black.*

Some people who read this book will say, What are the niggers complaining about? These guys made it . . . that proves any of them can make it if they try!

It proves nothing of the sort. *Every man whose story we have told is an exception. Most of them have exceptional intelligence. All of them have extraordinary patience, endurance, imagination, energy, drive—and luck. All of them had to sweat and strain and struggle many times as hard as their white counterparts for every sale, every achievement, every dollar.*

We know white men who are multimilllonaires, or distinguished business leaders, or presidents of large banks or manufacturing companies or utilities or railroads, who haven't one-quarter *of the ability of the men in this book.*

In America, lots of ordinary *white people make it. Why shouldn't an ordinary black man of average ability be able to make it, too? Why should he have to rise to heroic achievements in order to share in American life?*

Another thing is that these men who have made it, who have become millionaires, would have made it much bigger if they had been white. The man who made $1,000,000 might have made $5,000,000 or $10,000,000. The man who employs 200 people might have employed 20,000. Or he might have become President of General Motors.

If he had been white.

That's *what black people are complaining about.*